W9-ANH-434

TECHNICAL COLLEGE OF THE LOWCOUNTRY
LEARNING RESOURCES CENTER
POST OFFICE BOX 1288
BEAUFORT, SOUTH CAROLINA 29901-1288

C. P. Snow
Revised Edition

Twayne's English Authors Series

Kinley E. Roby, Editor
Northeastern University

TEAS 179

C. P. SNOW
Photograph by Mark Gerson.

C. P. Snow
Revised Edition

David Shusterman

Indiana University Southeast

Twayne Publishers • Boston
A Division of G. K. Hall & Co.

C. P. Snow, Revised Edition
David Shusterman

Copyright 1991 by G. K. Hall & Co.
All rights reserved.
Published by Twayne Publishers
A division of G. K. Hall & Co.
70 Lincoln Street
Boston, Massachusetts 02111

Copyediting supervised by Barbara Sutton.
Book production by Janet Z. Reynolds.
Book design by Barbara Anderson.
Typeset by Black Dot Graphics, Inc., Freeport, Illinois

10 9 8 7 6 5 4 3 2 1

The paper used in this publication meets the minimum requirements
of American National Standard for Information Sciences—Permanence
of Paper for Printed Library Materials, ANSI Z39.48-1984. ™

Printed and bound in the United States of America.

Library of Congress Cataloging-in-Publication Data

Shusterman, David.
    C.P. Snow / David Shusterman. — Rev. ed.
        p.   cm. — (Twayne's English authors series ; TEAS 179)
    Includes bibliographical references and index.
    ISBN 0-8057-6993-5
    1. Snow, C. P. (Charles Percy), 1905- —Criticism and
    interpretation. I. Title. II. Title: CP Snow. III. Series.
    PR6037. N58Z87 1991
    823' .912—dc20   91-9280

For my wife, Vi, whose support
over the years encouraged me to
complete this book
and for my daughter, Harriet,
who also encouraged me

Contents

Preface

C. P. Snow was one of the most controversial literary personages of the twentieth century. Few other writers since World War II have become such an object of attack or defense. A noted critic who labeled Snow a "frightening portent" of the future precipitated one of the most bitter controversies in the history of English literature. Snow himself, often described as a genial-appearing, friendly man, seldom hesitated to make his personal views known in his nonfictional writings in a direct, wholehearted fashion, and perhaps he thereby helped to stoke some of the fires built around him.

Probably the most efficient and fruitful method of approaching Snow's dominant viewpoints is to examine the two controversies aroused by his Rede Lectures in 1959 and his Godkin Lectures in 1960. This survey is made immediately after consideration of some of the highlights of Snow's life, especially those of the earlier years leading up to his period of fame. Both of these lectures, subsequently published as books, incorporated many of the views Snow had been expressing throughout the 1950s in essays published in various journals. In light of these two controversies, the novels, particularly the "Strangers and Brothers" sequence, have an additional interest quite apart from their intrinsic value as literature. A short chapter summarizing Snow's literary views precedes the discussion of all the novels. Though Snow's fame does not rest alone on his fiction, certainly his prestige as a novelist became the ultimate basis for much of the eminence he possessed.

In discussing the "Strangers and Brothers" series, it may seem peculiar to split up the treatment of the three novels of Lewis Eliot's direct experience into two parts separated by the lengthy chapter about the novels of observed experience. I saw no other way around the fact that *Last Things* not only is a novel of direct experience but also is certainly meant by Snow to be the final discussion of all Eliot's experience. To place a presentation of this book together with that on the two earlier novels of direct experience would be quite confusing to many readers. The best way out of the dilemma was to present a separate chapter on *Last Things*; the very title indicates the appropriateness of this method.

The reader may notice that at times I have been trying to establish at great length what sort of man Lewis Eliot is in the sequence of novels of both direct and observed experience. This treatment is due to the fact that though there are profound differences, Eliot may very well be a man much like his creator, C. P. Snow. Snow himself admitted the resemblance: "I would have thought that in depth Lewis Eliot is myself. In a good many of his situations, a good many of his external appearances he is not me, but in any serious and interesting sense he is."[1] This resemblance is mentioned, whenever pertinent, throughout my text. It is of paramount importance that the reader understand Lewis Eliot—and this would certainly be true even if we did not have the impression that he and Snow were similar in a number of ways—for the entire sequence of the "Strangers and Brothers" novels is nothing more than the story of Eliot's life as he presents it. To fail to comprehend Eliot would be comparable to reading the *Odyssey* without understanding the character of Odysseus, or *Don Quixote* minus any consideration of the nature of the title character of Cervantes's book.

After a short chapter 8 on the three later novels marking the end of Snow's novelistic career, chapter 9 of this revised edition deals with his later nonfiction. His reputation as a writer of nonfiction gradually became greater near the end of his life. His many essays on scientists, politicians, and writers, written mainly during the last two decades of his life, reflect his brooding over the many people whom he met during his active years, people who had made a tremendous impression on him. In addition to those whom he had met, there were the writers who had made the most impression on him during his years of literary creativity. Trollope probably headed that list, but as the essays in *The Realists* suggest, there were a number of others. Finally, *The Physicists*, which he was working on just before his death, deals with some of the scientists who were Snow's personal friends and also some of those who worked on the development of our century's most momentous scientific achievements. This lengthy chapter, followed by a much shorter conclusion, brings our review of Snow's works to an end.

For this edition, I wish to extend my thanks to Mr. Philip A. Snow, O.B.E, J.P., M.A., F.R.S.A., Lord Snow's literary executor, for his permission to quote freely from his brother's published writings and also from his own very helpful book, *Stranger and Brother: A Portrait of C. P. Snow.*

Acknowledgments

The author and publisher wish to thank the following who have kindly given permission for use of copyright materials:

Philip A. Snow, O.B.E., J.P., M.A., F.R.S.A., for use of his book *Stranger and Brother*, and for permission to use his brother's materials also; Mark Gerson, photographer, London, England, for photographs of C. P. Snow; Curtis Brown Group Limited, London, England, for use of the following books of Snow: *The Malcontents, The Search, Trollope: His Life and Art, Variety of Men;* Macmillan Publishing Company, New York, for the use of the following books of Snow published by Charles Scribner's Sons: *The Affair, A Coat of Varnish, Corridors of Power, Homecoming, In Their Wisdom, Last Things, The Light and the Dark, The Masters, The New Men, Public Affairs, The Realists, The Sleep of Reason, Strangers and Brothers, Time of Hope;* Macmillan Company, of England, for the use of the following books of Snow: *The Affair, A Coat of Varnish, The Conscience of the Rich, Corridors of Power, Homecomings, In Their Wisdom, Last Things, The Light and the Dark, The Masters, Public Affairs, The Search, The Sleep of Reason, Strangers and Brothers, Time of Hope, Variety of Men;* Little, Brown and Company, Boston, for the use of Snow's *The Physicists*.

The author also wishes to thank Mrs. Juli Crecelius of the Humanities Division of Indiana University Southeast for her excellent typing of the more recent part of the manuscript.

Chronology

1905   Charles Percy Snow born 15 October, Leicester, England: parents, William Edward and Ada Sophia Snow.

1925   Enters University College, Leicester. Writes *Youth Searching,* first novel, while undergraduate but destroys copies.

1927   Receives Bachelor of Science degree with First Class Honours in chemistry; stays on for graduate study.

1928   Receives Master of Science in physics. Enters Christ's College, Cambridge, as research student in physics.

1929   First published paper: on infrared investigation of molecular structure.

1930   Is awarded Doctor of Philosophy degree. Is elected Fellow, Christ's College (held to 1950).

1932   *Death under Sail*

1933   *New Lives for Old* (anonymously).

1934   *The Search*

1935   Is elected Tutor, Christ's College (holds post until 1945). On 1 January, conceives idea for "Strangers and Brothers" series.

1938   Is editor of *Discovery* until 1940.

1939   Is appointed to subcommittee of Royal Society to organize scientists for war effort.

1940   *Strangers and Brothers* (retitled *George Passant* in 1970), first novel in "Strangers and Brothers" series. Joins Ministry of Labour to organize scientists for war.

1942   Becomes Director of Technical Personnel, Ministry of Labour.

1943   Is made Commander of the Order of the British Empire (C.B.E.).

1944   Becomes Director of Scientific Personnel, English Electric Company (work performed in conjunction with government duties).

1945   Becomes Civil Service Commissioner (holds post to 1960).

1947   Becomes member of board of directors, English Electric Company. *The Light and the Dark.*

1949   *Time of Hope.*

1950 Marries Pamela Hansford Johnson, writer. *View over the Park*, a play, is produced.

1951 *The Masters*

1952 Son, Philip Hansford Snow, born.

1954 *The New Men*. Is awarded James Tait Black Memorial Prize for *The New Men* and *The Masters*.

1956 *Homecomings* (American title: *Homecoming*).

1957 Is awarded knighthood.

1958 *The Conscience of the Rich*. *The Search* is revised and republished.

1959 Rede Lectures, Cambridge; published later in the same year as *The Two Cultures and the Scientific Revolution*. Is awarded Honorary Doctor of Laws, University of Leicester; first of many honorary degrees and awards.

1960 *The Affair*. Godkin Lectures, Harvard.

1961 *Science and Government* (Godkin Lectures). *The Affair* is dramatized and produced. Becomes President, Library Association (England), and Rector, University of St. Andrews, Scotland.

1962 *The New Men* is adapted for the theater and produced. *Science and Government* is reissued with a new appendix.

1963 *The Two Cultures: And a Second Look* (expanded version of original book).

1964 *Corridors of Power*. Becomes Parliamentary Secretary, Ministry of Technology (until 1966). Is made life peer as Baron Snow, of the City of Leicester, in August.

1966 *Variety of Men*.

1968 *The Sleep of Reason*. John Findley Green Foundation Lectures, Westminster College, Missouri.

1969 *The State of Siege* (Green Lectures).

1970 *Last Things* ("Strangers and Brothers" concludes).

1971 *Public Affairs*

1972 *The Malcontents*.

1974 *In Their Wisdom*.

1975 *Trollope: His Life and Art*.

1978 *The Realists. A Coat of Varnish*

1980 Death of Snow, 1 July.

1981 *The Physicists*. Death of Mrs. Snow, Pamela Hansford Johnson.

Chapter One
Boy from the Midlands
Early Life and Education

C. P. Snow was born in 1905 in Leicester, a city in the Midlands, which is the industrial center of England; not far away are Birmingham, Stafford, Coventry, and Nottingham—cities that grew large as a result of the industrial revolution of the nineteenth century. Charles Percy was the second of four sons of William Edward and Ada Sophia Snow. William Snow was for a number of years a clerk in one of Leicester's shoe factories. If it is true that Snow's picture of Lewis Eliot's early life as described in *Time of Hope* (1949) is based to a large extent on his own, as some have said, then we can see that Snow's early years were spent in an environment that had little margin for cultural and intellectual development. Like the families of millions of other English factory workers, William Snow's family found its primary task to be the earning of a living that was often not much above the level of bare subsistence.

Though a factory worker, William Snow was probably not quite the ordinary one, for he was an accomplished organist, being a Fellow of the Royal College of Organists. Since this was so, the home atmosphere of the Snows may have been culturally somewhat above that of the average Midland factory family. Having been reared in an industrial environment, C. P. Snow, who has had much to say about the industrial revolution in his nonfiction writings, knows what that environment is like, at least in part, from the inside. The "in part" should be stressed because he never, as far as is known, did any work within an industrial establishment as an artisan or as an industrial laborer.

He was in this respect—having come from the working class—like several of his predecessors in twentieth-century English literature, such as D. H. Lawrence and Arnold Bennett. This list is not extensive; most of England's leading writers have come from upper-level or relatively prosperous families that have had little, if any, contact with the problems of the working class. These three—there are probably a few more, but not many—were boys who knew what it was to be born poor in an English society that was rigidly stratified and in which advancement was based to an enormous extent on class and family prestige.

In America, books such as those of Horatio Alger gave widespread dissemination throughout the late nineteenth and early twentieth centuries to the firmly held American belief that a poor boy could rise easily from rags to riches; American society in these periods was, in fact, so fluid that often a boy could relatively easily make the Alger stories come true in real life. In England, the rise was not at all easy, but nevertheless, some of the same mythology percolated into the minds of the English working masses. The way to do it, if at all, was felt in England to be through education: give a poor boy an education and he might possibly break out of his class and rise into the rarefied atmosphere above.

Snow has given us an intriguing portrait of his own grandfather, whose faith in the possibilities of education was great. Despite the hardships of industrial life in the nineteenth century, he became, like many of his class, inbued with the belief that the common Englishman was on the move upward, that life held promises that were never seen before by people of his kind. This view is so preeminently an element in Snow's own faith that we can well quote it in full:

I remember talking to my grandfather when I was a child. He was a good specimen of a nineteenth-century artisan. He was highly intelligent, and he had a great deal of character. He had left school at the age of ten, and had educated himself intensely until he was an old man. He had all his class's passionate faith in education. Yet, he had never had the luck—or, as I now suspect, the worldly force and dexterity—to go very far. In fact, he never went further than maintenance foreman in a tramway depot. His life would seem to his grandchildren laborious and unrewarding almost beyond belief. But it didn't seem to him quite like that. He was much too sensible a man not to know that he hadn't been adequately used: he had too much pride not to feel a proper rancour: he was disappointed that he had not done more—and yet, compared with his grandfather, he felt he had done a lot. His grandfather must have been an agricultural labourer. I don't so much as know his Christian name. He was one of the "dark people," as the old Russian liberals used to call them, completely lost in the great anonymous sludge of history. So far as my grandfather knew, he could not read or write. He was a man of ability, my grandfather thought; my grandfather was pretty unforgiving about what society had done, or not done, to his ancestors, and did not romanticise their state. It was no fun being an agricultural labourer in the mid- to late eighteenth century, in the time that we, snobs that we are, think of only as the time of the Enlightenment and Jane Austen.

The industrial revolution looked very different according to whether one saw it from above or below. It looks very different today according to whether one sees it from Chelsea or from a village in Asia. To people like my grandfather, there was no question that the industrial revolution was less bad than what had gone before. The only question was, how to make it better.[1]

C. P. Snow, the grandson of this artisan with the desire for education, made good through this means, but unlike the Horatio Alger heroes, he did so with hard, steady study and with a step-by-step advancement. He entered Alderman Newton's Grammar School in Leicester; on reaching Sixth Form (which is roughly equivalent to the American high school), his path was, in a sense, decided for him: since the school did not at that time have an Arts Sixth, Snow was obliged to specialize in science. He stayed on at the school as a laboratory assistant after graduation while he prepared himself for the winning of a scholarship to the University College of Leicester. There, from 1925 to 1927, he continued his specialization in science and was awarded the highest honors in chemistry. He remained at Leicester until 1928, having been awarded a research grant to work for a Master of Science in physics in the field of infrared spectroscopy. Then, upon being awarded a scholarship to Cambridge University, Snow entered Christ's College as a research student in physics.

Before Snow entered Cambridge, and while still a student at the University College of Leicester, he wrote his first novel; appropriately, it was called *Youth Searching*. It was never published, and he believed later that no copy of the manuscript was extant; in fact, he blushed to admit its name. Though he was preparing himself for science, because it seemed to be the most reasonable way to make a living and a career, he had already set his sights on becoming a writer: "I always knew—that is, from the age of eighteen or so—that I was going to be a writer. But I was a poor young man, I had to make a living fairly quickly. I knew that I was the sort of writer who had to nose his way among reality and learn his stuff as he went along. So therefore I was glad to have a scientific career and be ambitious in that career. But all the time the ultimate aims and the ultimate ambitions were in writing."[2]

As a youth, then, the many-sided, multifaceted life of C. P. Snow began. Whenever his name was mentioned, this multiplicity was usually stressed: that he was a novelist of growing fame; a man who made his mark in science; a government official; a Civil Service Commissioner; a businessman; a college don; and a man of public affairs—a list of accomplishments that is large and seemingly everextending. But we can easily see the two main prongs of his approach to life: science and literature. All the other tasks and accomplishments are peripheral; these two are central. His abiding interests have always been in these two fields, and in both he has spoken out sharply and bluntly—winning friends, making enemies, creating controversies. It is rare—in fact, almost nonexistent in human history—that a writer who takes literature seriously and whose literary work, in turn, is taken seriously by readers and critics should also be one who is deeply immersed in scientific endeavor. Therein lies Snow's strength and, as some say, his weakness—and our task is to examine both.

Cambridge and Whitehall

At the same time that Snow was writing the first novel in his "Stranger and Brothers" sequence, he was publicizing, as editor and essayist, the achievements of science. An essay of the 1930s discloses that the first excitement about knowledge for him, at the age of eight or nine, was reading in a children's encyclopedia an account of how atoms are constructed, for it "seemed to open up a new sight of the world." It "gave me," he wrote, "the first sharp mental excitement I ever had. It gave me the heightened sense of thinking and imagining at the same time."[3] We wonder just where and when the first excitement in creative literature started in Snow; since he decided to be a writer at the age of 18, he must surely have had some stimulus, some mental excitement, of a comparable order during his childhood. Science, however, claimed his first allegiance, and with his entrance into Cambridge in 1928, he entered the world of Ernest Rutherford (Nobel Prize winner in physics, 1908; from 1919 head of the Cavendish Laboratory), who for him has been the touchstone by which to a large extent he measured other scientists.

Snow's rise in Cambridge was as brilliant as it was rapid. A year after he entered Christ's College, he published, in conjunction with a colleague, a paper on infrared investigations of molecular structure; in 1930, he was awarded a doctor's degree in physics, and he was elected a fellow of his college. In 1935, he was elected a tutor. This period was to him one without parallel: "There has never been such a time. The year 1932 was the most spectacular year in the history of science. Living in Cambridge, one could not help picking up the human, as well as the intellectual, excitement in the air."[4] At the center of the excitement was Lord Rutherford, who had stimulated it with his monumental work in nuclear physics and with his discovery of the structure of the atom. To Snow, it was the age of Rutherford: "The tone of science was the tone of Rutherford: magniloquently boastful because the major discoveries were being made—creatively confident, generous, argumentative, lavish, and full of hope. The tone differed from that of T. S. Eliot or F. R. Leavis. During the twenties and thirties, Cambridge was the metropolis of physics for the entire world."[5]

Snow was probably alone among the better-known creative writers of our time, perhaps of any time, to find his great man in the person of a scientist, and significantly, he compared him, if only briefly, with two leading literary figures. The string of adjectives he applied to Rutherford is silently compared with that which might be applied to the literary men. Moreover, the tone of Rutherford had become that of Snow, one that was often extremely irritating to nonscientists. We adopt the tone dominant during our most impressionable years, and certainly the scientific Cambridge of the 1930s must have been exactly as Snow described it: an intoxicating place for a young, rising scientist.

The tremendous optimism, enthusiasm, and hope in the scientific Cambridge of the decade were undoubtedly like an oasis in the great desert surrounding it. No person who really lived through it could forget the despair, hunger, anger, and pessimism that marked the depression of the 1930s. Snow, however, gives us little or no glimmer in all of his writings that scientific Cambridge was aware of the deeply troubled world outside it. Snow himself was aware—we must make no mistake about that—of the discrepancy between the tone of scientific Cambridge, of modern science in general, and that of people on the outside: "people outside the scientific world often felt that Rutherford and his kind were optimistic—optimistic right against the current of the twentieth-century literary-intellectual mood, offensively and brazenly optimistic. The feeling was not quite unjustified."[6] Certainly, the reaction to the difficulties of the era of the rest of Cambridge—the Cambridge of the arts and the humanities—must have been not similar but quite different. And outside Cambridge itself, England was prostrate economically and in trouble socially. The spirit of scientific Cambridge, as Snow describes it, contrasts to that tone of the age. Nevertheless, we must understand why it was so if we are to understand Snow and his position in modern literature and thought.

It is in the nature of science itself, at least as we have known it to the present time, to be filled with optimism and hope. From its beginnings until today, science, with its insatiable curiosity to know, its intense desire to expand its boundaries, has had success after success; therefore, optimism and hope are component parts of the natural tone of science. The scientific Cambridge of the very late 1920s and 1930s would in all probability have been optimistic and hopeful even had there been no Rutherford. But with Rutherford, whom Snow regarded as greater than Michael Faraday (nineteenth-century discoverer of the laws governing the relationship between electricity and magnetism; called by many the greatest experimental scientific genius the world has known, according to *Encyclopaedia Britannica*), the spirit of optimism and hope was overwhelming.

Of all the kinds of people Snow lived among, the scientists were to him much the happiest: "Somehow scientists were buoyant at a time when other intellectuals could not keep away despair." People, he said, who are drawn to scientific activity tend to be happier in temperament than other clever people. For one thing, and extremely important, they do not think constantly of the individual human predicament: "Since they could not alter it, they let it alone. When they thought about people, they thought most of what could be altered, not what couldn't."[7]

The urge to write was powerful in Snow, and as he became imbedded more deeply into the scientific fabric of Cambridge, his desire to become a professional writer also grew. *Youth Searching,* his abortive attempt at a novel during his Leicester college years, was behind him. Shortly after being elected a fellow at Christ's, he wrote *Death under Sail,* a detective story that was published in 1932. From that moment on, Snow's way in life was "under sail." *New Lives for Old,* a science fantasy published anonymously followed quickly in 1933. The next year *The Search* was brought out. Three novels published in successive years gave a brilliant start to a second career that, like the first, came with astonishing quickness and with possibly even more success. These books were not best-sellers—Snow had to wait many years for that type of success—but he received enough critical encouragement to warrant continued pursuit of literature as a way of life. And when, on 1 January 1935, the idea for a long series of novels to be eventually called "Strangers and Brothers" came to him in Marseilles, he knew immediately what he had to do and began to do it. And he felt, as he said years later, "extraordinarily happy."

After writing *The Search,* Snow experienced a period in which he was "extremely miserable" because everything "personal and creative, seemed to be going wrong,"[8] but this interlude was brief. In fairness, we cannot gainsay the personal and creative turmoil he probably felt (for no one can adequately measure the troubles of another) in the few weeks or months that fell between *The Search's* publication and the onset of the idea for his novel sequence, but the period was, in the light of a whole life, a comparatively short one that should not be overestimated in importance. Success in writing came comparatively quickly, easily, to Snow, without setbacks of major proportions, without the pangs of years of frustration and failure that have beset innumerable literary persons. This factor can almost, in a sense, make him an epitome of the science for which he has become a chief spokesman; the prevailing tone of optimism and hope that was both science's and Snow's can be traced, at least in part, to the almost continuous successes that came to them.

In the second half of the 1930s, as Snow began writing the first novel of his sequence, England drifted toward war. To the acute political and military minds, it had been evident that Nazi Germany's designs would inescapably lead to conflict. One of the legacies of the age of Rutherford, according to Snow, was that England was able to utilize its scientists effectively during the prewar and war years, especially the younger scientists, like P M. S. Blackett.[9] In the autumn of 1939, shortly after hostilities commenced, Snow was appointed to a subcommittee of the Royal Society, England's leading organization concerned with the advancement of science; his task was to study the ways in which university scientists could best be utilized for the war effort. In 1940, Snow continued this work as an official member of the Ministry of Labour; that year also *Strangers and Brothers* (retitled in 1970 as *George Passant)*, the first novel of the "Strangers and Brothers" series, was published. The war years brought him additional responsibilities and honors. In 1942 he became director of technical personnel in the Ministry of Labour, with the specific job of coordinating the activities of Britain's scientists in the various laboratories and establishments set up for war. In 1943 he was made a Commander of the Order of the British Empire as a reward for his work in government.

During this invaluable period for him, Snow came to know well the inner maneuverings of government, and he used this knowledge of the "corridors of power" in his later novels. The ring of authority, of understanding and perceiving his subject from the inside, where power politics are made, was the unique contribution of Snow's war work to his writing. It was a fortunate circumstance that brought him into government, and if Snow had to delay his creative writing during the war years, the experience and insight gained were worth the postponement. Certainly, the novels published after the war, beginning with *The Light and the Dark* in 1947, owe much in one way or another to the almost six years their author spent in the official labyrinths of power. Many critics have insisted that the study of power is his major theme—power in its various ramifications as it affects society in its broader aspects, as well as in the lives of individual people. Although I agree with this conclusion, I also recognize that other themes occupy prominent places in his fiction. However, I concede that no other English novelist has written more about power.

The Years of Fame

Since World War II, the list of Snow's books, activities, and honors has become extremely long. The 30 years since 1945 saw him emerge from relative obscurity, from someone known only to the few British leaders in science and politics to someone known throughout the world. It is sometimes hard to keep our perspective in the correct focus when we look at this phenomenon, but we must recognize that fame came primarily because of his novels. Had he not become a leading novelist in the 1950s and 60s, he would not have carried the weight of authority he later wielded; therefore, any study of Snow has to be concerned with his fiction. Like no other literary figure of our time, however, Snow's extraliterary pronouncements threatened to obscure him as a novelist. An image was being built before our eyes of Snow the pundit, who pronounced wisdom on the vital matters of modern science, politics, education, culture, nuclear warfare, and the rise and death of civilizations.

To an impartial observer, Snow might have seemed extremely conscious of the place he has made for himself outside the sphere of his creative literary accomplishments. That he was completely sincere in what he was doing is of little doubt, but we often wonder whether a shrewd sense of business values is not perhaps a partial motivation for the often-shocking words that gained him much attention from the nonliterary world: publicity wins buyers of books. Even adverse publicity—and he had some of that—often stimulated the desire on the part of the curious to see just what his novels were all about. To many of the people attracted to him, he was not just C. P. Snow, the literary man who wrote a series of novels that were compared with Honoré de Balzac's *Comédie Humaine,* Émile Zola's *Rougon-Macquart* series, John Galsworthy's chronicle of the Forsytes, and Marcel Proust's *A La Recherche du Temps Perdu;* he became successively Sir Charles Percy Snow and Lord Snow, spokesman of the two cultures, publicist for the increasing importance of science in human life, warner of the dangers that lay ahead for humankind, advocate of increasing understanding between East and West, and blunt attacker of some of the idols of our time. Snow was indeed a public as well as a literary figure, and we must consider him in both capacities.

Chapter Two
Two Controversies
The Two Cultures

The germ of the Rede Lectures in 1959, later published the same year as *The Two Cultures and the Scientific Revolution,* can be found in a 1956 essay of Snow's entitled "The Two Cultures," in which he propounded substantially the same thesis: our society is marked by two cultures that are widely separated—the traditional literary culture and the newer scientific one. They are not only divided, but each exhibits a profound dislike of the other. The literary culture in particular, Snow claimed, shows its antipathy openly, for since the nineteenth century it has professed contempt for adherents of the scientific viewpoint. In the Rede Lectures, Snow expands on this subject and emphasizes his belief that the problem of the cleavage is not merely an English one but one that is common to the West as a whole; it is of the utmost importance that we recognize and overcome it: "I believe the intellectual life of the whole Western society is increasingly being split into two polar groups. . . . They have a common distorted image of each other."[1]

The Rede Lectures embody a number of points that have aroused strong reactions, particularly these: Snow charges that leading literary intellectuals of the twentieth century—such as D. H. Lawrence, William Butler Yeats, Ezra Pound, and T. S. Eliot—helped prepare a reactionary intellectual climate that has had a great deal to do with bringing about fascism and with it the ensuing concentration camps like Auschwitz. To Snow, scientists are closer not only to the realities of the present but also to the problems of the future than literary people are. Scientists have "the future in their bones" but the literati resemble the Luddites of the nineteenth century in their attempts to sabotage the basic structure of our industrial and scientific society. Snow implies that the tone of scientists is masculine, direct, virile, and wholesome and that the tone of the literary is feline, oblique, feminine, and unwholesome. His deep conviction is that though there have been faults in the scientific and industrial society, it has basically been good for humankind and has raised the standard of living in the West.

Though Snow insisted in several places in his lectures that his desire had been to bridge the gulf between the two cultures and to bring them together for the sake of the health of society, many did not accept him completely at his word. The literary adherents in particular considered Snow's tone too scathing to accomplish its avowed purpose and that the tenor of his remarks in general indicated his own deep-seated preference for the scientific as opposed to the literary culture, however much he protested his intention to achieve a mutual and harmonious understanding. In the bitter, ensuing controversy some of England's best known intellectual figures wrote communications to *Encounter,* the periodical that had published the lectures in June and July 1959, before they finally appeared in book form. As might be expected, both science and literature had their vigorous proponents, and the whole controversy was dubbed by one critic as the "Great Debate of our age."[2]

Two years later the debate was renewed when F. R. Leavis, one of England's leading literary critics, delivered the Richmond Lecture at Downing College, Cambridge, where he had been a don for a number of years. This lecture, published later as *Two Cultures? The Significance of C. P. Snow,* indicates that what provoked Leavis more than anything else was Snow's derogatory attitude toward D. H. Lawrence, whom Leavis had long regarded as the greatest writer of the century: Snow had committed heresy in sniping at Lawrence. Leavis's extremely virulent lecture exhibited his contempt for Snow both as a novelist and as a thinker. Snow, he stated authoritatively, is a mechanical writer whose novels read as if they had been written by a computer rather than a living man. Snow, he proclaimed, is a "portent" of the watering-down of our values as a result of the technological revolution that has come to dominate our society; Snow is "frightening in his capacity of representative phenomenon," the epitome of the Establishment; he promises "jam tomorrow," which is merely an extension of the materialization that is corrupting our whole society; and what Snow promises is a kind of "life impoverishment," an emptiness frightening in its implications for humankind.[3]

Leavis's attack is surely one of the more abusive polemics in the entire history of English literature and thought. Again, as two years before, others took part in the ensuing discussion, and this phase of the debate lasted for several more years and spread from England to America. Both phases of the affair make an interesting commentary on modern thought, and though the controversy had its titillating and even amusing moments, it should not be taken lightly. It may have had a salutary effect in that it brought clearly into the open the deep suspicion that has existed for more than a century between people engaged in literary pursuits and those engaged in scientific and technological endeavors. Between Snow and Leavis lay a profound gulf created by the important question as to how the individual now and in the future can develop his total potentialities for harmonious and vital living in a society that is increasingly becoming more industrialized through the agencies of science and technology.

One of the arguments used by several commentators in the debate was that there are actually not two cultures; the term, they said, was wrong at the start because we all belong to one Western culture and because the split is between two diverse groups within one culture. Snow had therefore unduly confused the subject and had caused much mischief by his lack of clear thinking. Perhaps this charge is correct, but quibbling of this kind over terminology cannot hide the fact that there *is* an intellectual bifurcation—a polarization of immense proportions between two very important groups in our society.

The danger is that, as Snow indicated in his *Second Look* (an addendum to the original published lecture), the world is increasingly becoming divided among ideologies, nations, and races. One of the most dangerous divisions, he maintained, is that between the rich and the poor nations; millions of people in the poorer nations are now on the verge of starvation, and many millions more will starve in the next few decades. Increasing industrialization is necessary, he said, to enable the poorer nations to tackle their problems in the right manner. Snow believed that a widening of the impasse between important groups like scientists and writers may serve to immobilize us at a time when the quickest action is needed. The main emphasis of the *Second Look* is the need for the spread of the scientific revolution all over the world. It is doubtful if Leavis and his followers and all those who opposed Snow's original thesis would ever agree with him. And if the groups within Western society are so polarized that they can never be brought together, what then remains for humankind? The prospect is not very inviting.

Tizard, Lindemann, and Churchill

When Snow's Godkin Lectures, delivered at Harvard in December 1960, were published in April 1961 as *Science and Government,* the controversy that arose was not so bitter as the one about *The Two Cultures,* but in several ways the second debate may have been more immediately far-reaching. It touched more closely on national matters in the recent past, and it had more implications for the immediate future of Western countries. In these lectures Snow explored the role of science in its relationship to government during World War II, and he made some sharp proposals about the role to be played by science in any future period of crisis.

Snow is on surer ground in *Science and Government* than in *The Two Cultures* in that he is writing, for the most part, about a crisis he had the opportunity of observing personally from a very close vantage point. Moreover, he personally examined many documents and papers connected with the scientific side of the 1939–45 war, and he discussed the subject with many of the people involved. During the war, Snow was in charge of selecting scientific personnel for war research in Britain, an exceptionally important task, for never before had scientists had such a major share in the determination of victory. Snow's job brought him very close to what he later termed the "corridors" of power, and this experience, as we have noted, gave him invaluable background material for his novels, as well as for this book about the politics of science and governmental affairs.

Science and Government is constructed around "two men and two choices": Sir Henry Tizard and F. A. Lindemann, who, as Lord Cherwell, eventually became "the right-hand man and grey eminence of Winston Churchill."[4] Close friends since 1908, Tizard and Lindemann became bitter enemies after 1936. Tizard had been in the ascendancy as head of a government committee to study air defense during the 1930s, and without Tizard's leadership, Snow claims, Britain would never have developed its radar chain in time for the Battle of Britain. But in May 1940, when Winston Churchill became prime minister, Lindemann became his scientific adviser, and Tizard was relegated to a comparatively minor scientific-military function.

The most important row between Tizard and Lindemann came in 1942 over the subject of strategic bombing. In that year, Lindemann, now a member of the cabinet, issued a paper claiming that the British bombing offensive must be directed essentially against German working-class homes. Although the ethics involved did not so much worry Tizard and a few others, Snow asks, "What will people of the future think of us? Will they say, as Roger Williams said of some of the Massachusetts Indians, that we were wolves with the minds of men? Will they think that we resigned our humanity? They will have the right." Tizard and his allies were more concerned that Lindemann's calculations about the effect of such bombings were too high. Tizard charged that Lindemann's claim that a total concentration of bombing effort would destroy 50 percent of Germany's houses was five times too high; indeed, P. M. S. Blackett, who in 1948 would become a Nobel Prize winner in physics, asserted that it was six times too high. Tizard, who pushed the minority view the hardest and claimed that a different strategy should be developed, was regarded as a defeatist, and a hysterical atmosphere developed that "had the faint but just perceptible smell of a witch hunt." Lindemann won, and strategic bombing was "put into action with every effort the country could make."[5]

Snow insisted that Lindemann's policy was a failure, just as Tizard and Blackett had predicted it would be. The bombing survey after the war revealed that Lindemann's estimates were 10 times too high. The best statement appears in Tizard's own words after the war: "No one thinks now that it would have been possible to defeat Germany by bombing alone. The actual effort in manpower and resources that we expended on bombing Germany was greater than the value in manpower of the damage caused."[6] Tizard believed to the end of his life, in 1959, that had he been granted a fair share of the scientific direction between 1940 and 1943, the war might have ended earlier and with less cost. "As one goes over the evidence," Snow states, "it is hard not to agree with him."

Snow extracts some "cautions" from these experiences of the two scientists. He insists that no country's governmental science is "freer" than any other's; nor are its secret scientific choices. "So we find ourselves looking at the classical situations of closed politics" in any society. The relationship between Lindemann and Tizard "is the purest example possible of court politics"[7]—the attempt to exert power through a man who possesses a concentration of power. Tizard's authority was over when he was called to No. 10 Downing Street in 1940, and Lindemann, as Churchill's chief scientific adviser, "had more direct power than any scientist in history." Roosevelt also had a "court," but no scientist ever became intimate with him, and fortunately for Americans, Snow says, Hitler in Germany kept his power to himself. The relationship between Churchill and Lindemann, admirable and noble in some ways, unfortunately resulted in bad judgments in public affairs: "Bold men protested to Churchill about Lindemann's influence, and were shown out of the room."[8]

Although Snow argued that there are no easy answers to the whole

THE LOWCOUNTRY
LEARNING RESOURCES CENTER
POST OFFICE BOX 1288
BEAUFORT, SOUTH CAROLINA 29901-1288

problem of the use of power in closed politics, he believed that there surely are some things we can and must avoid in the future: "I think most of us would agree that it is dangerous to have a solitary scientific overlord. It is specially dangerous to have him sitting in power, with no scientist near him, surrounded by politicians who think of him, as some of Churchill's colleagues thought of Lindemann, as the all-wise, all-knowing Prof."[9] Even if the scientific overlord is a Tizard or a Vannevar Bush, the "obvious dangers outweigh the vestigial possibility of good." Nevertheless, Snow believed, perhaps somewhat paradoxically, that scientists should be allowed to be more active in all levels of government. Scientists have something that our kind of existential society in the West desperately needs: foresight. "I am not saying, of course, that all scientists have foresight and no one else has," but enough scientists do have it. "For science, by its very nature, exists in history. . . . Scientists have it within them to know what a future-directed society feels like, for science itself, in its human aspect, is just that."[10] Administrators by their very nature, Snow thought, become masters of the short-term solution; therefore, we need scientists who have the gift of foresight concerned with government decisions.

In an appendix to *Science and Government,* published a year later, in 1962, Snow had some additional remarks that he deemed necessary as a result of the reviews, articles, and communications that had followed his book's publication. The main lesson he wanted to draw in 1962 seemed to matter more vitally than ever before: "The longer I think about the way decisions have been taken, are being taken, and will continue to be taken, the more frightened I get." We are forced to depend, "much more than is healthy for a society," on the scientific judgment in military affairs of a comparatively small number of people. Lindemann "proved himself, beyond any possibility of argument, dangerous and vindictive in action, outside the ordinary human run." The Battle of the Atlantic, which was decisive to the needs of victory, may well have been lost because of the diversion of long-range aircraft to the bombing offensive advocated by Lindemann and Churchill and finally adopted by the prime minister's cabinet. The primary lesson Snow again draws, though in even stronger terms, is that since Lindemann's scientific judgment was unusually bad, we must never again tolerate a single scientific overlord. "Whatever we do, it must not happen again."[11]

The foregoing statements of Snow's main thesis fail to do justice to the author's somewhat imaginative approach to his account of Lindemann and Tizard. The novelist, rather than the historian, is often foremost in the delineation of the two scientists, and this type of presentation has brought charges of bias and of a lack of objectivity upon Snow. It is possible that, as some say, Snow weakens his case by showing so graphically the personalities of the two scientists. On the other hand, for many *Science and Government* is remarkably enhanced by its method of presentation: Snow's case might not have been believed so readily had he left individual personalities out of the subject, for after all, Snow's objective is to demonstrate that a strong personality, like Lindemann's, can do irreparable harm to a nation in a period of emergency. Moreover, unless we subscribe to the belief that individuals count for little in human affairs and that the only determinants of history are strong impersonal forces, such as environmental conditions and economic developments, we cannot help feeling that the peculiar individual quirks of dominant people may often be of paramount importance in the shaping of national affairs.

Snow was attacked on many points by adherents of Churchill and Lindemann. Whether or not, however, Snow was particularly unjust to Churchill, as some declared, in attributing to him the naiveté of listening to only one scientific adviser, his warning against placing any scientist in a position of isolated power should not be dismissed lightly. The noted historian A. J. P. Taylor has summarized the controversy by asserting that Snow should have extended his remarks to warn against placing any individual in a position of isolated power, whether president or prime minister: "Clemenceau said that war was too serious a business to be left to soldiers. Nowadays it is too serious a business to be left to anybody."[12] Snow's novels, as shall be seen, reveal, among other things, the follies of those in power; indeed, they present a commentary on this aspect of Snow's argument in *Science and Government*.

Chapter Three
Snow's Literary Outlook

In *Two Cultures? The Significance of C. P. Snow,* one of the many derogatory statements made by F. R. Leavis against Snow was that he knew nothing whatsoever about literature. Since Snow expressed very decided views on literature in a number of places and indicated a wide range of reading in English and in European literature, what Leavis must have meant was that he did not agree with Snow's views. For example, Snow had committed the unpardonable sin of not thinking highly of D. H. Lawrence, and it may be true, as George Steiner suggests, that Leavis "cannot forgive Snow for suggesting that the English novel should have a future beyond Lawrence."[1] For Snow does have much to say about the future and the past of the novel.

In one basic aspect of the novel, Snow and Leavis are in substantial agreement: their dissatisfaction with the intensive experimentation with the form and the language of the novel in the twentieth century that is represented most dynamically by such writers as James Joyce and Virginia Woolf. Both Snow and Leavis spoke strongly against this type of experimentation, and both in this respect would have to be labeled conservative and, in the eyes of some avant-garde critics, even old-fashioned. To Snow, in particular, Joyce, Woolf, and their coteries have for the most part led the novel into bypaths of trivia, thereby alienating literature from the important intellectual life of our era. Their writing has led to what is called in the cant language of our time the antinovel, and according to Snow, Joyce in *Finnegans Wake* came nearer to writing the antinovel than any other writer.

Though Snow seems to believe in the vigor and strength of the novel and is optimistic about its future, he thinks that several times in the twentieth century, because of the alienation of some of its practitioners, the novel has looked as if it might fall into the "Alexandrian situation." By this phrase Snow means that when writers write novels, they divest themselves of any signs of using the intellect. His viewpoint in this respect is similar, he points out, to that of the American editor and critic Norman

Podhoretz, to whom many modern American novelists seemingly suppress in their fictions half of what they see and know.[2]

It is obvious that Snow believes fervently in the importance of communication in art and that the artist's main task is to transmit his vision of life as completely as he is able. The antinovel esthetic—which has become active in France and America since 1945 but is in retreat in England—believes not in communication but in the novel as an arrangement of words whose value is to be judged solely by whether the arrangement exists as the exact, consistent correlative of an internal "personalist" vision of experience. It matters little to this type of novelist whether his vision tells us anything much about the external objective world or whether what it tells has any correspondence to objective truth. To Snow, this aesthetic view is absurd: "it is rationalized into thinking which shows the characteristic of bad thinking, complicated, rococo, and often subtle in its decorations, but naive at the core. The basis for the rationalization is, of course, a naive comparison with nonrepresentational graphic art: and its result would be to make the novel not less significant, but also not more, than a somewhat minor graphic art."[3]

Snow thinks that this aesthetic in twentieth-century literature cannot be separated from a social view of life; it is a "syndrome of attitudes" springing from the same ultimately social root: "the romantic conception of the artist, the alienation of the intellectual, the aesthetic of the anti-novel, the abdication of the generalizing intellect, the hatred of the scientific-industrial revolution, the desire to contract out of society. This syndrome is seen at its most complete in writers like T. E. Hulme, Joyce, or Pound. It has been visible in a considerable sector of advanced literature all through the first half of the century. . . . (There is a) connexion which seems to be close, though not in individual practioners inevitable, between this sector of advanced literature and extreme social reaction—not conservatism, but extreme social reaction."[4]

Snow's views about literature are consistent with his own social views; he is on similar ground with what he had said in *The Two Cultures*. His attack is directed against those who would stand in the way of the advancement of the scientific-industrial revolution, and he attributes what he calls the "reactionary syndrome," leading to the "Alexandrian situation" in literature, to the impact of the scientific revolution: "For it seems that the scientific revolution has affected these people in two ways: (1) by the increase in complexity of social organization, which such temperaments have found abnormally hard to cope with; (2) by the direct

invasion of science into intellectual fields previously occupied by literature."⁵

Snow is scornful of contemporary critical techniques, especially those
practiced in the departments of English in universities: academic critics
study literary works as if they were merely verbal structures. Their type of
literary criticism, when applied to the novel, is much better adapted to
the consideration of novels whose range is narrow. According to Snow, the
novelists whom most writers would tend to accept as supreme practitioners of their art—"the real heavyweights," he calls them—are Leo
Tolstoy, Fyodor Dostoyevski, Charles Dickens, Honoré de Balzac, and
Marcel Proust, and they are fish too big and too elusive for this kind of
narrow criticism. A critic can't handle *War and Peace,* considered by many
the greatest novel in European literature, in this manner, for this novel
demands a variety of techniques to deal with it critically. The narrow type
of criticism can only catch the limited and narrow type of novel; the two
tend to reinforce each other.

The type of narrow criticism Snow is especially inveighing against is
the New Criticism, a type of criticism that became prominent in the
1940s and 1950s and that has still many adherents. The basic tenets of
the New Criticism are as follows: (1) the literary work is autonomous,
existing for its own sake; (2) since this is so, the critic should deal with it
objectively and should refrain from recourse to the author's biography,
the social conditions existing at the time of creation, and the psychological and moral effects on the reader to explain the work of literature; (3)
the distinctive method of the critic should be explication de texte; and the
critic should especially point out the complex interrelations and ambiguities that exist within the literary work. Conversely, the recent critics
whom Snow seems to like most are those who in general have moved away
from the New Criticism and have used broader approaches: George
Steiner, whom he selects for special praise; Harry Levin; Lionel Trilling;
Alfred Kazin; and Leon Edel.

The trouble with novelists and critics, Snow insisted, is that they are
caught in their own historic situation and find difficulty in transcending
it. He seems to be implying that both novel and criticism in our epoch
have been caught in a restrictive historic situation and have, through
inertia, been unable to portray life or art (as the case may be) in any but a
restricted manner. The range of the novel has deplorably been restricted
by the stream-of-consciousness technique, Snow thinks. Although most
critics regard this technique as a widening of the novel's range, Snow

disagreed: it can be nothing but narrow. The stream-of-consciousness method of narration gave the New Criticism, in its narrowness, exactly what it needed and wanted; therefore, the New Critics encouraged and shaped this kind of technique. What surprised Snow is that this method caught hold of literary sensibility so tenaciously.

Marcel Proust, whom Snow admires greatly (Snow's wife, Pamela Hansford Johnson, wrote a book about Proust), shows us another way to portray the flux of mental experience, and Snow compares Proust's method with Joyce's. The flux, Snow points out, is very largely nonverbal. Joyce's use of stream of consciousness is an attempt to find a verbal equivalent for the nonverbal flux: "The strategy is straightforward: adopt what looks like a naturalistic approach, write the verbal equivalent as thought it were the flux itself, discard the reflective intelligence (which will dilute the naturalistic approach), and try to make words suggest what scientists call a one-to-one correlation with the elements of the verbal flux."[6] Proust, however, would have regarded this strategy as naive and artificial; he uses the resources of the reflective intelligence and so evokes a flux of sensation.

Snow has little doubt that Proust's method is better than Joyce's because he believes that Joyce and other stream-of-consciousness writers had to abandon the reflective intelligence. Joyce, to Snow, narrowed the range of the novel; Proust widened it. Although the stream-of-consciousness technique is itself interesting as a device, a novelist needs something more.[7] Though Snow does not say so, we assume he is thinking mainly of Joyce's *Finnegans Wake* when he says that Joyce narrowed the range of the novel, for in at least parts of *Ulysses* and in almost all of his earlier works, Joyce does not abandon the reflective intelligence in order to concentrate on the stream-of-consciousness technique or on any other of the techniques he uses, and particularly in *Ulysses* he uses a great variety of approaches to the portrayal of life in Dublin. Moreover, we should observe that Virginia Woolf, another of Snow's targets, did not abandon the reflective intelligence in many of her novels and stories. We therefore wish that Snow had in this instance clarified his viewpoint by being more precise.

The novel in English, according to Snow, has been lacking in several important ways. For instance, it has never been strong in what he called "causal psychological insight"—the "insight which probes beneath the continuum of feelings." Such fiction does not tell us what it is like to be in a certain mood but asks what the mood is and why people are driven by certain motives. This causal insight exists in the fiction of both Tolstoy and Dostoyevski, for example, though in different fashions, and its existence makes for a complex and enriching interaction between their fictional characters and their immense social range. The novel in English has shown very well the continuum of feelings, but it has been lacking not only in causal insight but also in introspective insight: "The essence of introspective insight, which is not a common quality, is that at one and the same time one sees oneself with total intimacy and at the same moment as though one were some one else. Immersed in the stream of consciousness one can never achieve the second part of this illumination."[8]

Snow further maintains that two of the themes he himself dealt with in his novels—science and politics—cannot be adequately treated with the stream-of-consciousness technique. The only hope of suggesting what the experience of science is like is to use, as Proust did, every literary weapon at hand, including that of the reflective intelligence, though, as Snow points out, even then scientific experience remains one of the most difficult of themes; therefore, it has not yet been done well.

The theme of politics is less difficult in one respect than that of science because the difficulty of communication does not arise, according to Snow, since readers in general are better acquainted with the language and concepts of politics than with those of science. But in another respect this theme is more difficult because the technical problems are unusually complex. The power relationships between members of an organized society, which determine so much of our lives, are, like the theme of science, "forbidden" if the writer is committed to the stream-of-consciousness strategy, for he cannot write about politics without using causal and introspective insight. Further, Snow points out, since the power relationships of individuals are inseparably connected with a complicated social setting, the stream-of-consciousness technique, which is designed to present the solitary life, is inadequate in dealing with anything so complex.[9]

Snow's assault on the novel as practiced in English in the twentieth century—and particularly his attack on the stream-of-consciousness technique—reflects the determined viewpoint of a man who had early decided about the direction his own novels would take. He says that he wanted to deal with a number of themes when he started to write, and these included science and politics: "When I was a young man, they seemed to me quite good themes, i.e., themes the serious novel ought to be able to be capable of coping with. They still seem so." Of the two English novelists of the past who treated national politics in their books,

Anthony Trollope seemed best to Snow, for Trollope's presentation of parliamentary life "rang absolutely true," a reaction agreed to by ex–Prime Minister Harold Macmillan. Benjamin Disraeli, on the other hand, wrote about Parliament as if it were a kind of Utopian paradise that had little connection with the real world (a statement with which some would disagree).[10] Though Snow said the kind of politics he was interested in as a theme in his novels is more general than Trollope's, it is nevertheless apparent that he is much attracted to what Trollope did in the Victorian age to portray political life and to relate it to the general life of the English.

In connection with Snow's admiration for Trollope, there is an amusing sketch by Lionel Trilling about how he imagines (completely fanciful, of course) Snow launched upon his career as a novelist: it came about as a result of a wager at a club to prove that the novel as a literary form is not dead. It was decided by all concerned, including Snow, that he would attempt to write a novel, but it was not to be anything like the novels of Faulkner, Dostoyevski, Joyce, or Proust. The novel these clubmen wanted had to be lacking in symbols, myths, significant structure, and any strange, violent, or beautifully intense vision of life.

Snow, so the story goes, took stock of himself and found that the attributes he had for writing a novel were a set of old-fashioned notions about loyalty and generosity, a sense of social fact, a sense of the present in relation to a sense of the past, and a strong interest in "man in committee" as he lives the petty politics of life. Then Snow remembered that Anthony Trollope, the Trollope who wrote *The Way We Live Now* in particular, had begun writing novels with a similar set of characteristics. The implication left by Trilling in this imaginative, comic sketch is that Snow did pattern his writing upon the way set by Trollope. To Trilling, the significant thing, however, is that the situation of the novel in our time is not quite hopeless so long as we have Snow's novels. The plain, modest novels of Snow, which, Trilling says, engage our emotions and intelligence, give us, as Trollope's do, the sense of the reality, the verisimilitude of life, and the evidence of the vitality of the novel.[11]

Writing in 1959, Snow indicated that the English have more feeling for writing the realistic novel than Americans have, the latter having gone in for either symbolism or naturalism but not for realism. The nature of the American language, Snow claims, tends to be more abstract than the language as used by the English. The academic ties that many American writers have, if continued, will tend to make American writing "more convoluted, more packed with invented symbols and ironies, altogether

Alexandrian." Snow, whose books have sold widely in America and England, said he would not want to be an American writer, if it were within his power to make a choice: "It is simply that in England we know our audience. In America the writers don't really know whom they are writing for—apart from their fellow writer-scholars."[12]

An important factor in understanding Snow's novels is that he feels close to his audience, at least his English one; indeed, he probably feels much closer than most serious writers of our time do. Probably more important, Snow feels he has an important message to communicate to his audience, who for the most part will comprehend it and treat it with careful, if not always respectful, consideration (for as Snow says, there is sufficient diversity among this audience). He is a writer who definitely wants to communicate, and he wants to write in his own tone and to avoid, he insists, the device of the mask, the persona, or any other oblique method of presentation. (This attitude may be considered somewhat anomalous, for what else is Lewis Eliot than a mask?)

Snow's detractors on both sides of the Atlantic have considered him to be an Establishment man who wrote for an Establishment audience. This much-abused term is quite slippery, for there are differences of opinion as to what constitutes the Establishment; in general, perhaps, we can accept Snow's own statement about it: "One has to live in the English air to know by instinct and in detail what the Establishment means—but broadly, it is an agreement entirely unspoken and very largely unconscious, to preserve substantially the present web of power-relations."[13] Many of Snow's supporters would deny the allegation that he was of the Establishment by pointing out that his appeal is obviously to a wider audience than the necessarily very small Establishment provides. The Establishment net would certainly have to be stretched extremely wide to include Lionel Trilling and Alfred Kazin, to name two of Snow's perceptive readers and at least moderate admirers. These leading critics have subscribed to the dictum laid down by Henry James that the house of fiction has many rooms; therefore, they are able to appreciate Snow, as well as other writers such as Joyce and Faulkner, who are almost completely dissimilar.

The point that needs to be made is that though Snow may or may not have been an Establishment writer, the audience for whom he was, or seemed to be, specifically writing probably cannot be comprehended under such a term and is probably not very homogeneous, even if Snow himself may have thought so, though it is not extremely diverse or heterogeneous. His audience comprises readers on both sides of the

Atlantic who are mainly well educated, are of the middle-middle and upper-middle class, are fairly broad-minded and tolerant people, and are fairly sophisticated or urbane enough to appreciate his often slow-moving and generally quiet incursions into the realms of power politics played out in the areas of government, science, and academe, and who can also appreciate his revelations of middle- and upper-class mores. His fiction may appeal to the Establishment in England and America, but it seems to appeal also to quite a few of those who react strongly against anything smacking of Establishment—and this fact is a tribute to the art and mind of Snow.

His writing, however, will probably never appeal to young romantic rebels (except as a curiosity piece: an interesting example of how Establishment people supposedly live) or to those who have a predilection for experimental fiction; it will never have an audience among those who demand violent action and erotic, deviant, or unusual behavior that stimulates the senses; it will probably never be acceptable to the proletariat of any country; and it will probably never be read with enjoyment or understanding by the bigoted wherever they may be. A critic has called Snow one of the most tolerant novelists in generations because he is "a great deal more interested in studying and understanding character than in judging it."[14] This quality the avant-garde, the young romantic rebels, and the bigoted and the narrow cannot quite understand, and it sets Snow apart from most of his literary contemporaries.

Chapter Four
Early Novels

During Snow's active Cambridge period, from 1928 until the end of the 1930s, a period in which he was also becoming recognized as a scientist, he wrote and published three early novels: *Death under Sail* (1932), *New Lives for Old* (1933), and *The Search* (1934). This early work, when considered beside his later, reveals nothing very startling; nevertheless, it has several aspects that Snow's readers may not want to ignore.

Death under Sail

In an author's note written for a later, 1959 edition of *Death under Sail*, Snow relates that, when he was 21 and a student at a provincial university (Leicester), he wrote his first novel, *Youth Searching,* which "never got into print, fortunately for me and no manuscript now exists." *Death under Sail,* actually the second novel he wrote, was a signal to him that he should eventually give up his scientific career and become a novelist, an endeavor that had "always been my ambition." Snow could not say, he related later, why he wrote this detective story; his motives even in 1931–32 were obscure: "I suspect I had a sense that I was one of those writers who have to nose their way among experience before they know what they are good for. Anyway, I did write a detective story very much in the manner of the day." It was great fun to write, but he never had any intention of writing another, because he already knew what he wanted to do.[1] We can surmise that he already wanted to write the more serious kind of novel such as those he eventually did write.

Alfred Kazin has written about Lewis Eliot's constant concern in the "Strangers and Brothers" novels with the assessment of character; this fascination of the narrator seems to be derived from Snow's own similar interest. To Kazin, Snow's being chosen to administer scientific personnel during the war was appropriate because "he has an awareness of people such as only a poor and gifted boy who has had to depend for everything on his intellectual resources can develop; it reminds me of the sharp, rousing, malicious, but uncomfortably objective conversation of English scholars gossiping in commons rooms about each other."[2]

This awareness of people that led Snow to build his plots around character development is seen in *Death under Sail*. As William Cooper observes, what singles out this detective story from most others of its genre is "the fact that the plot grows out of the characters rather than the characters out of the plot. They are presented as interesting persons outside the puzzle."[3] This treatment of individual character, along with some better-than-average dialogue for detective stories, makes *Death under Sail* a fine beginning for Snow's career. To Cooper, it is a "remarkable beginning."[4] Although this statement is an exaggeration, I agree more with Cooper than with another critic, who thinks that Snow's first published novel shows no signs of the power and skill of the later novels and that it was not an especially promising beginning.[5] *Death under Sail* has a number of the typical "Snowian" qualities and, for me, sustains its interest to the end.

From the beginning chapter, entitled "Six Pleasant People," we are introduced to a group of unusual people on a sailing trip. The narrator is an odd character, chiefly because he is a retired man of 63 among a group of younger people in their twenties and thirties. The typical Snow touch is seen in the narrator's description of himself on the first page: "Every year I found it more of an effort to tear myself from my pleasant chambers, where I could indulge my bachelor habits, enjoy good food and sleep in comfort; but at sixty-three I was still prepared to submit to a little mild discomfort for the sake of friendly company. And I knew that at any of Roger's parties one was certain to meet some amusing young men and women." It is unusual for a young writer in his midtwenties to present his story through the eyes of an older man. Perhaps Snow wanted an older man—if there were a reason at all—to act not only as a kind of mature contrast to the sometimes madcap behavior of the younger characters but also as somewhat of a foil to the amateur detective Finbow, the dominant character in the book.

Finbow is in the tradition of the sophisticated, erudite solver of crimes, the amateur outwitter of the official detective bureaus, created by Edgar Allan Poe and carried forward through the nineteenth century by Conan Doyle and into the first three decades of the twentieth by many others in the genre, such as Dorothy Sayers and S. S. Van Dine. But Finbow is also in part the forerunner of Arthur Miles in Snow's *The Search* and of Lewis Eliot in the "Strangers and Brothers" series. Though he is not, like them, the narrator of the story, he has their same quality of close observation of people: "but chiefly," the aged narrator tells us, "he gratified what was apparently his only passion—the watching of men and women as they performed their silly antics for amusement. He watched in a curious, detailed, scientific way . . . of an amused and rather frightening detachment" (37).

Calmly and unemotionally, Finbow solves the murder—the "whodunit" aspect of every detective story—but any amateur detective of his genre could probably have done so as well. What makes Finbow most arresting is the quality and quantity of his dialogue as he observes the antics of his fellow human beings: "Old-established English traditions—there aren't any such things! They're usually extremely new, they're rarely English, and as for traditions—we always change them whenever there's a selfish end to be pursued" (131). "The only reason people preserve an air of mystery is because they have nothing else to preserve" (78–79).

One of the most interesting aspects of *Death under Sail* is the observations made, chiefly by Finbow, about scientists. Since writers usually write about things that most concern them, it is not unexpected to find that the young Snow did make several of his characters scientists. Roger Mills, the murdered man, had taken half the credit for the medical research of William Garnett because he had helped him financially: Mills had made his scientific reputation on the strength of Garnett's labors, though he, an utter fool scientifically, had done none of the work. Finbow, after learning the truth, says, "A scientist once told me that there was as much petty dishonesty and mean trickery in science as in high finance. I shall soon think he wasn't altogether wrong" (116). Discussing William Garnett, the excellent young scientist, Finbow talks of his emotional underdevelopment:

"He's an extremely hard, self-centred, ambitious young man who's going to get on in the world. He's emotionally underdeveloped in lots of ways. He's frightened of the girls, you notice: he hardly ever speaks to them. He gets no enjoyment from literature: he reads popular science. Like a good many scientists, he's still aged fifteen except in just the things that his science encourages."

"They're not all like that," I objected.

"Of course they're not," said Finbow. "Take old—" (and he mentioned a name known to everyone with a nodding acquaintance with modern atomic physics). "He's a large-sized man in quite a number of ways. But he's an exception; and William isn't an exception." . . .

"My dear Ian," Finbow broke in, "when I say a man's one-sided, you mustn't think I've got the same idea as the comic papers—absent-minded scientists who forget about their meals, and that sort of rubbish. Actually, an experimental scientist like William is pretty well-bound to be thoroughly competent at sailing yachts and mending cars. I mean psychologically one-sided: I mean he's at home with *things,* at home with anything where he can use his scientific mind—but very frightened of emotions and people, utterly lost in all the sides of life which seem worth while to most of us. He can run a society, because that's really an absolutely inhuman pastime, although most people don't realize it; but he could never run a love affair. Now do you see what I mean?" (121–22)

This is a particularly interesting observation about scientists because of Snow's later treatment of scientists in his novels and also because of his later viewpoint on scientists and nonscientists in his nonfiction works. Since Finbow is a personage in a novel, it would be fallacious to attribute with surety his views to the author; nevertheless, since Snow was at the time trying to make his mark as a writer and to leave science as a profession, we can perhaps believe that Finbow's views were not far from Snow's. Very probably Snow did believe that his fellow scientists, with exceptions—and very probably also the exception mentioned by Finbow (the "name known to everyone") was Rutherford—were "at home with *things*" but were one-sided psychologically. *Death under Sail* probably indicates at least one very good motive for Snow's desire to break away from science: he desired to enter into "all the sides of life which seem worth while to most of us."

New Lives for Old

Snow's second novel, *New Lives for Old,* was published anonymously, and he has given two reasons for not wanting to put his name to this novel of science-fantasy: "One, I was very dissatisfied with it. I wasn't under any strong temptation to own to its authorship. But the second was a practical reason. I was in for a job and I thought, the climate being somewhat different from what it is now, that a novel of that kind wouldn't help my chances. It was a job which for practical reasons I badly wanted."[6] Cooper claims that "it seemed possible that the publication of the book might lead to his being spoken of as too bright." Actually, as we now realize, according to Cooper, publication under his own name would not have made any difference to Snow's career.[7] Quite probably Snow was excessively sensitive to the attitude of his colleagues, as the remarks made by Finbow in his detective novel of the previous year would indicate. But in *New Lives for Old* the two scientists, Pilgrim and Callan, make some scathing comments about the stupidity and complacency of university dons. If they were actually as inadequate as Pilgrim and Callan state, then perhaps Snow may not have been far from wrong in claiming that his chances would have been hurt had the book carried his name.

He should not, however, have been so dissatisfied with the novel itself. Though, of course, his first two novels are in different genres and hence difficult to compare, the second work is in some respects greatly superior to *Death under Sail*. Indeed, more interesting characters are found in *New Lives for Old;* the idea of the book not only is more imaginative but shows in its development a greater understanding of the processes by which society operates, and this novel must certainly have been more difficult to write. Intriguing also is that this is the only Snow novel until late in his career (he came back to its method of narration in *The Malcontents*) not written in the first person; for a young writer, Snow handles the third-person-omniscient method reasonably well. Moreover, this book reads as smoothly as his detective novel, despite long stretches of authorial commentary, too much talk on the part of the characters, and a plot that falls apart in the last 40 or 50 pages. Often a fascinating mixture of fantasy and realism, the narrative holds up surprisingly well until perhaps the concluding pages. Though Snow wanted to let the novel be forgotten, it deserves to be reprinted under his name.

This novel, published during the lowest stages of the Great Depression, reflects the pessimistic view of society prevalent in left-wing and in liberal circles of the period; in a sense, this novel was therefore, a tract for the times. The story concerns the discovery of a process of rejuvenation that will not only extend the life span of most people some 30 or more years (after they have reached their sixties) but also give them the physical properties of fairly young adults. The development in society subsequent to the discovery becomes catastrophic. Rejuvenation, we are told numerous times, has only hastened the process of the British capitalist system's decay and its final collapse during a Communist revolution; but since all the seeds necessary for that debacle were already present in the system, its fall would have come inevitably without rejuvenation.

The leaders of the government in England are portrayed as corrupt incompetents who lack the necessary vision and ability to keep society moving in a smoothly organized manner and to see that the poorer classes receive a fair share of the world's goods. Rejuvenation hastens the process of division of the classes since only the wealthy and the privileged classes can afford it; the poor, who are only able to live the normal life span of sixty or seventy years, become increasingly angered when they observe the shameless spectacle of the upper classes living new lives and enjoying the sex hunt which has always been the mark of the young. The family and traditional morality break down when people of more than sixty years of age behave in a manner that the really young feel is unbecoming to their elders' years. Society in its every aspect is dislocated, and the book concludes with a successful but very bloody Communist revolution.

There are four fairly vividly realized characters: Billy Pilgrim and David Callan, the scientists who discover the way to rejuvenate the race; Vanden, a novelist; and a charming female, Alison Byrne, who becomes the mistress of both Pilgrim and Vanden after their rejuvenation. Snow's two scientists and Vanden often express their contempt for the world's leaders; their remarks, plus the whole picture of a society in shambles, may conceivably have made the young writer nervous when he contemplated publishing the book. Only science itself is depicted without attack in this gloomy and corrosive picture of society, but it is made clear that, while science is of immense importance for humankind, those engaged in scientific pursuits are human like everyone else and not all are as wise as they could be. As Pilgrim observes, scientists are "like each other in exactly one way: that they do some scientific work. Otherwise there's no more resemblance than there usually is between human beings."[8]

The Search

The Search, published in 1934 (revised slightly and reprinted in 1958), is in several ways an excellent novel that is not inferior to at least a few of the "Strangers and Brothers" novels. Its critical notices have been generally favorable and in a few cases enthusiastic; in fact, one critic considered it a better novel about scientists than Sinclair Lewis's *Arrowsmith*.[9] Certainly *The Search* and *The New Men* are, along with Lewis's, among the better twentieth-century novels that deal with scientists, and Snow's novels are more authentic because they were written by a scientist who had actually worked in the profession he was writing about. Many of Snow's scientific friends, including Rutherford, told him that his account of science was in essence true.[10]

The Search is greatly superior to the two novels preceding it for a number of reasons, but mainly because it is about something the author actually knew: the struggles, disappointments, and success of a young scientist. This novel, according to Robert Greacen, "must surely have been partially based on the experience of the author and his friends. Such telling details, related with the zest of a still young man, is [*sic*] not to be conjured up out of the air."[11] Like all of Snow's later novels, *The Search* is at least partly autobiographical, and a close connection must exist between the autobiographical element and the narrative method the author uses. The first-person angle of narration came easily to Snow, and there probably is a good psychological reason for it: he was probably writing about the things and people he knew.[12] *The Search,* in any case, possesses the intimacy and immediacy—that sense of being a personally meaningful story—that mark Snow's later and better work.

The novel concerns Arthur Miles, a scientist who searches for an understanding of himself—his relationship to other human beings—and the conflicts that arise when the ideals of science, those by which he has organized his life, are betrayed. It has been maintained that *The Search* represents a trying-out of the themes and techniques of the "Strangers and Brothers" sequence, but though Snow, of course, had not consciously made such an attempt, one of the stories Snow told over and over again centers on the search for a personal integrity and a social morality.[13]

The narrative begins with a young boy's excitement in looking at the stars and his introduction, through means of a telescope presented to him as a gift from his father, to the world of science. It is difficult to read this vivid account of the boy's desire to know the mysteries of the physical universe without believing that the experience was derived from Snow's own but slightly transmuted recollections of himself. Arthur Miles soon shows himself moving rather easily from childhood desires to early scientific success at King's College, London. The young scientist, whose specialty in physics is in the comparatively new field of crystallography, also finds success in love in the person of a young history student named Audrey. For the first time in his life he is shaken out of himself, or at least he thinks he is: " 'I must be a very selfish man,' I thought. 'No human being has really mattered up to now. That's just the fact. The only thing outside myself has been my work. Is this girl going to *upset* that?' "

But soon after he has fallen in love with Audrey, he leaves London for a research career at Cambridge. Audrey is not forgotten, but she lies at the periphery of his attention while Arthur describes for some pages the exciting atmosphere of Cambridge in the years when the great Rutherford was engaged on such tremendous work as the disintegration of the atom. The excitement of scientific discoveries is to Arthur the world of romance. Pages like these, though undoubtedly presenting an accurate account of how most young scientists on the rise surely must feel in the presence of greatness, are really not very near to the lives of the general run of humankind. Consequently, what seems to Arthur to be enthralling is to most people tedium, and several of the earlier reviewers of *The Search* emphasized that the novel was clogged with expository pages that seemed out of place in fiction. The justification for these pages, of course, is that they show us just what makes Arthur Miles develop into the man he later becomes.

Near the end of part 1, Miles discovers that a hypothesis on which he had been conducting an experiment is accurate except for one X-ray photograph. He asks himself what would have happened had he not taken this photograph, for the evidence would have been overwhelmingly accurate except for this. He is tempted to suppress the faulty evidence, but he overcomes the temptation and finally records the error:

From that day I understood, as I never had before, the frauds that creep into science every now and then. Sometimes they must be quite unconscious: the not-seeing of facts because they are inconvenient, the delusions of one's own senses . . . Sometimes, more rarely, the fraud must be nearer to consciousness; that is, the fraud must be realised, even though the man cannot control it. That was the point of my temptation. It could only be committed by a man in whom the scientific passion was weaker for the time than the ordinary desires for place or money. Sometimes it would be done, impulsively, by men in whom no faith was strong; and they could forget it cheerfully themselves and go on to do good and honest work. Sometimes it would be done by a man who reproached himself all his life. I think I could pick out most kinds of fraud from among the mistakes I have seen; after that afternoon I could not help being tolerant towards them. (94–95)

But though Arthur receives a temporary setback, he is soon working on his experiments and telling the reader just how difficult the struggle is to arrive at success in science. Finally, his first great success comes, and he feels a delight in "The Moment" (the title of the last chapter of part 1). To him, his success is like a great religious experience. We were told earlier that Arthur did not believe in God, that he had never had a religious life. But now: "once, when I was young, I used to sneer at the mystics who have described the experience of being at one with God and part of the unity of things. And that afternoon, I did not want to laugh again; for though I should have interpreted the experience differently, I thought I knew what they meant" (104).

In part 2 Arthur tells his readers that his ambition is very great. He delivers a paper to the Royal Society and thinks that by the time he is 35 he ought to be a Fellow of the Royal Society (F.R.S.), perhaps sooner. Like the author of this novel, Arthur is elected as a fellow in his college at

Cambridge. Then suddenly, unexpectedly, in the midst of the glow of his first great success, his mother dies, and Arthur goes home for the first time in 18 months. He feels almost nothing: "I was making no pretence at grief. I had felt almost nothing, and I could not bear to act my sadness. Why I could not dissimulate I did not know. It would have eased their [his relatives'] minds—yet it was out of my power" (113).

Arthur is surely a cold one, but he is at least honest with himself. He cannot feel grief even when he recalls the picture of his mother sitting by his bedside when he was a child. Instead, he feels freedom because he had been worrying during his early research days that he would eventually have to support his mother. He comforts himself that she had been given pleasure by his success, but why he needs to comfort himself, since he feels no grief at her death, is beyond the reader. A few days later, he meets Audrey, who tells him she's sorry about his mother. " 'It doesn't matter,' I said. 'You know, there was never anything between us.' " And then he blithely asks her to celebrate with him the winning of his fellowship. Audrey says she does not want to marry him even though she thinks she is in love with him; his work is too much of an obsession: "It'd be as bad as marrying a man with a faith. It *would* be marrying a man with a faith. You're a religious, my dear. . . . And religion doesn't leave much room for anything else. You oughtn't to marry. Perhaps you ought to be a celibate" (120).

Arthur feels he is in love with her, but all the time he gives himself reasons that he should not marry, the main one being that his fellowship would probably be over in six years and his future after that uncertain. Later, after a stay in Germany, Audrey tells him she is to marry Charles Sheriff, a fellow scientist with whom Arthur had been friends in his early days in London. Arthur, slightly stunned, tries to win her back. He proposes that Audrey have an affair with Sheriff for a month and then return to him. But Audrey insists on marrying Sheriff, whom she says she loves. Before leaving Arthur finally, however, she spends a night of love with him.

Though the reader may lack sympathy for Arthur at this point in the novel and may even feel that Arthur has been given what he has deserved, the reader may nevertheless admire him for his honesty as he bares his heart—he admits his selfishness, his coldness, his excessive engrossment in his scientific work. But the reader's possible awareness of his honesty may be qualified by such passages as this: "Occasionally my regrets had, I think—or perhaps I hope—an unselfish side. I was also sorry for her, that we had parted. I like to think this pity came from the other side of self-comfort. We had fitted so well, I thought—and that was true. Making all the allowances for jealousy I could, I still was not able to believe that Sheriff would match her moods as well as I had done. . . . [A]ll the depths and light and shade that were Audrey's—he could no more enter them than do my work" (151). After reading other, comparable comments, we wonder whether such a man when thwarted in love could make many allowances for jealousy, as he claims. Arthur seems to be an insufferably smug, selfish, and egotistic prig. As with Lewis Eliot, we find difficulty in knowing how we are to react to Arthur: are we to take him as being completely frank, or are we to read what he says as ironic, as devious and misleading? The same problem confronts the reader of *The Search* and of all the "Strangers and Brothers" novels. How are we meant to react to the narrator?

Another character in *The Search*, Hunt, an economist who had been friends with Arthur and Sheriff in London, tells Arthur what is really wrong with him with regard to Audrey: "What is distressing you is—that she's gone. That she won't come back. That she'll be happy. . . . [Y]ou're hurt because you lost her; but you're hurt much more because, in a way, you wanted to lose her, and you're tormenting yourself with that." Hunt tries to impress upon Arthur his belief that what is needed by humankind more than anything else is knowledge of the causes of human motivations, of human behavior: "These causes, that count more than anything else—and they are as mysterious to us as your science to a pre-paleolithic man. . . . It still seems to me, and more strongly than ever, that we're lost without that consciousness. . . . We've come at a time when it is most necessary" (159–60).

Arthur says he was impressed by what Hunt tells him, and he seems to see and understand. Later in part 3, however, when he is wondering whether he should carry on his scientific work in the same way as before or launch into new paths, he thinks, "But as I write, I am wondering uneasily how honest I have been. It is so easy to blame it on Audrey. Should I have really taken a different course, if she had been with me?" (174). Hunt had seemed to convince him of his emotional dishonesty, but now he seems to be wondering uneasily about it. We simply do not know how to interpret Arthur, and the cause of our bewilderment can surely be placed on the author, who juggles Arthur's viewpoint: at one time, he is looking more objectively at himself after everything has happened; at another time, he is bringing the viewpoint to a time nearer to an event's actual happening or even at the moment of its happening, as in this quoted passage. Similar shiftings of Lewis Eliot's viewpoint occur in the "Strangers and Brothers" sequence; the attentive but confused reader wonders whether it is clumsiness on Snow's part or an element in his overall design.

In part 3, Arthur moves back to London, having received a better position at University College. Incredibly, not having learned his lesson with regard to Audrey, he writes to her and arranges to meet her. Much to his satisfaction, he finds she has been disillusioned with Sheriff: he is a liar and cheat. But she is still in love with her husband—"captured in love" is Arthur's phrase. Arthur, however, soon forgets about her when he is involved in another new position, a possible appointment as director of a newly formed Institute for Biophysical Research. A number of pages are devoted to details about the five-man committee of scientists who have been selected to form the institute. Man in committee is one of Snow's most constant subjects in his later novels; here, for the first time, we see such a situation rendered—but Snow's depiction is not as illuminating as it sometimes is later. The committee members argue at great length about such a matter as whether the institute will be located in London, Oxford, or Cambridge. It is true that man in committee reflects the petty failings of human nature, and that important decisions are often determined for petty reasons. But the young Snow had not yet learned the best way to highlight the more revelatory matters and to pass over lightly the least.

Man in committee is a subject seldom depicted heretofore in the novel. Has there been any major novelist who has dealt with it? Snow seems to have stumbled upon it while writing *The Search,* though it may be based on a committee he had personally known. Arthur's professor in London tells him, "You're too much impressed by Committees. . . . When you've served on as many as I have, you won't treat them so respectfully" (225). We do not know whether this is also a fitting statement about Snow as a young man like Arthur. In any case, he has mined this field in fiction that, especially in some of the later novels, provides a number of interesting moments.

Arthur thinks he will certainly become director of the new institute; he feels that at last he will be an important figure in the scientific establishment. But suddenly his hopes are dashed. An experiment he had proclaimed as successful backfires because an assistant had given him a wrong fact and he had been too careless to check it. The committee rejects him as director; Austin, who has backed him and whose protégé Arthur has been, "felt that my future was not as certain to be brilliant as he once hoped, and had to withdraw the support he tentatively thought of

giving" (267). Though the scientists who have judged him and found
him wanting may have acted in the wider interests of science but may
have been motivated by petty reasons (as another old professor of Arthur's
tells him), what they do is good because he has "committed a crime
against the truth. . . . Now if false statements are to be allowed, if they
are not to be discouraged by every means we have, science will lose its one
virtue, truth. The only ethical principle which has made science possible
is that the truth shall be told all the time" (273). Arthur is grievously
distressed, but he sees the justice of this view.

In the last chapter of part 3, entitled "End of a Journey," Arthur
travels to the Continent and indulges in a long struggle within himself, a
search to understand himself. Should he continue in science, which would
mean he would be forced to accept a lesser position than he expected at
the age of 30, or should he go into some other field? He feels that though
he had been devoted to science, that devotion has now faded. There are,
he decides, three main, conscious reasons for becoming a scientist: that
science benefits the world; that it represents the truth; and that it is
enjoyable. The last reason, he decides, is the commonest of all, but it is
not good enough for Arthur: "I should always need faith in the results
before I could enjoy. Human intricacies I might enjoy for their own sake.
But not scientific problems, unless they were important to me for
something richer than themselves" (280–82).

At the end of his soul-searching, Arthur thinks: "I wondered . . . if
this is how priests felt, when their only obstacle to success in the Church is
a troublesome disbelief in God" (283). There is, of course, a great
difference between Arthur's plight and that of a priest troubled by
disbelief: Arthur's is forced upon himself by his own serious mistake and
by the knowledge that he would not achieve success as easily as he had
hoped. Had he not failed in his experiment so foolishly and had his
success not been delayed, we can believe that Arthur would have gone
blithely on through life without one thought of doubt, content to remain
in science. There is thus no real comparison between Arthur and the
priest, but there is no indication anywhere that Arthur recognizes this
difference. It is also revealing that Arthur delays giving up science; he goes
back to the institute and is elected assistant director, and he settles down
for at least three years of work, at the end of which time he feels he will
have regained his former standing in science. When this time comes, he
will be ready to leave science for good: "I wanted to leave science only
when I had retaken my success." No, the comparison between himself
and the priest who genuinely wrestles with his disbelief is not valid at all.

Ultimately, Arthur's "search" is highly factitious, and we cannot refrain from feeling that he is somewhat of a fraud. If he is supposed to be the scientist-as-hero, as several have said,[14] then he is a poor hero. There is nothing heroic about either him or his "search," and we doubt whether Snow intended to portray him as a hero. What Snow is trying to portray, rather, is the difficulty thrown in the path of a scientist who aims for success and who gradually realizes that fraud has no place in the search for scientific truth. His honesty is mainly to himself only in that he finally realizes that he has been in the wrong occupation, that he would never be, at best, more than a "very good second-rater" (299), and that for the sake of his own personal happiness he had better get into some other field, which he finally decides is writing.

This type of honesty is certainly not heroic, and it is incredible to think that anyone could regard Arthur as a cultural hero. R. G. Davis says that in *The Search* science comes off badly,[15] but it is not so much science as scientists that come off badly. One impression left by *The Search* is that if scientists themselves are often fallible creatures, science itself is greater than its practitioners: it represents in its totality the search for objective knowledge of the universe, the knowledge without which truth is warped. But as Arthur comes to realize himself, the truth of science is only a limited, though very necessary, part of what we need to arrive at "truth."

The last part of the novel deals with the beginnings of Arthur's success in writing; a book he is composing about European politics, called *The Gadarene Swine,* later achieves a limited success. At the same time that he pursues his new career, he masterminds the scientific experiments of Sheriff by giving him the ideas he no longer needs himself. Arthur also marries a girl named Ruth, but his help to Sheriff affords him a sense of smug satisfaction because he is the gracious befriender of Audrey's husband in front of his former flame. Indeed, there are several hints that if Audrey would take him back, he would leave Ruth without much compunction. At the end of the book, Sheriff, unwilling to wait for success to come after long, hard, honest work, makes a deliberate mistake: he suppresses false facts in order that his experiment can be proclaimed a success and thereby gain him a coveted university position. "He had committed the major scientific crime (I could still hear Hulme's voice tricking gently, firmly on)" (338).

Arthur is now in a dilemma, and he decides to write a letter exposing Sheriff to the scientific world. He has it in his hands, as he realizes, to wreck Sheriff's career, or at least to sidetrack it for a while just as his own scientific career had been. Then, having written the letter, he tears it up.

"No, he should have his triumph to the full. Audrey should not know, she had seen so many disillusions, I would spare her this" (342–43). Arthur is consoled by the knowledge that eventually some scientist, somewhere, will expose Sheriff's falsehood to the world, for scientific truth must ultimately prevail. But for Arthur the scientific passion is over at last: "Yet I was free of a cloud that for so long had come between me and the future; I was liberated from all the faiths and superstitions, and at last there was only the honesty I should try to keep myself" (342).

The ending is very confusing, and as these thoughts of Arthur's should reveal, he is a very confused man. If science is the radiant search for at least part of the truth, then why does Arthur claim that he is "being liberated from all the faiths and superstitions"? It is hard to see how Arthur's claim for personal honesty can be reconciled with his failure to expose Sheriff. That Sheriff may eventually be exposed because the truth of science will ultimately conquer cannot justify Arthur's action, though he finds satisfaction in knowing that he will not be the instrument of this exposure and that he is cutting the tie that has bound him to science. Isn't Arthur really lending himself to a fraud? How can what he does be construed as really honest? Isn't he really following the path of his desires and then trying to rationalize it?

In his prefatory note in 1958, Snow cautions his readers not to mistake Arthur for himself: "Arthur Miles is not much like me. . . . I was educated as a scientist, as Miles was: but I never had his single-minded passion, and in fact knew my own ultimate vocation from the time I was eighteen." He adds that "Miles's intellectual attitudes are simpler than mine were." This statement is true, but partially confusing: Arthur's passion for science is only single-minded briefly, for he loses it quickly at a fairly young age; his ultimate vocation, writing, comes just a little later in life than in Snow's. It is hard to believe that we are supposed to be wholly sympathetic to Arthur and to agree completely with what he tells us; his simplistic intellectual attitudes are surely quite different in many ways from Snow's—especially those in 1958.

Our strictures against Arthur should not invalidate the interest this book should have as a revealing commentary on the scientific life as practiced in this century. This novel broke new ground, so far as its subject matter was concerned, and it surely must have given Snow the impetus to continue writing novels.

Chapter Five

"Strangers and Brothers":
The Early Novels
of Direct Experience

The structural design of the "Strangers and Brothers" sequence is quite extensive and unusual. The entire sequence covers much of the life of Lewis Eliot, the narrator, who was born in 1905, the same year as his creator—one of a number of reasons for assuming that Eliot is a persona or mask for Snow, though dissimilarities exist. Snow has divided the sequence into two main parts: three novels of Lewis Eliot's direct experience, *Time of Hope* (1949), *Homecomings* (1956), and *Last Things* (1970); the rest, eight in all, are novels of his observed experience with "flickers of inner experience." Many characters and some incidents keep recurring throughout the series, but all of them are viewed through Eliot's mind as he has seen them at various stages of his career. The inner design "consists of a resonance between what Lewis Eliot sees and what he feels."[1] The simplest way to deal with the sequence would be to discuss the novels in the order of publication; however, a better understanding of Eliot (and perhaps of Snow) and of what he was trying to do throughout his life can be acquired by separating the novels in the manner indicated by Snow.

Time of Hope

The third in the sequence to appear, *Time of Hope,* the first novel of direct experience, treats of Eliot's life from 1914 to 1933. The narrative begins when he is a boy of nine, shortly before the beginning of World War I, and concludes when he is becoming established as a lawyer and has tried to separate from his first wife, Sheila Knight, but has found that he cannot, that he has a strong compulsion to continue in his marriage. The title refers primarily to the period during the 1920s before the troubles of the 1930s brought disillusionment, and when young people in Britain felt a wave of optimism about the future. The war "to make the world safe for democracy" and "to end all wars," in Woodrow Wilson's phrases, had ended, and now, mingled with a feeling of revolt against the older generations, hope for humankind existed. As George Passant, Eliot's friend, tells him, "The next few years . . . are going to be a wonderful time to be alive. Eliot, my boy, have you ever thought how lucky you and I are—to be our age at this time of all conceivable times?"[2]

The title also refers to George Passant's personal hopes and to Eliot's: despite grave setbacks at the end of the book, they both have, in their individual ways, a fund of optimism that, we are led to believe, may help them overcome future obstacles in their paths. We see in the later books of the sequence, however, that as the treacherous years pass by, the terrible events that unfold usually darken minds and change optimism to either pessimism or to a more realistic, less romantic appraisal of the human condition; a few of the characters, on the other hand, remain incurably optimistic.

George Passant is one of the latter type—Eliot refers to George's "impervious optimism"; Eliot, who has had much less optimism than George from the beginning, is one who wavers back and forth between optimism and pessimism, between hope and despair, and seems to be, as the sequence progresses, trying to shed his illusions and to confront life as free from them as a human being possibly can be. Eliot to a great extent is, at the end of his narration in the final book, a man to whom a moderate, balanced appraisal of the human condition has finally come, a man who has made his adjustments to the world in what is described as a realistic manner, though not without great personal pain and discomfort.

Like Arthur Miles, Eliot is narrating his story as an older man. But Eliot has a much larger, more varied story to tell, and he does it in a number of books. In *Time of Hope,* Eliot states that if he had his life to live over, "I would chance my luck as a creative writer, in the hope of leaving some sort of memorial behind me" (381). The "Strangers and Brothers" sequence is this memorial: an attempt to portray his life in fiction, using the first-person narration throughout. He relates both what has happened to himself personally and what important events in the lives of friends and acquaintances have made a great impression on him at various times. His narration ends near the time of the writing of the final book, when Eliot, like Snow, is a man well past middle age (at the time of publication of *Last Things,* Snow was 65).[3]

Some critics have wondered that Eliot is able to compartmentalize the various aspects of his career, to keep so many separate and different stories going, and to bring some to the forefront in one book and to relegate them to the background in others while focussing attention on new ones. Such critics have thought this method of narration to be somewhat artificial and unlike what happens in life. On the contrary, it reflects precisely what does happen in life. The narrative is, of course, sometimes confusing and occasionally tedious when Eliot weaves into his narration several different stories at the same time and jumps from one to the other. Much that seems irrelevant here and there in the total context of the sequence finally does become relevant, but some parts (though not many, considering the scope of the whole sequence) appear to be mere padding. In the number of things that have impinged on his life, Eliot's has certainly been a very rich and full one, and though to some there seems at times to be an air of artificiality, of contrivance about it as he piles up myriad details about different aspects of his life, this accumulation of details is one of the things the reader should accept without undue reluctance.

Our abandonment of resistance—the willing suspension of disbelief, in Coleridge's phrase—is not difficult if we realize that in almost every life, particularly in that of a man who has had a long public career, there is contact with many events and people interesting enough for stories. Further, as we all know, some events and people jostle us much more at some periods of our lives than at others; they arouse our interest at one time and not so much at others. The difference is that most of us tend to forget many of our experiences, whereas Eliot apparently has forgotten very little, though it is problematical as to whether he tells his readers everything he knows: there are long lapses of time within each story—in some cases, several years—and surely things must have happened that are not revealed. His mental recall is exceptionally great—and this ability to remember much that the ordinary person would forget is one of the marks of the true creative writer. He has fulfilled what Henry James told the novice writer: "Try to be one of the people on whom nothing is lost!"[4]

Each book in the sequence can be read separately and can be enjoyed for itself, but the individual impression of each volume is greater if we read the entire sequence.[5] Nowhere is this cumulative effect stronger than in the books dealing primarily with Eliot's personal life. His second marriage to Margaret Davidson, in particular, beginning with *Homecomings,* is more revealing when we know the full, unhappy story of his life with Sheila.

Three women have been important in Eliot's life. His mother, Lena Eliot, is the first, but we only get glimpses of her in part 1 of *Time of*

Hope—about 90 pages. The father, Bertie, is almost a nonentity; he is an abject failure in business, is not able to keep his family above the poverty level, and apparently has not vividly impressed his personality upon either his wife or his eldest son, Lewis. The latter's childhood is dominated by his mother, who has instilled in him her own fierce desire for recognition, which constitutes success to both. The most revealing scene in this part of the book is the one in the secondary schoolroom when Eliot presents a 10-shilling note in front of the class. The children have been asked to donate money for the war effort (it is 1917), and despite her poverty, Mrs. Eliot insists on having her son present more than anyone else: "She was not content with doing 'as well as other people.' Her imagination had been fired. She wanted me to give more than anyone in the form. She told herself that it would establish a position for me, it would give me a good start" (50). Eliot is humiliated by a cruel teacher who says, in front of the class, "I wonder you can afford it . . . I wonder you don't feel obliged to put it by towards your father's debts."

But Eliot does not tell his mother what had happened; he invents a story "to save her from a bitter degradation." The lie, he says, "showed the flaw between us." Time and again, throughout this book and later, Eliot's mind reverts to what he feels has been his dominant reaction to his mother: his sense of withholding himself from her, of being detached, a spectator. This sense is one he must fight within himself constantly in both *Time of Hope* and *Homecomings.* He cannot be a true brother to his friends unless he can shed this feeling, he believes; nor can he be a true son or husband. He is a stranger.

The sense of being a stranger, coupled with his intense urge to succeed, one derived from his mother and from the poverty and humiliation of his childhood, motivates Eliot's behavior throughout *Time of Hope.* When he is asked in 1923, at the age of 18, about what he wants in life, he first replies that he wants to see a better world, but for himself, he goes on to say, he wants success, which means not to spend his life as an unknown, and then he wants love (115–16). Unfortunately, for a number of years he is in love, but it is not reciprocated. The story of this tragic love affair concludes in the first section of *Homecomings,* but it is much more intensely told in *Time of Hope:* this is almost the peak of Snow's writing, and it, combined with the imaginatively realized first section of the same novel, makes *Time of Hope* one of the better novels in the entire sequence.

Eliot and Sheila are an ill-mated pair. A man with a more-than-ordinary drive for success who at the same time finds it difficult to give of himself completely needs a woman who will meet him more than halfway. Sheila Knight cannot, because she too is a stranger. Snow's portrait of this unhappy, tormented, neurotic (possibly schizophrenic) woman is extremely vivid. Eliot speculates occasionally on the amount of will an individual must exert to overcome the forces within and without that seem to be arrayed against one's happiness. He has the belief at times, one expressed in this novel and in others, that the individual is caught in a deterministic universe, that willpower amounts to little. Eliot does not always think like this; it is one of the many ideas that he keeps bringing out and examining in his reminiscences of his past life. With the possible exception of his reflections on Roy Calvert in *The Light and the Dark,* nowhere else does he seem to feel the full force of this deterministic view as when he tells about his life with Sheila.

Though she endlessly humiliates and frustrates him, he takes her behavior with seemingly endless endurance, and this unhappy state of affairs continues through their period of courtship (if we can use so quaint a term for the period before their marriage) and through their married life, until it ends with her suicide. Eliot is beset by so many ambivalent feelings about Sheila that it is often difficult to keep up with them; basically, however, he is alternately repelled and charmed by proximity to Sheila or even by the thought of her. At times, he is a masochist, absorbing blow after blow and coming back for more, hating himself every minute because he cannot avoid what he knows he should. At other times, she brings out a cruel streak in him; he becomes sadistic ("sadic" is usually Snow's version of the word, and he uses it often) in tone and spirit but not often in action. Once he does commit what is a virtual rape of Sheila, so forcibly does he take her (and in general, their physical relationship, as he says in *Homecomings,* has "the one-sidedness of rape").

Sheila is basically an honest person, for she warns Eliot many times before and during marriage about what she is (rather what she thinks she is) and about why she will not make him happy. Because of her honesty, our sympathies often go out to her at the same time that we wonder how Eliot can endure their relationship any longer, and we can sympathize with him because of his ordeal.

Though they are dissimilar in many ways, their sexual natures set them apart more than anything else. Eliot wants her in the flesh, and this aspect of marriage lures her not at all: she is frigid, and knows it. Her torment is that she can never satisfy any man or be satisfied in turn. A statement of gossip, bruited about by Eliot's friends (in *Homecomings*), of her possible homosexuality is discounted by Eliot; nevertheless, a discerning reader would have to say that this may be, at least in part, what is wrong with

Sheila. Her excessive interest in Roy Calvert's "innocent" love at 15 for
Jack Cotery (briefly mentioned in *Time of Hope,* but the central situation
in part 1 of *Strangers and Brothers*) may be revealing: the entire
significance of the story for her "lay in the emotion of the boy himself,"
and she says "I wonder what it was like." She says also, most revealingly,
"I wish it had happened to me at his age" (160). Many years after
Sheila's death, her father tells Eliot in *Homecomings:* "She had become
strange before ever you met her or she brought you to my house. . . .
When I told her she was pretty, she shrank away from me. I remember
her doing that when she was six or seven. . . . I used to enjoy saying she
was beautiful. I can see her eyes on me now, praying that I should stop."[6]

There is ambivalence, however, in her nature, and Eliot must endure
her almost constant strivings to find a man who will make her happy. He
is torn by intense jealousy of her interest in the "misfits, waifs, and strays"
that lure her, for she is not attracted at all by the successful, the ordinary,
or the seemingly normal man. A Freudian would make much of this
attraction, which is described in the following passage about her as a girl
in her early twenties: "she would find some teacher . . . timid with
women or unhappily married . . . She had a very alert and hopeful eye
for men whom she thought might fascinate her. In getting to know them,
she rid herself of her self-consciousness; instead of shrinking into a corner,
as she did in company, she was ready to take the initiative herself, exactly
as though she was a middle-aged woman on the prowl for lovers. . . . I
knew that she herself imagined some implacably strong character, some
Heathcliff of a lover who would break her will—but they were all weaker
and gentler than she was" (210).

The pattern for the relationship of Eliot and Sheila is very similar to
that of Marcel and Albertine in Proust's *Remembrance of Things Past.*
When we note that Snow's admiration of Proust is greater than for any
other twentieth-century writer and that Eliot mentions Proust so often in
the course of his narration, we are tempted to conclude that Snow's
conception of the relationship of this ill-fated pair comes directly from
Proust. Eliot and Sheila are Marcel and Albertine, transmuted into
English life and with a few variations. Eliot, like Marcel, with all his
attempts at comprehension, never seems to quite understand what is
bothering the woman he loves. As Pamela Hansford Johnson wrote
(before she married Snow), the difference between Eliot's respective
attitudes toward George Passant and Sheila "is precisely the same as the
difference between Marcel's attitudes towards Charlus and Albertine.
Where the women are concerned, both narrators are too deeply involved

for the judgment that is tempered by pure, objective interest and amusement."[7]

Sheila tells Eliot before their marriage, "I believe in joy" (239). But there is little joy in her; she is one of the most joyless characters in the twentieth-century English novel. She has even less hope (and this is certainly one of the ironies of the book's title), except in some vague sense of hope that she acquires in Eliot's ability to help her somehow, but she does not know exactly how. Neither does Eliot know, and both go pathetically through the motions of marriage for many years, with Eliot giving as much as Sheila will accept and with Sheila giving little beyond her presence in his home. He is possessive in the extreme, and she resists his possessiveness with ferocity. She is egocentric, and he reproaches her bitterly because of it, but in his own way, he is almost as egocentric: he is driven by his fierce desire for success, and he constantly accuses her of standing in his way when he wants to move upward, though she has plainly told him she could never be of service to his ambition.

On many pages of *Time of Hope* he relates how tormented he is that Sheila is preventing the success he knows would certainly be his did he not have her to hold him back, and he wishes there was some way he could get rid of her. But when she does want to leave him for Hugh Smith, Eliot drives Smith away in a ruthless use of power, which he admits to the reader is a terrible thing to do. This act is probably the most awful use of his cunning and wits against Sheila's chances for happiness during their years of married life, but it is not the only one.

Time of Hope nears its end when Eliot decides they must separate for the sake of his peace of mind and to save what is left of his career before it is irrevocably wrecked. But then, while waiting for her to leave, which she insists on doing, he suddenly decides that he cannot allow her to go: her spirit is too frail to withstand the buffets of life alone. "She would move from hotel to hotel, lonely, more eccentric as each year passed. . . . I could not bear to let her. There was no more to it than that. Whatever our life was like, it was endurable by the side of what she faced. I must stay by her. I could do no other" (413).

But that there is more to it "than that" the next few pages make clear; he realizes that his misfortunes are of his own making and that some deep inner compulsion drives him to stay with Sheila:

But I already knew that my bondage to Sheila was no chance. Somehow I was so made that I had to reject my mother's love and all its successors. Some secret caution born of a kind of vanity made me bar my heart to any who forced their way within. I could only lose caution and vanity, bar and heart, the whole of everything I was, in the torment of loving someone like Sheila, who invaded me not at all and made me crave for a spark of feeling, who was so wrapped in herself that only the violence and suffering of such a love as mine brought the slightest glow.

My suffering over Sheila was the release of my vanity. At twenty-eight, walking in the garden on that night after I had tried to escape, they were the deepest parts of myself that I had so far seen. It was not the picture that others saw, for I passed as a man of warm affections, capable of sympathy and self-effacingness. That was not altogether false—one cannot act a part for years; but I knew what lay in reserve. It was not tenderness that was to stop me sending Sheila away, at this time when I knew the cost of keeping her and when my passion was spent. It was simply that she touched the depth of my vanity and suffering, and this was my kind of love. (414–15)

Eliot's kind of love as depicted in *Time of Hope,* like Marcel's in Proust's great work, has the deep tinge of the unhealthy, the warped; it is not Sheila alone who may be the subject for the analyst. Sheila tells him once "You're not as nice as people think" (243). The picture that emerges of Eliot in this novel is that he is a man of many sides, complex; he is, moreover, engaged at times, possibly most of the time, in presenting a mask to the public while underneath he may be considerably different.

We are again, as we were in considering the narration of *The Search,* confronted with the question of the narrator's veracity. Eliot is seemingly baring himself to the reader's gaze, recounting the joys and misfortunes of his life, telling of the good things he has done as well as the most ruthless and horrible. On the surface, his seems to be the frankest of all confessions; but everything that we read is filtered through his own consciousness, and nowhere do we get the chance to see him directly as others see him. Kazin speaks of the "interpretative wariness" of Eliot's mind; this ability to examine, to dissect, to size up people—an ability he has learned from his childhood on—is an excellent cognitive quality that serves him in good stead in his dealing with the society of ambitious and successful people he meets in various corridors of power.[8] Does this "interpretative wariness" operate fully when he is telling us about himself? How can we be sure that, as in the corridors of power, he is not manipulating us for the sake of his own hidden purposes? The answer is that given this type of narration, we can never be sure, but as attentive readers, we must be alert for the nuances of his filtered narration.

Because *Time of Hope* has fewer subplots than most of the other novels in the sequence, it gains in unity and intensity. The attention of the narrator is concentrated almost exclusively on telling the story of his own childhood, the period of his law studies, the first years of law practice, and his relationship with Sheila, which progresses along with the other two aspects of his life. In actuality, it may be said that this novel has no subplots at all; however, interspersed within the details of Eliot's life to 1933 are vignettes of various people Eliot has known during the period: George Passant, whose life is dealt with in greater detail and to much better effect in *Strangers and Brothers* and in *Homecomings;* Mr. and Mrs. Knight, Sheila's parents; Eliot's Aunt Milly; Mr. Vesey, the head clerk at the education office where Eliot works before going into law; Marian, the girl who unrequitedly loves Eliot; and best of all, Herbert Getliffe, the attorney under whose direction Eliot obtains his first training. These vignettes, or short portraits, do not become so extended in this novel that they constitute separate stories distinct from Eliot's rendition of his own life. The narrative gains strength from this lack of distraction.

Homecomings

Homecomings, the second novel of Eliot's direct experience, begins in February 1938 and ends in July 1951. There is a hiatus of five years from the time of the conclusion of *Time of Hope.* Part 1, entitled "Homecoming," continues the account of Eliot's life with Sheila and concentrates on what happens in 1938 until Sheila's suicide in December.

The English title in the plural is the appropriate one; the title of the American edition, *Homecoming,* is not suitable, because it jars with the fact that the novel is shaped to a large extent around a comparison of the bleakness and agony of Eliot's first homecoming in the book's first chapter (which stands symbolically for all the unhappy homecomings he had had during his childhood and later in his first marriage) with the joy and hope he experiences in his homecoming with Margaret, his second wife, at the conclusion of the book. The last part is called "Another Homecoming," and this title helps indicate what Eliot has in mind as he constructs the second section of his own direct, personal experiences. When we realize that this pattern of homecomings gives the novel a great measure of unity, we can see that the comment of some critics that the book is disjointed because the first part really belongs with *Time of Hope* is erroneous.[9]

This realization is not, however, the same thing as saying that *Homecomings* is as unified as *Time of Hope* or that it is as good a novel. One reason for its comparative inferiority is that Margaret is never as interesting a person as Sheila; as one critic has said, the elusive personality of Sheila—neurotic, destructive, and pitiable, yet oddly engaging—is caught and realized beyond that of any other female character in Snow's fiction, and in comparison with Sheila, Margaret is a "mere cypher."[10] One fault in this novel, then, is that after Sheila leaves the book, Margaret, though portrayed as an intelligent, forthright woman, is never able to arouse sufficiently our attention. Snow does better in portraying the warped, the misfit, the eccentric than he does with the merely good or the nearly normal. Yet cannot the same be said of most novelists? And certainly if Eliot himself, the narrator, ever manages to hold our interest throughout the sequence, he does so because he exhibits qualities that at times seem to deviate from those which most people would consider normal or ordinary.

A few pages after the opening of *Homecomings,* Eliot recapitulates his earlier complaint that he had broken his career in trying to look after Sheila and that she was able to "tantalize" him for years because he loved her and she did not return his love. But she could not love anyone: "she tried to find psychiatrists and doctors who would tell her why she could not" (5). Nothing has changed in the five-year interim between the novels. We are told that Eliot's own peculiar nature sought such a marriage. The root of his nature, "from which the amiable and deceptive parts" grew, "was not so pretty." "At the springs of my nature," he says, "I had some kind of pride or vanity which not only made me careless of myself but also prevented me going into the deepest human relation on equal terms." And he is again obsessed with "the question, which now found itself quite clear: *what shall I do with Sheila?*" (Snow's italics; 48–49).

In the last year of Sheila's life she becomes fitfully engaged (she cannot maintain a steadfast interest in anything outside herself) in aiding the career of R. S. Robinson, a tricky, unscrupulous publisher who had once been prominent and successful but who is now existing by the ability of his wits to capture the financial help of gullible women. Robinson is one of Snow's finest portraits; he is brought to life vividly in just a few pages. He is the last of the "strays" whom Sheila has picked up in her life: Eliot now calls them "lame dogs" and says she can be selfless only with them: "they gave her a flash of hope" (8).

Not only does Sheila invest money in Robinson's flimsy publishing concern, but he has flattered her, as he does all his female benefactors, into thinking that she has literary ability. She tries to hide her writing from Eliot, but one day he surprises her. She slams the exercise book, into which she tried to write, and cries " 'It's not fair.' . . . like an adolescent girl caught in a secret." Nothing much comes from this pathetic woman's attempts, and her disintegration moves quickly to its climax. She gives up Robinson, realizing that she has been tricked; Robinson has also spread gossip around that is derogatory to Sheila—that she is unbalanced and that she prefers women. It is his unique way of repaying benefactors: his "fibre made him savage anyone who had been of use to him" (44).

Sheila's last attempt at salvaging her life is to obtain a job that will begin on 1 January. As the time moves closer to that date, her anxiety increases; she tells Eliot she can't do it. Eliot tells her, on the fateful morning of 20 December, that "if you get out of this, you'll get out of everything else in the future, except just curling up into yourself. . . . It's better for you to come through this, even if it means a certain amount of hell." And as he relates, "I was speaking sternly. I believed what I said; if she surrendered over this test, she would relapse for good and all into her neurosis; I was hoping, by making my sympathy hard, to keep her out of it. But also I spoke for a selfish reason. I wanted her to take this job so that she would be occupied and so as least partially off my hands. In secret, I looked forward to January as a period of emancipation" (73–74).

His emancipation comes sooner than expected. Next morning, when he returns home after a night at his club, he finds that Sheila is dead from an overdose of sleeping tablets. His emotions are as mixed as those he had felt when advising Sheila the day before: "I seemed at a distance from my own pain: somehow, dimly, numbly, I knew that grief and remorse were gnawing inside me, twisting my bowels with animal deprivation, with the sensual misery of loss. And also I felt the edge of a selfish and entirely ignoble fear. I was afraid that her suicide might do me harm; I shied from thinking of what kind of harm, but the superstitious reproach hung upon me, mingled with remorse. The fear was sharp, practical and selfish" (79–80). The curtain thus rings down, amid Eliot's mingled feelings of grief, remorse, and relief, on a most unhappy, harrowing marriage.

Part 1 takes up 91 pages. The last four parts cover about 300 pages and have three main themes: Eliot's love for Margaret and his subsequent marriage; Eliot's successful work in government; and a phase in the life of George Passant (intertwined with the second theme) during which he joins the government office as Eliot's assistant and finally is dismissed and sent back to the provincial town. The space of time dealt with is 10 years, from 1941 to 1951, from wartime England to the postwar world.

Very soon after Eliot meets Margaret the thought of marriage enters his mind, but he scrutinizes her carefully "to make sure there was no resemblance [to Sheila], to be convinced that anyone I so much as thought of was totally unlike what I had known" (102). It is not long before they are cohabiting together, but Margaret resists legal marriage itself. She is not sure of his attitude toward her and toward marriage itself. "You were standing outside all the time," she says. "Are you looking for the same thing again?" He tells her that he hopes not, but later he feels "that it was natural I should trust myself so little about another marriage after the horror of the first" (139). Margaret dislikes the dilemmas of conscience and egotism that come to those who are in the official world, the corridors of power. Though Eliot is now burrowing into this world successfully, she is convinced he would be a better man without such dilemmas (147).

Margaret decides to leave Eliot after she hears from Gilbert Cooke, his assistant in his government post, that Sheila had committed suicide. When she confronts Eliot with the charge of withholding the truth from her, his reaction is to vow to get rid of Cooke because of his malice, though as Margaret points out to him, Cooke had meant his talk only as idle gossip. She tells Eliot, "With those who don't want much of you, you're unselfish, I grant you that. . . . With anyone who wants you altogether, you're cruel. Because one never knows when you're going to be secretive, when you're going to withdraw. With most people you're good . . . but in the end you'll break the heart of anyone who loves you" (163). In the last chapter of part 2, she tells him she is to marry Geoffrey Hollis, a young physician. It is now 1943.

Part 2 is entitled "The Self-defeated," which is indicative of Eliot's realization of what he had been during his relationship with Margaret. It is revealing to note also that near the end of their affair, he starts dreaming of Sheila, but before the dream is ended, he discovers she is really Margaret. As a result, he realizes that points of identity exist between them and that there are even facial resemblances. The titles of the third and fourth parts are no less indicative of his conception of himself during the three or four years without Margaret until he becomes her lover again: "Condition of a Spectator" and "The Undetached."

Shortly after the end of the war, Eliot and Margaret find that they are still in love and embark on a clandestine affair. She is a mother and seemingly a fond wife of a man she admires, but she cannot fight her strong love for Eliot. She wants to hide their affair, but Eliot argues that secrecy and lies would mean the corrosion of every human relationship. After a delay to allow Hollis to pass his examinations as a specialist, they inform him of their intentions. Margaret gets her divorce quietly, and Eliot marries her in the late summer of 1947. He has now acquired a family because Margaret obtains custody of her child, Maurice. Eliot's only child is born in September 1948 and is given the name of Charles George Austin—the George after Passant.

The presentation of Eliot's love affair and marriage with Margaret has a thinner emotional texture, as one critic has pointed out, than that of his relationship to Sheila, not only because Sheila is more interesting than Margaret but also because during the period with Margaret he is, or seems to be, almost wholly absorbed in the world of affairs. Their relationship is presented as rather perfunctory, as on a level with one of his absorbing encounters in his official life. The melodramatic illness of Eliot's child is perhaps introduced near the end to give the relationship more weight.[11] This illness, however, which should be moving, is far from convincing.

The climax of *Time of Hope*, on the other hand, is much more convincing: it seems right, despite the slight element of surprise at the end (Eliot's sudden decision to stay with Sheila), because we have been adequately shown throughout that novel just what kind of marriage they have had and what they themselves have been for a long while. But in *Homecomings* we have scarcely been told about the birth of his son before almost three years elapse and we are plunged into a narration of the illness, whose only conflict or high point (and a slight one it is) is Eliot's unwillingness for a short while to have Geoffrey Hollis, Margaret's ex-husband, called in to assist Charles March in treating the child. Things happen like this in real life very often, but an exact imitation of life is in itself not enough: the imitation must convince; it must seem right. This last part, which does neither, is a glaring weakness in *Homecomings*.

A fortnight after the child's recovery is assured by Hollis, Eliot and Margaret walk homeward from his office together, and Eliot has supposedly learned in a manner convincing to him, as he had stated earlier (while waiting for the birth of his son), that in "a true relation—I had evaded it for so long—one could not absent oneself, one could not be above the battle, one fought it out" (338). He could not be a spectator; however benevolent, he could not be detached. He had to accept the irony of receiving help from the man (Hollis) whose life he had wronged; supposedly this incident also proves that he cannot reject the hand of friendship whenever and wherever offered, even if extended not wholly unselfishly: Hollis had the moral initiative in helping those who had wronged him, and for Eliot and Margaret, who were, in a sense, "in his hands," their feeling of resentment and shame is swept away by their gratitude (397).

And they return home together, and now the dread he had felt many times in his life before is gone. "It was a homecoming such as I had imagined when I was lonely, but as one happening to others, not me" (400). This ending, which rounds off the second main movement of Eliot's life, complements or contrasts, as we have noted, with the dreaded homecoming at the beginning of this novel (and also with the homecoming at the beginning of *Time of Hope*). Eliot's state of mind is now seemingly one of peace and happiness: he has come home in a true sense. Did we not know that Eliot will have more crises to face in later years (ones treated in the novels published before *Homecomings*) and that there is especially to be another novel of direct experience, we would be tempted to say, "All's well that ends well," or to enunciate some similar phrase of benediction.

Large segments of the second, third, and fourth parts of *Homecomings* are about Eliot's work in government, his public life in the corridors of power, and they are therefore similar to what is in most of the novels of observed experience. Here we meet Paul Lufkin (later Lord Lufkin), the business entrepreneur for whom Eliot had worked for a few years as a law consultant up to the period of the first few chapters of this novel. Sometime in 1938, around the time of the Munich crisis, Eliot joins a government department that supervises the semisecret and secret scientific establishments, such as the one at Barford where the early work on atomic fission (treated in detail in *The New Men*) is being conducted. Here also are Thomas Bevill, the minister of the department, and Hector Rose, the permanent secretary, and under these two Eliot works directly as chief of a section; by 1941 he "had made, in those anonymous couloirs, some sort of reputation" (98).

Several dilemmas of conscience and egotism come to Eliot in *Homecomings*. One has to do with Lufkin, whom Eliot admires as a business leader; he and Rose, of those Eliot knew in the early years of the war, were the ones with the most aptitude for power. In "the great political divide" before the war, Lufkin, Rose, and Bevill had been supporters of the Munich settlement and were therefore "on the opposite side." Yet after war came, Lewis had to acknowledge that the three were as "whole-hearted as men could be. Compared with my friends on the irregular left, their nerves were stronger" (123). This surprise is one of many that come to Eliot in his experience in the corridors of power, and he learns he cannot always tell from the political views of those engaged in public affairs just how they will react during moments of crisis. These Tories, who seemed before the war not very strong in their opposition to

Hitler, were among the staunchest opponents of Nazism after the war began.

Eliot's dilemma is that Lufkin wants a government contract to supply material to the Barford establishment; he presses Eliot and Cooke, both of whom are grateful to Lufkin for past favors, to act in his behalf. They recommend, however, that the contract be awarded to another firm that has a greater supply of the engineers needed. The chapter entitled "Gigantesque" deals with the meeting of the government officials and Lufkin. Later on in the war Eliot realizes that he had been wrong in keeping Lufkin out. He makes amends for one of his worst official mistakes by recommending Lufkin for a subsequent government contract.

Another dilemma is the one previously mentioned: Eliot's decision to ask for the transfer of Gilbert Cooke, who has been a strong supporter of his, just because of personal animosity aroused by Cooke's gossip about Sheila. In this act Eliot behaves in an ignoble manner, as Margaret points out to him, and makes another mistake. The most interesting and painful dilemma is that which concerns George Passant, whom Eliot recommends to succeed Cooke. *Strangers and Brothers* (written earlier) had told the story of Passant during the 1920s and early 1930s, culminating in a scandal that had almost wrecked his career and that even now tarnished his reputation. When Eliot recommends Passant at the end of 1943 to Rose, Passant is still a law clerk in a provincial town. For 20 years he has made no improvement in his status. Rose is impressed by George's intellectual ability and by his high examination record, but he tells Eliot there must be something wrong with a man who has been content with a fourth-rate job.

Despite Rose's strong opposition, Eliot insists that Passant be hired. "It was war-time . . . my job was regarded as exacting and in part it was abnormally secret. In the long run I had to be given my head. But I knew that I should have to pay a price." The price is that he has offended his superior, who tells Eliot that his insistence on Passant is an error in judgment. "If I had been a real professional, with a professional's ambitions, I could not have afforded to." To many of his friends, Eliot reflects, his interest in success and power is "forbiddingly intense." "And, of course," he adds, "they were not wrong: if a man spends half his time discussing basketball, thinking of basketball, examining with passionate curiosity the intricacies of basketball, it is not unreasonable to suspect him of a somewhat excessive interest in the subject." Yet now, in 1943, he thinks that his preoccupation with success and power is waning. Though his interest in power had started off "greater than that of most reflective men," it was "not a tenth of Lufkin's or Rose's, nothing like enough to last me for a lifetime." Sooner or later, he felt, he would become a writer, and even now he is keeping notebooks and is writing in them late at night. "It gave me a kind of serenity; it was like going into a safe and quiet room" (194–96).

During the remainder of the war, George Passant serves the department and Eliot loyally and in an extremely able manner; at the same time, he is enjoying London life with all the gusto of his strong sensual nature. When the war ends and it becomes necessary for the heads of departments to decide on the future disposition of their principal employees, it seems to Eliot that George must be retained. Passant's recapitulation of his accomplishments to Rose and the other committee members who sit in judgment on him is nothing less than masterly, and to Eliot it is unthinkable that any fair-minded man can reject him. But Eliot fails to take one important point into account: he is not always dealing with fair-minded people, and "Rose was not the man to forget his own judgements." Eliot is shocked when Rose makes undue use of his power to convince the committee that Passant should be dismissed on the ground that there is a finite chance that they would be making trouble for themselves in the future if they retained so "powerful, peculiar and perhaps faintly unstable personality," especially one George's age. Eliot loses his temper: "I said they were too fond of the second-rate. I said that any society which deliberately makes safe appointments was on the way out" (317). He accuses them of being prejudiced, but he loses and Passant must go.

Eliot is wretched; if he were in a position of greater power, he could have saved his friend and others who are worthy. He pronounces judgment on those who are in power: "The men I sat with in their offices, with their moral certainties, their comfortable, conforming indignation which never made them put a foot out of step—they were the men who managed the world, they were the people who in any society come out on top" (318). But he is faced with the sad task of telling his friend of his dismissal. George, after initial rage, reacts with his "invulnerable optimism." He has had three interesting years, he tells Eliot, and he produces some ingenious and unrealistic interpretations of why Rose and the others find it necessary to let him go. To Eliot, George seems to be a happy man: "it was the happiness which comes to those who believe they have lived according to their nature." And so George can joke about himself as Eliot sadly watches his departure on the "last train to a provincial town."

This section is certainly one of the better parts of an uneven novel. Snow makes us "see" Passant in the final period of his London days; rather than just reflecting about him, as he often does about people, through the penumbra of his own emotional feelings, he makes us "see" Passant as a quixotic, somewhat naive, self-deceived, and even clownish figure who is very much out of touch with the world of power politics in London, and who is content to go home to the little town after his three-year splurge in the big city. There is an inevitability about Passant's departure (we wonder if his name was chosen deliberately: he is one whom more astute and stronger people pass by) that is curiously effective: it is the inevitable fate that comes to many good, though flawed people who are cut down by outside forces too strong to overcome.

Yet in a way, Passant's fate is partially of his own making. If George had been different—a shrewder, a more astute, a more aggressively pragmatic individual—he might have survived in London and made a success on the world's terms, and Eliot's dilemma would have been more happily resolved. Though the novel ends on a note of happiness and renewed hope for Eliot, it is hard to forget that Passant and Sheila have been cut down—weaklings in a hard world. They are two of Snow's most impressive creations of character.

If Eliot is correct that George is at harmony with himself at last (though the portrait of him in *Strangers and Brothers* may be at variance with this view), we cannot for long retain a feeling of sadness at his failure; perhaps he is the luckiest of all in being finally out of the vicious atmosphere in the corridors of power. George may be intended as a kind of counterpoise to Eliot, who, though sometimes condemnatory, is not for long content to remain out of the struggle for success and power. For Eliot, there has not yet come such luck as has come to George; Eliot is still a man divided within himself, torn between what he wants to be and what he is, despite the happy and peaceful atmosphere at the end of the book.

Chapter Six

"Strangers and Brothers": The Novels of Observed Experience

Strangers and Brothers

Strangers and Brothers (whose 1940 title was changed in 1970 to *George Passant*) is meant to be the first novel of observed experience in the sequence.[1] The action, which occurs between 1925 and 1933, is dominated by the character of George Passant. The scene is a provincial town in the Midlands where Passant works as assistant solicitor and chief clerk in a law office; on the side, he gives evening lectures on law twice a week at a local technical college, the town's only semblance of an institution of higher learning. Passant is 26 in 1925, and Eliot, who has been attending his lectures, is 20.

The narrative line of this novel is comparatively simple: part 1 is about Passant's saving of Jack Cotery from the loss of his scholarship at the college and his thereby gaining a minor triumph; the name of this part is, appropriately, "The Triumph of George Passant." The other parts deal primarily with Passant's indictment, along with that of Cotery and a young woman named Olive, on charges of conspiracy to defraud and to obtain money by false pretenses. A trial takes place; the accused, being found not guilty, are set free; but Passant's reputation is tarnished. In part 1, Eliot is still living in his hometown, and as one of Passant's protégés, he is a direct observer of his activities and a participant in the Group (always capitalized) that Passant has gathered around him. In the last three parts, Eliot is living in London, but as Passant's friend and as a rising young lawyer, he is called in to be the chief attorney for the defense in the conspiracy case.

In part 1, Jack Cotery is threatened with the loss of his scholarship and his job because Roy Calvert, Jack's employer's son, has given him as a present a silver cigarette case. Unfortunately, a note of excessive endearment sent by Roy, a boy of 15, to Jack has been read by Mr. Calvert, who interprets the letter as evidence of Jack's corruption of his

56

son and demands that the college not renew Jack's scholarship. (This story, told by Eliot to Sheila in *Time of Hope,* aroused her sympathy for Roy and her wish that at his age she could have had a love like that happen to her.) When George Passant makes an impassioned plea in Jack's behalf, the college renews Jack's scholarship for one more year. It is only a partial victory, for Jack has lost his job, but George and his friends decide that a great victory has been won that is worthy of celebration.

Cooper's claim that this novel is the most difficult of the sequence is based partly on his view that George Passant is a psychological rarity, one unlike any other character the reader may have experienced.[2] Only comparatively may this novel be considered difficult, and only because George is a fairly difficult human being to understand. That he is a psychological rarity cannot be given credence: tormented, bifurcated individuals like George are strewn throughout the pages of literature— Hamlet and Raskolnikov are outstanding examples. George is not on their scale in the intensity or grandeur of authorial conception. He is at best a very minor Hamlet or Raskolnikov set in the world of the twentieth century, but he is vividly realized nevertheless. (Cooper calls him "triumphantly realized.")[3]

The reader may be struck by the difference between George in this book and in *Homecomings.* It may be true (as we are told in the later book) that George as a middle-aged man in 1946 has finally found a deep sense of harmony in his nature and is contented at last to return to the provincial town and to his job, menial at best, in the law firm, where he will stay for much of the remainder of his life. This view, however, is greatly at variance with him as seen in *Strangers and Brothers,* where he is portrayed as being at odds with himself and with certain aspects of society, and there is no indication at the conclusion that he will ever resolve his difficulties. We might also add that much later, in *The Sleep of Reason,* he is very much the same person as in this first book.

Early in part 2, Lewis Eliot refers to George as one of "the rebels of the world" and then observes that George has a deep respect for the solid law firm of Eden and Martineau, but this attitude is natural, Eliot thinks, because rebels are not indifferent to authority and institutions.[4] Some would find Eliot's view of what constitutes a rebel shallow, and George is certainly not a rebel in the usual sense of the word, whatever Eliot may think. But a few elements of George's nature are antagonistic against the narrow provincialism of the town's older generation. Young men like George could be found in every medium-size or large city in England and America in the years after World War I: those who chafed at the mess the older people had made and who felt that a new freedom was needed for the young. People "get on best when they're given freedom," George tells his Group early in the book, "particularly freedom from their damned homes, and their damned parents, and their damned lives" (16). This statement seems to be the extent of his rebelliousness; there is no indication that he wants more than a possibly mild kind of democratic English socialism, and we can imagine him as a devoted follower of Ramsay MacDonald's Labour party in the 1920s. In politics, he is probably much like his creator, but he lacks Snow's intellectual grasp of Labour's platform.

George's Group meets on weekends at a place in the country they call "the Farm"; they talk vaguely of a new freedom, and George holds out hope to them, expressed in the most general and unintellectual terms, of a better new world in which social justice will prevail and in which the younger generation will be free of the heavy-handed restrictions of the elderly. They do not plot revolution; they seem to have no desire to tear down governments or institutions. Their animosity is directed solely against what they conceive to be the narrow Victorian conventions of their elders in politics, religion, and morality.

Though George is praised by Eliot for his intellectual ability, George's comprehension of the individual and of society is primarily on the intuitive level and is not based on an intensive study of the major thinkers who have dissected the world of the past or the present. Though he is intelligent and has a good grasp of the practical applications of the law, enough at least to be able to lecture to novices in a provincial town, no intimation is given that he is aware of the broader philosophical implications of legal thought. Eliot says several times that of all the men he has known, George is built along the lines of a great man, and he quotes other members of the Group to the same effect. But we are never told or shown what constitutes George's greatness, and it is extremely doubtful that these young people know much of the lineaments of greatness. It does take courage for George, a law clerk in a small town, to take up Cotery's defense against the power structure of the college, especially since there is a tinge of sexual deviance about the charge, and perhaps this act, to Eliot, reveals George's potentiality for greatness.

Eliot himself, moreover, soon sees that George's triumph is a very limited one, for he has actually been outmaneuvered by the governing committee in giving Cotery only a one-year scholarship. Whether intended as part of his design by Snow or not, what the rest of the novel actually depicts is not only the pathetic defeat of Passant but also the error of Eliot's high regard for him—the deficiencies in Eliot's early judgment of George. The story of Passant, in one respect, is a study of the dangers of ambition in its incipient stages and of how easy it is for the traditional, conventional forces in society to undercut the urge for power when it appears.

George has grandiose, though vague plans to use his Group to further his ambitions. Despising what he calls the bellwethers of the town (the term *Establishment* had not yet been coined), he takes great pride in his ability to lead the unconventional young; he needs the Group as much as they seem to need him, because a leader always needs followers. The only older person he respects is Howard Martineau, whom he refers to as the "only spiritual influence in the whole soulless place." Unfortunately for George, Martineau, upon whom he has been depending to take him into the firm and thereby help him achieve his monetary goals, turns out to be a disappointment. Martineau throws up his partnership and eventually leaves the town as a religious itinerant, determined to save his own soul and happy to abstain from the pleasures of the senses; he becomes known as Old Jesus. He is in direct contrast to George, who has turned away from his parents' religion and who delights in sensual pleasures to the point of debauchery.

Most leaders have their defects and make mistakes because of them that are often fatal, and so it is with George Passant. That George's optimistic confidence may be only a mask can be seen occasionally. Eliot calls George's confidence that he is indispensable to his law firm "optimism gone mad." George replies that he had to have his triumph in the case of Cotery because "I've never had much confidence, and I knew it would take a triumph to prove to myself that I've a right to do as I please." Besides, he asks, what would happen to everyone in his Group if he went away? Eliot replies, "One or two of us you've affected permanently. . . . But the others—in time they'd become what they would have been if you'd never come." "I won't have it," George exclaims, "Good God above, I won't have it. . . . I refuse to contemplate it" (85–86). Earlier, when one of the girls in the Group says she believes that George would have done something big had the Group not made things pleasant for him, Eliot sees, in one of his numerous sudden flashes of insight (which to some critics have been annoying devices in Snow's technique because Eliot has too many of them), that the Group has been a defense for George to protect him from the uncomfortable and superior world.

Eliot's insight in this case is correct. Having drastically broken away from his parents' influence (and Eliot sees several times George's heated arguments with his parents over money, religion, and his general behavior, of which they disapprove), George has had to make his way altogether on his own. He regards the world of the respectable, conventional bourgeoisie, the bellwethers of society, as being against him in his efforts to move upward. Every triumph he can obtain, no matter how small, confirms George in his belief in his own ability. If he suffers defeats, these will mean that he lacks the quality needed to defeat both his parents and the bellwethers, the people who are holding down the young like himself. George will not recognize the realities of almost every situation he is in, because he demands triumphs everywhere and because he refuses to admit the possibility that some times he will fail. For these reasons, when George clearly sees (as Eliot later discovers through a reading of his diary) that the business ventures Jack has led him into are probably shady, if not fraudulent, he refuses to stop, though he knows he ought to do so. He cannot admit failure and poor judgment; he cannot bear to think of the loss of the Farm and his leadership of the Group upon which he has based his hopes. George, like most would-be leaders, believes that the mere thought of the possibility of failure is to admit his innate inferiority in the eyes of the world.

What happens to George in the latter parts of *Strangers and Brothers* is pathetic because it destroys all his attempts to prove himself the leader he aspires to be. Eliot uses the right adjective later on, years later, in referring to George's "impervious optimism," though there is no indication on the surface of Eliot's narration that he has recognized the undercurrent meaning of his terminology: Eliot seems to give the impression that George's optimism is so firmly ingrained in his nature that nothing can ultimately shake it. But George's optimism is really a bold attempt to mask his deep dissatisfaction with and his lack of confidence in himself. Any personal failure must be rationalized as the fault of his enemies, the bellwethers—and George does plenty of this type of projection. His optimism must be, for the sake of his own inner needs, "impervious" to criticism.

George has other defects, and these are closely connected with his main defect. How is it possible to separate his excessive association with prostitutes over a period of years from his real lack of confidence in himself and from his imperviousness to criticism that would undermine the mask he wears to face the world? George asks in his diary, "Why am I so attracted by prostitutes?" No simplistic answer can be given, but we can suggest that one cause of his sexual debauchery is that prostitutes do not question motives or anything else about him: his relationship with them is strictly on a cash basis. He is a man with strong physical drives; though he says he wants real love, and in fact at one time seems to be considering marriage with a girl named Daphne, nothing ever comes of it. He never marries. Prostitutes are safer for George; they do not make demands.

Another defect is that despite his low income and his need for money, he often squanders what he does have. Eliot notices this trait and wonders at it. George cuts his parents' allotment for Jack's sake and then throws away the little he has left on his sensual pleasures. Squandering money indiscriminately as George often does may very well come from the same desperate internal needs—to indulge himself in an attempt to erect a carapace against the demands of life.

When Eliot receives, in December 1932, a phone call asking him to come to the aid of the accused trio, he is reading Thomas Wolfe's first novel (162). Whether this fact has any symbolic significance is unclear and probably doubtful, but the title of the book (unmentioned), *Look Homeward, Angel,* is appropriate: Eliot, whose career has been inching forward in areas far apart from George and the Group, is now called upon to look homeward to help the man who has done the most to give him his start in life.

Though Eliot is involved with his own professional affairs as well as with his devastating marriage, he cannot resist his desire to aid George. "Not by virtue," Lewis had stated earlier, "but simply by temperament, I was bound by chains to anyone who had ever really touched my life; once they had taken hold of me, they had taken hold for good" (143). A reasonable answer to those who are skeptical of Eliot's penchant to compartmentalize his life throughout the sequence of novels: to become actively engaged in someone else's affairs, often over a long period of time, and to be at the same time engaged in activities of his own or of entirely different people. Eliot is simply one of those very rare persons who can find time to take part in a multitude of activities, especially if they concern persons whose lives have taken hold of his imagination or, as in the case of George, his emotions. He is bound to George by great emotional ties; this bond explains also, more than anything else, why he recommends George during the war for a position in his government department (*Homecomings*).

Eliot takes charge of the case during its earlier stages and becomes aware of the animosity among the bellwethers of the community toward George and his Group. Because of this animosity, Eliot is forced to allow an older attorney, Herbert Getliffe, to present the case to the jury, who, he is told, will be prejudiced against younger people and particularly so if their attorney is of the same age.

It is evident that in this case the legal aspects are overshadowed by moral questions. Particularly damaging to George is his confession in court that his Farm had become a "haunt of promiscuity." Getliffe, however, cleverly makes the most of it, but what he says is damaging to George's dignity and to his desire to establish himself as a man in control of his own destiny. Getliffe's speech is primarily about the difference between the generations, and in presenting it he agrees with the jury's prejudices while at the same time showing them Passant's innocence. Passant, he declares, is a child of his time: "he represents a time and generation that is wretchedly lost by the side of ours." We had something solid to hold on to, he asserts: our religion, a decent hope for the future. These young people are children of their time; if they wasted lives, blame the times, not them. We're not trying them for being wasted; we're not trying them for their fatal idea of freedom, he insists in conclusion.

The effect of what has happened in the court, even before the jury's verdict of not guilty on all counts, is devastating to George and his followers. George receives notice of his dismissal as a teacher in the college; Rachel, a follower, has been asked to leave her job. But George insists on taking full responsibility: "I am utterly prepared to answer for my soul." He does not want the responsibility shifted to the fact that he is a child of his time, as Getliffe had suggested. Eliot says to himself that Getliffe was not altogether wrong, but what he saw was only half-true. George "could not be generalized into a sample of the self-deluded radicalism of his day."

But while George was in the dock, Eliot reflects, he had felt toward George much the same as Olive had (who meanwhile had told Eliot privately that George, led by Jack, was indeed guilty of deception and fraud in raising money). "I flinched from the man who was larger than life, and yet capable of any self-deception; who was the most unselfseeking and generous of men, and yet sacrificed everything for his own pleasures; who possessed formidable powers and yet was so far from reality that they were never used; whose aims were noble, and yet whose appetite for degradation was as great as his appetite for life; who, in the depths of his heart, was ill-at-ease, lonely, a diffident stranger in the hostile world of men" (308).

The novel concludes as George and Eliot walk together into town. Eden has promised to take George back into his firm, but he has little or no chance of ever becoming a partner. George is bitter because of the insinuation that everything he has ever done "was because I was a sensualist," but he has hope for the future. He insists he'll not give people the satisfaction of living as they do. He plans to leave Eden's firm after a few months and try to work his way through to a partnership elsewhere; he'll show everybody that what has happened will not prevent him from going on. Eliot, however, thinks, "It was himself in whose sight he needed to be seen unchanged. In his heart a voice was saying: 'You can't devote yourself again. You never have. Your enemies are right. You've deceived yourself all this time. And now you know it, you can't begin deceiving yourself again!'" Yet in the last sentences of the book Lewis concludes: "both he and I were still eager for what life would bring. He could still warm himself and everyone round him with his own hope" (319–20).

A vexing question arises: how are we to interpret this ending and, in fact, the whole conception of George Passant? It can easily be seen that Eliot is not merely a recorder of what happens, that he does often present his own reflections, and that he makes frequent value judgments. But what makes it difficult to know what Snow is trying to do is that he presents Eliot as recording the pros and cons of what he sees and hears in seemingly the same manner; likewise, Eliot makes pro and con value judgments about many of his characters, like George Passant, and about what happens so that the reader is confused about where Eliot really stands. Snow, through Eliot, refuses to take his stand; he leaves Passant to our judgment, but we are left wondering at the conclusion of this fascinating portrait of Passant, undoubtedly the best that Snow has done, just what our reactions are supposed to be. We wish that Snow had shown Passant through at least a few other eyes than Eliot's; it does not help matters much that we are given a few pages of Passant's own diary, for Passant reveals a balanced ledger of the good and the bad in himself.

I said in my concluding remarks about *Homecomings* that Passant is a good man. He has many defects of character, but his goodness is not entirely canceled by them. In another context and in another age, such a person as Passant (if he had been, of course, of aristocratic lineage) would have been considered a heroic character in the traditional mold who has suffered a fall by reason of the fates and his personal defects, such as his hubris, the Greek word for excessive pride in one's abilities. That Eliot considers him in this light can be seen by some of his comments about Passant, such as his references to him as one who is larger than life and as one who has left his mark for goodness on the lives of at least a few of his followers, especially on Eliot himself. To Eliot, this goodness is probably all that counts ultimately, for if he had believed that the bad in Passant voided the good, he would not have offered George his second chance years later.

What is extremely doubtful, however, about a man like George is that he would ever have resolved his personal difficulties to the extent of being at ease within himself and content with his lot in life as a clerk in Eden's office. "I don't want to stay there as a subordinate and watch myself grow old," he tells Lewis in one place (119). And in his diary he writes: "It will not be so easy to die in obscurity as I once thought" (210) and "if I neglect that work [his helping his friends], there is nothing left of me except an ordinary man and a handful of sensations" (208).

Eliot's belief in George's ultimate contentment (see *Homecomings*) is the result of his blindness; he is deceived once again by the mask that George presents, as he leaves London, to hide the grief in his own heart, for one of the themes of the sequence of novels is undoubtedly that self-deception, the maintenance of illusions, is strong in the human heart. We find it in Eliot and in Passant; they both are paradigms of a common human failing—people's ability to shut their eyes to truth, especially if they are ever instilled with the quest for power, be it large or small. George is ultimately left at the end of this book, and again at the end of *Homecomings,* as "an ordinary man and a handful of sensations." I find it difficult to believe that this fate would ever suffice a man like George, though life twice (and possibly three times, if we consider what happens in *The Sleep of Reason*) batters him to that abject state. This fate is his pathos—or tragedy (depending, of course, on our outlook).

The Conscience of the Rich

The Conscience of the Rich (1958) should really be the second novel in the sequence, as Snow indicates in his Author's Note. He also says that the resonance between what Eliot sees and what he feels will now be clearer to his readers; that the theme of possessive love is introduced through Mr. March's relationship with his son, a theme that reappears in *The New Men* and in *Homecomings;* and that through Charles March, Eliot observes both the love of power and the renunciation of power.[5]

One of the things that should intrigue a reader who comes to this novel immediately after reading *Strangers and Brothers*—and also after reading the two earlier novels of Eliot's direct experience—is the close parallel between George Passant and Charles March. These two men have in their different ways aided Eliot's early career as a lawyer, but George's direct influence ends where Charles March's begins. At the conclusion of the bar examinations, for which George had spent long hours in preparing Eliot, the long friendship of Charles and Eliot actually begins to take root, though they had had a casual acquaintanceship during their student days in the Inns of Court. The examinations take place in the summer of 1927, and in January of the following year Eliot is introduced to the rest of the March family; this connection, through Charles, leads to acquaintance with several leading figures in London law firms who give Eliot his first important cases, thereby helping him up the first difficult step in his chosen profession. Other parallels between Passant and Charles will be noticed later.

The Conscience of the Rich has one inherent difficulty not present in any other novel in the sequence: Eliot is an observer of the behavior of a Jewish family, a difficult theme for a non-Jew. Snow succeeds reasonably well in capturing the flavor of the March family, and he does so in his most objective manner. Had he been less objective, he might have failed, for an outsider who tells the story of any ethnic group must tread warily lest he distort his subject because of any bias he may have, whether pro or con. Though Eliot develops a keen appreciation of the Marches, he tells their story as an almost completely impartial and reserved observer; restrained by nature, he is now even more so.

The Marches are not just an ordinary Jewish family; they are unique in belonging to the highest level of Anglo-Jewish society, and Eliot sees for the first time the opulence and glitter of the lives of the very wealthy. The Marches are extremely conscious not only of their position of social leadership in their narrow milieu but also of their Jewishness, which sets them apart from the rest of English life. They have maintained their position and attitudes for generations, but now, in the twentieth century, the younger Marches are becoming more integrated into non-Jewish life than any members of the family ever had before and are breaking away from family traditions.

Eliot observes and presents their story as the realistic, objective recorder of a family whose ways are quite foreign to all his upbringing. Knowing the Marches is a great extension of his experience of human behavior; he had known only one Jew in his life before meeting Charles March—a little boy who had stayed in his grammar school for only a year or two. Indeed, Eliot could not even remember that his parents and their friends had ever mentioned a Jewish person in their conversation. Eliot does not learn that Charles is a Jew until Charles invites him to his home: "It might interest you to see the inside of a Jewish family."

Eliot observes only two other members of Charles's family closely—
Leonard March, the father, and Katherine, the daughter, who is four years
younger than Charles. Over the years, however, Eliot is invited to many of
the March family functions, and he meets other members of a large clan,
particularly Sir Philip, the older brother of Leonard March and the head
of the family. He also attends the Friday-night dinners when 40 or 50 of
the Marches often gather together to celebrate the sabbath in the
traditional Jewish manner; he attends the coming-out dances when the
unmarried March boys and girls are put on display for prospective
spouses; he spends numerous days and nights with the Marches in their
London home at Bryanston Square and, during the summers, at their
country estate. It is not long before Eliot becomes, or seems to become,
the closest confidant of all members of the Leonard March family; when
they accept him as almost one of their own, he becomes privy to their
most intimate family discussions.

Like George Passant, Charles March is in conflict with his father. With
George, the problem had been his inability to accept his father's narrow
Christian religiosity; with Charles, his father's assertion of his Jewish way
of life galls. Charles, as Eliot soon learns after meeting the family, is a
complex individual struggling with conflicting demands of his nature and
environment. Born into a Jewish family of wealth and tradition, Charles,
at the age of 22, suffers primarily from "the conscience of the rich"—the
guilt feeling at having wealth that is not used for the good of
society—and also from an intense self-consciousness at being a Jew in a
Christian world. Since Eliot had not known Charles in childhood, he is
unable to show the development of these strong drives; he can only
observe them full-blown as they dominate Charles and influence his
behavior from 1927 on. But from the portrait he gives of Leonard March,
it is easy to see that Charles might have been quite different had his father
been less dominating and possessive. It is the yoke of the father that
Charles is trying to throw off; this is to Charles the only way he can assert
his manhood and be an individual in his own right.

The plot of this novel concerns three conflicts between Mr. March and
his children; in all three the father loses. The first conflict comes after
Charles has proved to himself his ability as a lawyer in his first case in
court; he loses, but the judge compliments him on the able manner in
which he has handled himself. Mr. March sits in the court and is filled
with pride at his son's achievement. That night, when he should be
extremely happy, Charles tells Eliot he does not feel free, because the law
represents to him the part of his environment that he cannot accept: "If I

stayed at the Bar, I should be admitting that I belonged to the world . . . of rich and influential Jews. . . . If I stayed at the Bar, I should get cases from Jewish solicitors, I should become one of the gang. And people outside would dismiss me, not that they need so much excuse, as another bright Jew" (40).

An astonishing remark. Does Charles mean that what motivates him is his shame at being a Jew, or that, being of a rich and influential Jewish family, any success he obtained in the law would be suspect, would not be proof of something done through his own merits? He probably means the latter, and this interpretation is probably Eliot's, although, from his objective manner, absolutely right on this occasion, we cannot tell just how he reacts. He records only that "I was swept on by his feeling" and "yet with a tinge of astonishment or doubt," but he makes no value judgments about what he has heard. That Charles's motives are not of the purest can be seen from several other statements he makes to Eliot at other times, such as when he says, "There've been times when I've disliked other Jews—simply because I suffered through being one" (100).

Yet, we are never clearly shown in the book just how or why a very wealthy boy, who has led a sequestered life (as we are told in several places), would ever be made to suffer so terribly. All Eliot records about the last remark is that Charles suffers the "kind of shame we all know, but which had been more vivid to them [the Jews] than to most of us: the kind of shame which, when one remembers it, makes one stop dead in one's tracks; and jams one's eyelids tight to shut it out" (100–1). Eliot's reaction is too bland and even obtuse at this point; some readers may feel that a stronger response would be more satisfying, since the kind of shame Charles is talking about is entirely different from the "kind of shame we all know." Put succinctly, Charles is really ashamed of being a Jew, but Eliot does not seem to comprehend.

Charles's motives in going against his father's wishes are not unmixed, and soon after he has told his father that he wants to leave the law, he reveals to Eliot another side of his nature: he has a strong sadistic instinct. This characteristic, Eliot says, links them both together: "To be impelled to be cruel, and to enjoy it. Other young men could let it ride, could take themselves for granted, but not he. He could not accept it as part of himself. It had to be watched and guarded against" (120). Charles has confided his extreme Jewish sensitivity to Eliot, but never to his father. To Mr. March, he represents himself as disliking the law and as desiring to do something more useful to society. Later, when Charles decides to become a physician because he feels he ought to go into some other profession and not be an idler, "he gave the same justification—the desire to be of some use, the need to be secure" (111).

Mr. March, unaware of Charles's other motives, is bewildered by his son's decision. He argues on the only plane he can understand and on the basis of his own view of family tradition. For a March to be a doctor is unthinkable—it is to him a menial trade; the Marches have been bankers, statesmen, merchants, or lawyers. To him, it is nonsense to say that these honorable professions are not useful: "Why are you specially competent to say that one man's life is useful and another's isn't? . . . I suppose that I'm expected to believe that my brother Philip's life isn't as useful as any twopenny ha'penny practitioner's" (113). Mr. March "could not credit that a balanced man should want to go to extravagant lengths to feel that his life was useful. He could not begin to understand the sense of social guilt, the sick conscience, which were real in Charles" (114).

Charles's conscience is indeed "sick" in more than one way: though truly motivated by an intense desire to make himself a useful member of society, he is also strongly moved by the cruel wish to wound his father and, through hurting him, subconsciously to strike at the Jew. A Jewish anti-Semite is a not-uncommon phenomenon, but Leonard March— though portrayed sympathetically as an eccentric, garrulous, generous, and often amiable elderly man who has a deep, passionate love for his son—is also depicted as a stubborn, petulant, sometimes stupid reactionary and as a tyrannical, blundering father who seldom hesitates to override and mock his children's wishes. Though Charles strikes hard at his father, while professing affection for him, he is also striving for his own mental health, which he knows he needs to obtain; he desires to be a "balanced" man. By the close of the novel, we are to believe that, though cut off from his father and sister, he is well on his way to achieving that balance. A reader might be inclined to be skeptical, as he is in the case of George Passant's ability to resolve his difficulties at the end of *Homecomings*.

The second conflict is less devastating to Mr. March because it concerns Katherine, who, though loved by her father, does not ever occupy as tender a spot in his heart as his son does. Charles "was always my favorite child," he tells Katherine when she asks him how "to explain the contrast between his gentleness over her own marriage, and this fantastic harshness to Charles" (198). The conflict with Katherine concerns her marriage to Francis Getliffe, a Cambridge scientist in the same college where Eliot is teaching law part-time. Francis, Herbert Getliffe's half-brother, is a non-Jew, and Mr. March and the rest of the family, except for Charles, who favors the marriage, are upset and oppose the marriage at first. But the opposition is a mild one; at the wedding Mr. March is talking blithely to guests of "my son-in-law at Cambridge." He buys a house for the newlyweds and in all ways apparently accepts his gentile son-in-law into the March family; he even eventually defends Francis against his brother Philip's criticism. We later see Mr. March playing happily with his grandchildren, and he is pleased that Katherine's second son is named after himself.

The third and final conflict in the book, the most terrible one of all, is devastating to both father and son. It concerns Ann Simon, a very attractive and intelligent Jewish girl, daughter of a prosperous London doctor, whom Charles marries after the conflict with his father over his profession has been settled. Mr. March briefly and mildly opposes the marriage because he believes Ann was responsible for Charles's decision to quit the bar and enter medicine. He has dominated Charles so much during his son's childhood that he refuses to believe him capable of making such an important decision by himself. Nevertheless, when Mr. March sees that Charles is determined to marry Ann, he consents with only a little grumbling: Ann, after all, is Jewish; she comes from a prominent family (though not on the same social level as the Marches); moreover, she is liked by Sir Philip, to whose wishes his brother Leonard usually defers.

An intriguing factor in Mr. March's attitude toward Ann is that she is so attractive that when she enters a crowded room all heads turn in her direction; Mr. March himself, Eliot believes, has an immense erotic attraction toward her in spite of his age and his belief that she has harmed his son. This attraction-repulsion principle, according to Eliot, is so strong in Mr. March that when Ann lies ill in 1936 (the culmination of the great conflict), Eliot is sure that Mr. March desires her to die and suffers torments because of his wish. If what Eliot thinks is true—it is one of his many sudden psychological insights, about which some readers have been skeptical—one element that causes Mr. March's harshness to Ann and Charles is his own subconscious desire to separate the couple because of sexual jealousy: there is certainly more than a hint of this tangled web of sexuality in Eliot's reflections about the whole affair.

This last conflict between father and son is built around a type of intrigue plot that is injected into some of Snow's novels, especially the more recent ones. Everyone knows that Ann is a left-wing liberal in her thinking; earlier in the novel Mr. March has argued with her about her views; and Eliot learns that she is a member of the Communist party when she asks him to join. Though his sympathies are with the Left, he refuses to join the party. Ann has been giving information to a Communist paper, the *Note,* about some shady financial dealings having to do with inside knowledge of governmental armaments contracts and implicating a few junior ministers in the Tory government department of which Sir Philip March is parliamentary secretary, and Herbert Getliffe is also involved in part of the financial operations.

The Marches are fearful that the scandal, if the *Note* persists in continuing its revelations, will destroy Sir Philip's political career; it also alarms them that Francis Getliffe's half-brother is implicated—the affair, if not hushed, will bring scandal that may tarnish the whole March family. When Mr. March, Katherine, and Francis want Eliot to bring pressure on Ann to stop the paper from publishing any more articles on the subject, Ann contends that what she is doing is necessary because the only way England and the Jews will be safe from Nazi aggression is to get rid of the present Tory government. She cannot stand the complacency of the older Marches, Leonard and Sir Philip, who believe their world is invulnerable and permanent; they refuse to believe that there are reactionary forces in Europe capable of doing much damage to the world they've known; they are stubbornly living in the past and, for all their worldly knowledge, are stupid old reactionaries. Eliot and Francis, though left-wingers and in substantial agreement with Ann on this point, do not believe that a scandal sheet like the *Note* is the way to make England realize its peril.

Ann seemingly is finally convinced that the paper must stop its story for the sake of the family; further, Eliot learns that she has private documents that if used, will bring the *Note,* edited by an unscrupulous journalist, Humphrey Seymour, up against the libel laws and possibly cause it to be put out of business. Just when it appears Ann may do something, she suddenly becomes ill with pneumonia and is in danger of death. During her illness, she tells Eliot that though she is not ready to leave completely her work with the paper, Charles is to be told that he should have a free hand to do as he wants with her documents. It may seem incredible that Ann, who is supposed to have such a wonderful relationship with Charles, her husband, would not choose to divulge this information to him but chooses to tell Eliot instead. But in Snow's novels we are always to believe that Eliot is such a marvelous confidant of almost everyone, someone whom people instinctively feel is completely reliable, that they automatically gravitate to his side—and in this case, of course, Ann and he have been very close and sympathetic friends.

Now the pressure is on Charles. In a stormy scene with his father and his sister, Charles refuses to lift a finger to save the family honor and the career of Sir Philip, who has told Eliot and Mr. March that though he had made some financial killings in 1929 in the business firm that is implicated in the scandal, he did so honorably, without making any use of governmental knowledge of contracts; moreover, Sir Philip, upon joining the present Tory government, has divested himself of all his business connections and has had nothing to do with the present transactions. Charles is in a real dilemma: he can help his family and save his father from unhappiness, but he will be making a decision that he feels is Ann's alone to make. He will not tell her what to do, since, after Eliot has relayed to him her wishes, Charles has told her how he feels. Mr. March threatens to cut Charles out of his will; previously, when Charles had insisted on marrying Ann and in going into medicine, he had withdrawn from Charles a financial settlement that all of his children were supposed to get.

Mr. March also appeals to Charles's affection, but Charles is adamant. When Mr. March accuses Ann of being responsible for what he considers Charles's "unnatural attitude," Charles answers: "I am responsible for everything I've done." Further: "I tell you this. If she had died [she is now on the way to recovery], I wouldn't have raised a finger to save you trouble. I should have let it happen" (313–14). He will not be deterred, he says, by the misery that will be brought upon his father; by the knowledge of family disgrace; by the fact that he will have to live on what he makes in his medical career plus his wife's money (inherited from her father); and by the kind of loneliness he will have if he is cut off forever from his father and his sister, who has sided with Mr. March. "I can endure that kind of loneliness." he says.

The final article in the *Note* appears that mentions Sir Philip March. There is a strong suggestion of anti-Semitism, mentioned by the *Note* previously, in the affairs of upper-class Tories, and this possibility is seen in the culmination of the intrigue plot when, ironically, Sir Philip, comparatively innocent of any wrongdoing, is asked by the government to resign while it promotes Alex Hawtin, who has been guilty of the dishonest financial manipulations, as well as of having fascist connections, to full cabinet rank. This event happens in 1936, two years before the Munich deal of the Chamberlain government with Hitler. Obviously, in manipulating his plot in this manner, Snow, a Labourite, evidently felt that the incumbent Tory government was capable of any underhanded enormity. He may be correct, but anti-Semitism in England has not been confined solely to right-wing Tories. *The Conscience of the Rich* is one of the better novels in the sequence. The portrait of Mr. March ranks high among Snow's characters. It would have been easy enough to make him a stereotype Jew, as many other writers before Snow had done, but it is to Snow's great credit that he is portrayed in depth, in the complexity of full humanity—a rare feat even in modern literature, as at least one critic has maintained.[6] Snow's is a sympathetic, yet often comic treatment of an elderly man whom time has passed by, an anachronism in a world that is too complex and whose currents of change are too swift for his ability to cope with them.

Charles, on the other hand, is somewhat of a failure as a character, but such an eccentric as Mr. March might make anyone seem pale in comparison. Charles is a Passant-like character, but without George's full-bloodedness. Both have struggled to be free, and both have fought in their own ways against the tyranny that tradition, security, and conventionality seek to impose on the young. Like George, Charles affirms at the end that he accepts his own responsibility, but both know in their innermost heart that freedom is bought at a heavy price and may never be entirely secure for them. Both are cut off at the end from what they will really need to give them the balanced life they have sought, and they have both been betrayed by irrational inner impulses.

It is indeed true that Charles finds the useful and the good life he has sought, and we are told that he has even devised a minor, successful technique for the treatment of diphtheria, about which he has written a letter to a medical journal; this kind of success brings him a measure of contentment. But still he tells Eliot that medicine is to him generally a tedious occupation, for it does not give his restless and inquiring intellect the scope it needs. In the last scene in the book in which Charles is shown, he is finally aware of the implications of being cut off from his father and of the pain he has caused him: "I've done this, sometimes I can't believe it. It sounds ridiculous, but I feel I've done nothing. . . . At other times . . . I feel remorse" (331–32). Eliot, wisely, pronounces no final judgment; he is tolerant of other people's mistakes, he says, because he has made similar mistakes of his own.

In conclusion, good as this novel is, the narrative method has one fault that is confusing and inconsistent. When Ann lies ill, Eliot knows for certain most of the thoughts that run through Mr. March's mind about desiring her death. Now it is possible for Eliot to guess—but that is quite another thing and not what he says. He tells us with certainty that Mr. March wants her to die, despite the fact that Mr. March is doing everything within his power to assure her the medical aid needed for her recovery. Moreover, it is inconceivable that on such a delicate subject as desiring a daughter-in-law's death, anyone like Mr. March—or, for that matter, almost everyone else—would disclose to Eliot or anybody just what he has been thinking.

We feel that Eliot cannot be so prescient. Snow evidently wishes to combine the omniscient method with the first-person narration, or he may be the forgetful author who, in his excitement, has overlooked the fact that his narration is supposed to be confined to one man's necessarily limited vision. Knowing what is in Mr. March's mind is the most flagrant example of this omniscience, but there are several others no less annoying in this book; we noticed it previously in the earlier books, already discussed, but never so obtrusively. Unless we are to believe that Eliot actually possesses the kind of preternatural insight that Roy Calvert claims for him (seemingly in jest to Winslow) in *The Light and The Dark*[7]—"white man's magic," he calls it—its use is unacceptable in a realistic novel restricted to one point of view. Undoubtedly one of Eliot's strong traits is his great interest in people's motivations, and every now and then Snow has him make interesting and acute observations; still, when the narrator violates our credulity, we are inclined to rebel.

The Light and the Dark

The third novel of observed experience, *The Light and the Dark* (1947), is the second of all the novels in the "Strangers and Brothers" sequence Snow has published. In one respect, it is his most unusual one because it is his only attempt to write a tragedy; Roy Calvert is his "sole serious attempt at a tragic hero"; it is Snow's "black novel," the "fruit of the war years."[8] It is not altogether successful, for various reasons, but it is nevertheless one of the most distinctive of all Snow's books. *The Light and the Dark* is the first to have in large part a Cambridge setting in the college where Eliot is one of the dons during the 1930s. Unlike *The Masters,* however, this novel brings in the larger world setting, for it shows England's drift toward the tragic events of the war years. The time span is from 1935 to 1943.

Roy Calvert is the young man who, in several of the other books, was mentioned briefly as having given Jack Cotery a silver cigarette case, thereby provoking a minor scandal in Eliot's native town and motivating

George Passant's first attempt to fight the town's bellwethers. The gift
was all innocence on Roy's part, being merely a gesture of the admiration
a younger boy often feels for an older companion, and in this book we see
that apparently deviant sexuality has had little or no part in Roy's
makeup; a notorious lover of women, he often carries on his activities so
blatantly that he arouses the animosity of the staid and respectable dons,
who also dislike him for other reasons. He brings acute dismay to his
good friends at Cambridge: Eliot, Arthur Brown, and Vernon Royce, the
old Master, who are trying to advance his career as a research scholar who
has promise of great distinction in the field of Oriental philology.

The title *The Light and the Dark* comes from Roy's study of the
Manichees (often Manicheans), a third-century Christian heretical group
whose main doctrine was that man's nature is a dualism between the soul,
which has sprung from the Kingdom of Light, and the body, which has
derived from the Kingdom of Darkness: "In its cosmology, the whole of
creation is a battle of the light against the dark. Man's spirit is part of the
light, and his flesh of the dark. . . . The religion was the most subtle and
complex representation of sexual guilt." No work of the Manichees was
found for centuries; our sole knowledge of them has derived from their
enemies, the more orthodox Christians. But Snow says that a psalm book
and a hymnal written in a Coptic dialect were found in Egypt during the
twentieth century, and a liturgy in an unknown variety of Middle Persian
called "Early Soghdian" was discovered in Turkestan; all these works were
by the Manichees. Roy Calvert's work is a translation of the Soghdian
liturgy; he later prepares a grammar of the Soghdian language (45–47).
He is the only man in the world to decipher Soghdian, and the few
scholars who are able to judge regard his achievements, even when he is in
his mid-twenties, as a landmark in linguistics.

At 25 Roy should have everything to make a man happy: wealth, an
established position in the academic world (which he needs not for a
livelihood but only for prestige), good friends, and love (he is desperately
sought after by Joan Royce, the Master's daughter, and by Rosalind
Wykes, a beautiful home-town girl whom he eventually marries). But
Roy is temperamentally unable to achieve happiness or to sustain it; his is
"a nature marked out by fate": "he had the special melancholy which
belongs to some chosen natures . . . he was inescapably under the threat
of this special melancholy, this clear-sighted despair in which . . . he saw
the sadness of man's condition. . . . He was born with this melancholy; it
was a curse of fate, like an hereditary disease. It shadowed all his life"
(49). The technical term for Roy's nature, manic-depressive, is used

several times in the book. He fluctuates madly between moments of ecstatic exultation and deep gloom, between periods of light and often mischievous comedy and dark despair. Though his malady is undoubtedly real, Roy appears at times to be little more than a case of arrested adolescence, one who has never properly matured, and somewhat of a poseur.

Of all the novels of observed experience in the sequence, this one is the most subjective; almost as much of Eliot as a suffering and emotionally charged person appears here as in the two early novels of direct experience. The reason is that Eliot identifies himself so deeply with Roy. He had felt for both Passant and Charles March but not to the same degree of intensity as for Roy. In Roy's unhappy condition, which sometimes seems to approach madness, Eliot sees a reflection of Sheila's plight, which, it must be remembered (see *Time of Hope* and *Homecomings*), is going on at the same time. They are parallel cases in Eliot's life, and Roy tells him that it is hard on Eliot to have to look after two people—himself "as well as poor Sheila" (173). Eliot also has known periods of despondency, loneliness, and illness, and seeing these things happen to Roy, he is shaken "with resentment, fear and pity, with horror and unassuageable anxiety, with wonder, illumination and love" (366).

To some readers Eliot's excessive solicitude toward Roy may not ring quite true; it seems to be overdone and quite peculiar. The general objectivity with which Eliot narrated the stories of Passant and Charles March is here largely abandoned; instead, we find a welter of emotionalism, of rhetoric about how Eliot reacts toward Roy's troubles at various moments (as seen in the passage just quoted). His friendship with Roy, he says, was the deepest of his life (43) and to know Roy was one of the "two greatest gifts" in his life (366). Eliot does not say what the other greatest gift was. (Perhaps his love for Margaret, but surely not for Sheila?)

Roy affects Eliot so deeply that he almost seems sometimes to go out of his mind with anxiety; in fact, he says several times that he is ready to collapse from worry. Sheila seldom evoked the amount of rhetoric in the two early novels of direct experience that is applied to his feelings for Roy in *The Light and the Dark*. Friendship is a good thing, and Eliot portrays himself as a good friend, but when a friend's troubles arouse much more emotion than a man's wife's, the reader may well ask if the situation is not an odd one. The difference, of course, may be explained on the simple basis that Eliot never cares for Sheila as much as does for Roy. His anxiety for Roy is for Roy's sake; his anxiety for Sheila is for his own selfish sake. But even this simple explanation leaves some things unanswered.

Though we are told again and again that Roy is immensely gifted, only rarely do we actually see his gifts demonstrated. To some critics, *The Light and the Dark* is a total failure, primarily because though we are told a great deal about Roy, he nevertheless remains completely unrealized as a character; we don't feel that Roy is the remarkable man Snow tries to make us believe him to be.[9] This critical judgment is excessive, but it does have some justification. Roy is realized vividly at some moments, though not for his great gifts and in spite of the overdone rhetoric, and though the novel is not one of the better ones in the sequence, it is certainly not a complete failure.

In justice to Snow, it must be said that it is extremely difficult to portray a person who is supposed to possess remarkable ability in intellectual matters; only a handful of novelists have succeeded in doing it well. We constantly expect Roy to say brilliant things, but he almost never does. Roy is actually best shown in those scenes in which he seems to be more of a young smart aleck than anything else, and in these instances we get just a faint glimmer of his misplaced ability. Several of these scenes are varyingly comic, but they are excruciatingly mortifying for Roy's friends, not only because they may bring Roy recklessly close to disaster in his career but also because they indicate (especially to Eliot) the near madness of Roy's nature—his inability to control his impulses in a rational manner.

A case in point is the scene in which Roy insists on bringing up the name of a dead scholar, Erzberger, before an audience assembled to honor the seventieth birthday of Sir Oulstone Lyall, one of the two noted linguistic scholars who had been instrumental in recommending Roy for appointment as a don. Gossip had been bruited about for years that Sir Oulstone had not done any original work of his own but had dishonestly based his reputation on manuscripts left him by Erzberger. Roy's insistence on implying publicly that Sir Oulstone is a fake is not the type of thing a grateful and sensible scholar would do; he is like a silly undergraduate. Of course, the possibility exists that he may not be grateful to Sir Oulstone, but he has told Eliot that he really desires to be appointed as a college don.

Another, much more comic scene is the one in which Roy delivers a speech in English, though he is a very competent German linguist, before an audience of professors in Nazi Germany. The professors, who pretend to understand what Roy is saying, nod their heads and applaud at intervals. As a final touch, much to their consternation Roy answers in fluent German the last question asked by his audience. In several other good scenes the crueller side of Roy's nature is shown, such as the scene in which he sympathizes with the aging bursar, Winslow, for his son's failure in the college examinations and then, not having the good sense to stop, or impelled by the demonic in his makeup, tells the unhappy father that nobody really cared anyway that his son failed, because Winslow is universally disliked. Roy's loss of control evokes from Winslow the comment later to Eliot that Roy is "seriously unstable."

Winslow's judgment is correct, but he does not go far enough; instability is only one element in the syndrome of Roy's nature, or illness. He has a sadistic, vindictive streak that is very powerful; he is immature throughout much of the book; and he is easily influenced by demagoguery—in short, he shows little, until perhaps near the end, that would make him appealing to most persons of mature judgment. But undoubtedly Roy must be a complex individual, or so we are told, and we do occasionally see his great generosity, his charm, and his general goodness of heart to those he especially likes. Unfortunately, scenes like the one just mentioned, though vivid and skillfully written, do not serve to enhance Roy as a man of great ability; they do not usually afford us a view of Roy's many-sided nature, despite Eliot's assertions about Roy. It is more apparent in this novel than in many of the others that Eliot's personal judgments about a character are not conveyed as dramatically as they should be.

The scenes dealing with the Germans are among the best in the novel, and in these we see Roy's shallowness as a thinker about social matters; he expresses a crude pragmatism that is almost an exact echo of the Hitlerian viewpoint. Eliot, we have been told, is a a left-wing liberal who is not as socialistically inclined as his friend Francis Getliffe, but he, like Getliffe, possesses a strong anti-Nazi view and an awareness that England is drifting inexorably toward war. He is therefore disturbed to hear that Roy is becoming a great social success in Berlin and that he has made several unfortunate remarks that have convinced the Nazis he is on their side. To Roy's credit, however, Eliot also hears that he has told the Nazis that their Jewish policy is insane. All the rest of their policies Roy apparently accepts.

Eliot and Joan Royce, who loves Roy, are harrowed by the news of Roy's Nazi sympathies: "since we were living in a time of crisis [it is early in 1939, after the time of Munich] . . . it was bitter to find an opponent in someone we loved. Both Joan and I believed that it hung upon the toss of a coin whether or not the world would be tolerable to live in. And Roy was now wishing that we should lose" (236). Roy is not alone in sympathizing with the Nazis; if he were, the Munich betrayal would have been impossible. Several of the older Cambridge dons, Eliot shows, are of the conservative right wing, and they feel there is little to be feared from the Germans. None of those Eliot knows, however, has gone so far as Roy in showing open sympathy with Hitler. When in March 1939 Eliot is invited by Roy to visit him in Berlin, he suspects there is a hidden purpose, but he nevertheless goes. His suspicions are confirmed: Roy has brought him to Germany to convert him to Nazism.

For the first time in their friendship, Eliot has an argument with Roy—"it was painful, passionate, often bitter." Roy tries to convince Eliot that history is on the side of the Nazis, that the future would be in German hands; there was a chance that "they would create a brilliant civilisation." "If they succeed," Roy says, "everyone will forget the black spots. In history success is the only virtue." Eliot loses his temper with Roy: "Inflamed by anxiety and anger, I accused him of being perverse and self-destructive: of being intoxicated by the Wagnerian passion for death; of losing all his sense through meeting, for the first time, men surgent with a common purpose; of being seduced by his liking for Germany, by the ordinary human liking for people one has lived among for long" (248).

Feeling as Eliot does, he is on his guard with Roy's Nazi friends, such as Dr. Schäder, a minister in one of the Third Reich's departments. When Schäder speaks of power, Eliot answers by affirming a view that is highly significant in light of his subsequent experiences with people in power: "No one is fit to be trusted with power. . . . No one. I should not like to see your party in charge of Europe, Dr. Schäder. I should not like to see any group of men in charge—not me or my friends or anyone else. Any man who has lived at all knows the follies and wickedness he's capable of. If he does not know it, he is not fit to govern others. And if he does know it, he knows also that neither he nor any man ought to be allowed to decide a single human fate. . . . I should say exactly the same of myself" (253).

Eliot is determined that he is not going to be influenced by Roy's pro-Nazi views because he also wants to preserve their friendship. But the war intervenes to prevent Roy's folly from going further, which might even put him in trouble with the English authorities, and he returns to England. During the period leading to the war and for a while thereafter, Roy's melancholy seems to deepen, and what has been called Eliot's "mother-hen" anxiety about Roy[10] increases. Roy's trouble is that he lives without faith though he is one person who desperately needs it. Roy's "wound" is that "he could not throw off his affliction by losing himself in faith, he could see nothing to look forward to" (307). He tells Eliot after the war commences that he had never really been able to accept the Reich: "It was a feeble simulacrum of his search for God" (328). The adjective *feeble* is exactly right, but we doubt whether it is being used ironically in the text.

Inadvertently, when asked by Roy what is the most dangerous of all jobs in wartime, Eliot replies that it is flying. He thus feels guilty and physically giddy when he later learns that Roy has enlisted as a pilot in the British air force. In the course of the ensuing pages to the end of the novel, we are given some glimpses of England at war, and Snow manages to work in one or two of his views that were to be developed much later, in *Science and Government* (1961). Eliot by this time has a government job and has become aware of the internal workings of the government in wartime. For one thing, he has been behind the scenes in the bitter dispute about the bombing "master plan," and he accepts the view of the opposition party within the government that the bombing pilots are being sacrificed needlessly in the decision to destroy the German cities when better use could be made of them elsewhere. Roy, as a pilot, agrees with him, but this agreement is not surprising and might be regarded suspiciously in light of his former attitude toward Germany.

On the subject of bombing there is one revealing short scene in which Roy and Eliot point out to Arthur Brown at Cambridge their knowledge that the planes have not been very successful in their missions. Brown, surprisingly for a historian, does not realize that a government manages the news in time of war: he believes implicitly in the official reports of "pinpointing targets" and "factories going up in sheets of flame," and despite his friendship with Eliot and Roy, he looks suspiciously on what they have to tell him. But it is possible (though nothing is said) that he does not trust Roy, because of his former pro-Nazi leanings. Eliot reflects, "For a man so shrewd in his own world, he was curiously credulous about official news. (I remembered Schäder's remarks on how propaganda convinced everybody in time.)" (358–59). The implication is frightening: if a Cambridge historian can be so easily manipulated, how much easier it is for a strong government to mold the commoner to its will—even in the most democratic of countries.

The last part of this book ends, as so many of Snow's novels do, on a very quiet, anticlimactic note. Roy has married, has a child whom he loves, speculates about her future, and tells Eliot that he is afraid to fly on clear nights because he is now afraid of death—and that is the last we see of him. Eliot is told by telephone about Roy's death, and he recounts how he could not sleep for many nights after; the last chapter is about a memorial service held for Roy at the college. It should be moving, but is not. The irony that Roy seems to have changed at the end of his life—to have lost his melancholy, to realize he has something worth living for, to have lost his death wish—does not strike with the full force it should. But perhaps things do happen this way in life—perhaps this is the way the real often does take place. We expect, however, a heightened vision of the nature of human behavior, of the cosmos beyond humanity, or of light that penetrates the remoter aspects of the human heart—but nothing like that happens. The conclusion of this book might very well be described with the identical language of the concluding section of Arnold Bennett's *The Old Wives' Tale*, "The Way Life Is." The difference is that in Bennett's great novel we are left with the overwhelmingly horrible and ironic hollow sense of the futility of human strivings; in *The Light and the Dark*, no such forceful impression is rendered.

The Masters

The Masters (1951) is unquestionably Snow's best novel; it has been the most highly praised—and for very good reasons. It has the advantage of being the most self-contained novel, as one critic puts it, for it possesses the unities of time, place, and characters to a greater degree than any of the others.[11] The whole story takes place in one Cambridge college in a single year, 1937, and the action involves a limited group of characters who are, with several exceptions, members of the college faculty. The action is severely limited to a single proposition: who will be the new Master after the old Master dies?

Snow's strong points are most in evidence in this novel. His knowledge of power politics has found in *The Masters* its best subject: the struggle for power in the narrow college circle possesses, as Trilling says, a considerable amount of implied meaning, and this conflict serves handsomely as a paradigm of political life in general.[12] Another of Snow's strengths is his ability to create elderly or middle-aged eccentrics and exotics; since many of the characters fit this description, Snow's gallery of portraits is probably the most interesting he did.

Roy Calvert is much in evidence in *The Masters*, and he seems to have a larger measure of maturity than he exhibited in *The Light and The Dark*, though he is not the most dominant character in this book but merely one among the many who are concerned with the central issue. Evidently, in the interim between the two books, Snow gave some additional thought to his obsessed young scholar; quite probably, we might surmise, had he dealt with the subject of the earlier book at a later time, he would have treated it somewhat differently. To Roy in *The Masters* he gives the most memorable statement on the necessity of choosing the right kind of man for Master: "I want a man who knows something about himself. And is appalled. And has to forgive himself to get along."[13] It seems incredible that one who could arrive at that acute state of discernment in 1937 could ever have fallen for the empty and diabolic promises of Hitler, but such speculation is extraneous to any analysis of *The Masters*.

Eliot apparently agrees with Roy as to what is needed in the new head of the college, for they both back Paul Jago and are opposed to Crawford. To them Jago, a literature scholar, is infinitely preferable to Crawford, a biologist, because the former exemplifies Roy's qualification for Master. He has the most self-awareness of all the observed characters in Snow's novels, Roy Calvert excepted; portrayed as a man of deep humility, he occasionally, as a reaction to his feeling of humbleness, is given to brief flights in the other direction, that of what the Greeks call hubris.

These glimpses of the possibility of hubris in Jago are explained by Eliot and his other friends not as integral to his real nature but as concomitants of his desire to help his wife overcome her sense of deep inferiority. Jago's devotion to this pathetic woman is admirable, and it is especially so because she is portrayed as a tiresome, dull, querulous person, one utterly lacking any of the qualities needed in a Master's wife. Jago's flights of hubris are therefore not really basic to his own nature but a result of his own compassion and other good qualities. Some, however, find this attitude suspect; his opponents, particularly the malicious Nightingale, use these manifestations of Jago's nature to attack and undermine his candidacy. Not understanding him—not being able to realize, as do Brown, Calvert, and Eliot, the discrepancy between the reality and the appearance of his nature—they believe Jago would be harmful to the college as Master, or in any case, not so valuable as Crawford.

A basic weakness in *The Masters* is the great lack of attention that is paid to Jago's opponent, Crawford. In a book that gives abundant details to the minute nuances of behavior exhibited by the cast of academic characters, we are surprised that so few are given to Crawford. He is just a colorless name whom we hear about frequently but see only very briefly, except in 3 or 4 chapters out of a novel that totals 46; indeed, he has less than 150 lines of dialogue, totaling about 4 pages in a large book of more than 350 pages. We are told that he is the most famous among all the college's dons, is a leading figure in the Royal Society, and is one of the world's great biologists. We are shown his supporters scurrying madly around for support in his behalf, but we never see him personally as panting for the job or as suffering any of the agonies of spirit exhibited by Jago. Crawford maintains throughout an Olympian aloofness; he is seemingly content (or so we often hear) to become Master and just as content if he does not. If this is part of a paradigm of power politics, it may be a flaw, for candidates for high office are only rarely so indifferent when they come in sight of election. Does victory ordinarily come to the person who stands so aloof? The book is greatly imbalanced because it concentrates on exhibiting Jago and because the convolutions of the plot are almost wholly concerned with what Jago does and what is done in reaction to him. Nevertheless, Snow so skillfully presents this one-sided view of college politics that apparently no one else seems to have noticed what has been omitted.

We may well ask (though the question is probably unanswerable) why Snow chose to present his story in this manner: to show in great detail the squirmings and twistings within the nature of his literary scholar, Jago, but to refrain from presenting his scientist, Crawford, in anything comparable in extent. When the inevitable final vote comes and Crawford is elected, we feel that the dons have probably elected the right person after all because Jago has been shown to possess great flaws of character and because Crawford has not been sufficiently characterized. If we had seen Crawford as intensively, he too might have revealed serious flaws. Although Eliot and Calvert several times express their conviction that Crawford is too conceited and indifferent to individual human values to be a good Master, we ought to see him in action and speech comparable to that given Jago. (Jago's wife is also shown a number of times in detail, but a reader might well wonder after finishing this novel whether Crawford has a wife: he has, and she is mentioned once, on p. 98, but otherwise she is totally absent from the story.)[14] Because of this imbalance, we are not surprised later in the sequence (in *Corridors of Power*) when we learn that Eliot now realizes Crawford was the right choice after all. Lest there be a charge of bias in favor of the scientist and against the literary person, however, it should be noted that if *The Masters* has a villain, he is another scientist, a chemist, Nightingale.

Nightingale, though trained in scientific objectivity, is motivated by personal feelings that are anything but objective; in fact, his behavior demonstrates that on a college campus, or in any other place where human beings are assembled, reasonableness in decision making is inherent neither in the species nor in any single group or occupation. Education does not confer common sense on people; nor does it automatically confer objectivity and freedom from following the direction of one's own supposed personal interests. This fact is one of the paramount views presented in *The Masters.* In one way or another, all the dons support the candidate of their choice for reasons not wholly logical, and the most illogical selection of all is Nightingale.[15]

At first Nightingale supports Jago because of his own chagrin at being excluded from the Royal Society while Crawford has long been a member. Despite the fact that Nightingale's career, except for the very early period, had been undistinguished by any important contribution to chemistry, he somehow believes he deserves recognition. What irritates him is that Crawford has been behaving superciliously toward him: "There's not been a day pass in the last three years when he hasn't reminded me that he is a Fellow of the Royal and I am not. . . . He reminds me that I've been up for election six times, and this year is my seventh" (45). Nightingale is suspicious of everyone, however; he morbidly festers in envy whenever anyone else in the college obtains recognition: "Suspicion and envy lived in him. They always would have done, however life had treated him; they were part of his nature" (48).

Despite Eliot's active dislike of Nightingale—he is the one man in the college toward whom Eliot feels a strong dislike—he does nothing to discourage Nightingale in his hope that when Jago becomes Master, he will appoint Nightingale to an important post. But Eliot is not alone in not discouraging Nightingale's hopes; Brown, the manager of Jago's party, and Jago himself, though secretly determined to keep Nightingale from a future position of power, allow Nightingale to nurse his ambitions because they are fearful he will support the other side. This situation is not a pretty one; politics on the college level is just as full of chicanery as any politics on any other level. To Jago's credit, it must be noted that he suffers from a sense of guilt that he has had to stoop to chicanery in his dealings with Nightingale, to be, as he tells his supporters, *"despicably* tactful," to prevaricate "so shamefully." Brown and Eliot apparently suffer from no such qualms. "You had to do it," Eliot tells Jago. "I call it statesman-like," says Brown (145).

They cannot hold Nightingale, however, by their vague commitments, and it isn't long before he announces his support of Crawford. He tells Jago's supporters that he has good reasons for switching his allegiance:

that Jago is acting like the Master even before the present one is dead; that Mrs. Jago is also putting on airs; and that Calvert, a supporter of Jago, is giving the college a bad name by his sexual behavior. "What were [Nightingale's] true motives," Eliot thinks, "as I stared at him through my anger." "Nightingale suffered meanly, struggling like a rat, determined to wound as well as be wounded. . . . I could understand his suffering. . . . I was not moved by it, for I was cut off by dislike" (161). In searching for Nightingale's real motives, Eliot comes to believe that Crawford is the type of man Nightingale would like to be, and though Crawford, "impersonal even to his friends, would be the last man to think of helping" Nightingale, he somehow lives in hope that he would get something from his switch, perhaps Crawford's help in getting him into the Royal Society (160–62).

The managers of Jago's campaign for election—in fact, the prime motivators for it—are Arthur Brown and Charles Percy Chrystal, an interesting pair. Productive scholars, like creative people in most fields of endeavor, seldom have the time or inclination to engage in active politics, and all three who are most intensely *within* the power struggle have for a long time been nonproductive. Like Nightingale, Brown and Chrystal have left their period of scholarly activity far behind them; for 20 years they had become influential in the college solely by virtue of their political manipulations: "they had complete confidence in their capacity to 'run things.' Between them, they knew all the craft of government" (32). They were not ambitious for personal honors, and in this they were unlike almost all of their colleagues.

Several critics have maintained that something false exists in the picture Snow gives of his college dons, because they are excessively concerned with the honors they hope to receive and with "presenting bottles" of wine to one another. This view will not bear up, though perhaps such critics may be justified in believing that an immense amount of the normal activities of dons has seemed to escape attention as a result.[16] Snow should not be carped at in this respect. He is not attempting to present the daily life of a college; nor should he be expected to do so. Rather, he is concentrating on a political campaign and, as a result of this concentration, can be expected to show people only from a limited point of view.

When we recognize this necessary limitation, we can see that Snow was immensely right in portraying men in the grip of a political struggle as overly concerned with personal honors and with wining and dining one another. Had Snow not shown a large portion of his college dons as being afflicted with the urge for honors, Nightingale's personal concern with his election to the Royal Society, upon which hinges a large part of his political behavior, would have seemed merely eccentric and unmeaningful. Had Snow not shown them wining and dining, he would have been false to the true picture of politics as known throughout history: wining and dining are precisely what most people do to excess when they want to win friends to their cause. It is naiveté to fail to recognize that in politics nothing is given without expected recompense.

Chrystal and Brown (particularly Brown, who is the cleverer and the more conventional of the two) are more realistic in their thinking than Nightingale because, having been unproductive in their scholarship, they are sensible enough to realize that honors on any large scale will not come to them; therefore, Nightingale's folly is to expect honors without having earned them, and for this reason he is rightfully scorned by Crawford. Chrystal and Brown must resort to excessive attention to one of the chief methods open to them as politicians to influence people; by wining and dining their colleagues, they try to right the balance of influence that has been tipped in the direction of those who have reputations extending beyond the narrow confines of the college. This technique is all the more necessary for them than for Crawford's followers because Jago also lacks Crawford's outside reputation.

The choice of Chrystal's name is certainly odd, but it is probably idle to do much speculating about it, as several have done. Who knows why Snow chose not to reveal Chrystal's first two names (the same as his own) until the final vote for Master, when Chrystal, who had been edging away from Jago, comes out for Crawford? Does this mean that Chrystal's shift from the humanist to the scientist is a subconscious indication of Snow's own preference for the scientist? And is not there a similarity between Snow and Chrystal (snow consists of crystals)?[17] But there are really two turncoats in the book, and both of them turn to Crawford; however, since one is a scientist who is also ignominious and foolish (Nightingale), it is hard to see that there is anything significant about the names. Also to be noticed is that one of Jago's staunchest supporters, who never wavers, is the rising young physicist Luke, a man of great integrity. Luke differs on this matter with Francis Getliffe, who has made Luke his protégé and to whom Luke owes his appointment as a college fellow.

Luke and Eliot, who are both left-wing liberals, support Jago because they believe he is the best man for the job, even though Jago, like Brown and Chrystal, is an extreme conservative in politics at a time when England is becoming extremely sensitive to the international situation and the college, like the rest of the nation, is being divided over the Spanish civil war and over the growing power of Hitler. Luke and Eliot cannot understand why Getliffe should prefer Crawford, mainly because he is also a liberal of the left-wing variety. In the struggle for power, whether it is on the college level or on the national and international level, Snow seems to be implying, people seldom behave as we expect them to: they are not automatons but human beings, who often behave irrationally and often against their own best interests or their more logical interests. Though in most of the other books in the sequence Snow touches on this viewpoint, *The Masters* implements it.

Of all the characters, Chrystal seems to have the most mixed motives. Pledged to Jago from the first, he gradually moves in the other direction and finds plausible reasons for it; the chief one is that with Jago as Master there would be less chance for the college's "gaining in riches and reputation among solid men" as with Crawford. Chrystal is a hero-worshiper of the solid members of society, the people who hold money and power; his own humble power in the college, acquired through 20 years of internal politics, would be more secure with Crawford. But more than anything else, Eliot explains, it is probably Chrystal's vanity in desiring the spotlight that ultimately accounts for his change of mind; he, more than anyone else, will be the one upon whom the election hinges, since it has become obvious to all that the election will turn upon the change of one vote. Whereas Chrystal is eventually the central figure in the outcome of the election, perhaps one critic's speculation about his name is near to the truth: "Snow, if he intended anything at all, desired to show in Chrystal's choice the mysteries and inexplicables involved in human decisions, and used his own name to indicate everyone's involvement."[18] Apparently, human decisions are not "as clear as crystal."

The New Men

Snow was awarded the James Tait Black Memorial Prize in 1954 for his achievement in writing *The New Men* (1954)[19] and *The Masters*. The difference between their subject matter is striking: in *The New Men*, center stage is occupied by a group of men engaged in what some think to be the most momentous undertaking of the twentieth century—the development of the atom bomb. Though *The New Men* has such a sober subject, it is for the most part a novel that, like *The Masters* and several others in the series, treats the interactions of a group: they have been dubbed ensemble novels.[20] Surprisingly, the leading character of this ensemble is

Eliot's younger brother Martin. Throughout the entire series there are a number of revealing clues that Snow probably did little advance planning of it as a whole and that almost all the novels are improvisations, but no clue is more indicative than the use of Martin in *The New Men.*

In the four novels written before this one there is only one brief mention of Martin (in *Time of Hope*); Eliot has gone his way as if his brother had dropped from the face of the earth. But we are now told that he had always loved Martin with the strongest kind of possessive brotherly affection, that his mother on her deathbed had told him never to waver in his attention to Martin's needs, that Martin had been at Cambridge with him for a number of years, and that Eliot had sacrificed a great deal to see that Martin received his education and his start in physics.

A close reader of the previous novels would probably find it difficult to escape the feeling that either Eliot has not told us as much of his past life as he could have or else, what is more probable, that Martin is now being created (for the brief mention of him previously can hardly be considered a creation) by the author because Martin is needed for this individual novel. Having produced him, however, apparently out of thin air, Snow brings Martin back into most of the novels written later; having made so much of Martin in *The New Men,* he could not be so implausible as to drop him again from his brother's life.

The theme of possessive brotherly love is certainly important in *The New Men,* and it presents an interesting parallel to the possessive parental love in *The Conscience of the Rich* and to the possessive conjugal love in the several novels that deal with Eliot and Sheila. But this theme is far overshadowed, as it should be, by the relationship of the atomic scientists to their creation, the atom bomb. What should these lords of science, these modern Pygmalions, these new men do when they realize the startling truth: that their Galatea possesses frightening implications for humankind? When they see the hideous consequences the bomb has on Hiroshima and Nagasaki, and realize that their government and its allies may eventually be responsible for the doom of humankind, can they keep silent? Should they keep silent? This dilemma is faced by the nuclear physicists at Barford, Snow's name for the English nuclear establishment.

It is unfortunate, perhaps, that such a momentous subject is partially diluted by too many peripheral themes, for in addition to that of possessive love, there is also the theme of espionage (plus any number of scattered details about various people, whether necessary to the plot or not; some of these amount in substance to additional or minor themes).

Snow interweaves the large themes together in a workmanlike way, but we get more than an ordinary sense that too much is being attempted—and this fault is common in most of Snow's later novels. Life is often full of such diverse dilemmas happening simultaneously, but need fiction imitate life with exactitude?

By the title *The New Men* Snow probably means to suggest that the nuclear physicists may be the vanguard of a race of human beings sometime in the future who will be able to manipulate with greater proficiency than heretofore the technological advances that our knowledge will achieve. But judging from their results in this novel, there is hardly cause for much optimism. The upshot of the book is that "the new men" are unable to withstand the cleverer manipulations of the old men (not in the chronological sense of personal age) who have always been in the government saddle, particularly in the foreign affairs offices and in the military. If, as Eliot observes, it is true that there is an "unassuageable rapacity" in the hearts of those who have a "love of power," whether it be for power on the lowest scale or on the very highest, and if it is also true that people do not alter substantially because of larger social issues that may face them (278–79), then the cause of those of goodwill in science, or whatever other field, is ultimately doomed to disappointment. Is there, then, no defense against the rapaciousness of power-hungry individuals? Must those of goodwill abdicate and leave the field to their opponents? This aspect of the subject is diluted or muddied by Snow's concentration on the particular dilemma of Martin and his relationship with Eliot.

Martin's dilemma is that he has been so much under the domination of Eliot that he feels he must independently do something of sufficient magnitude to help him escape from under this yoke. At the same time, he recognizes in himself, with mounting concern, his own excessive desire for power. He is at first only Walter Luke's assistant on the atomic pile, but due to Luke's illness from radiation poisoning, he later becomes virtually the unofficial leader of the nuclear scientists. Sensing his opportunity to advance over the heads of older and more distinguished scientists, Martin insists on pressing the case against Sawbridge, a young nuclear physicist who has been accused of delivering atomic secrets to an enemy, presumably the Soviet Union.

Though the whole Sawbridge affair is not made entirely clear, it is evident that Luke and Eliot, and some of the others who have been drawn into a consideration of the case, believe that Sawbridge, though having been indiscreet, has not done a sufficient amount of harm to be prosecuted to the fullest extent. But Martin, sensing power within his grasp, is so ferociously adamant against Sawbridge that Eliot is dismayed; he watches Martin "without sympathy," for it seems to him that Martin has become the exact counterpart of Sawbridge: though each is on the opposite side of the fence politically, one pro-Soviet and the other pro-England, both seem to possess "the closed mind, the two world-sides, persecution, as facts of life" (255).

Martin succeeds in having Sawbridge sent to prison for a lengthy sentence. With Luke ill for an extended period, it appears that Martin is almost certain to become the top man; he is not a distinguished scholar; nor does he give promise of becoming one (in fact, Eliot and everyone else see that Martin will never be more than a humdrum mediocrity in physics), but he has pleased Bevill, Rose, and other government functionaries by his intensive pursuit of Sawbridge. Martin seems to be one they can understand and work with, one they can dominate easily, and a scientist willing to carry on their narrow political aims without complaint or without being unduly bothered by qualms of conscience about the use of the doomsday weapons of war or by what they regard as impractical and sentimental visions of human brotherhood. He appears also to be utterly cynical, at least to Eliot, and willing to climb at other people's expense, and his ambition the denizens of the corridors of power understand and are prepared to cope with.

There is a rash element in Martin, however, that comes as a surprise in the last part of the book. While the war in Europe is on and while other nuclear scientists want to voice their protest about the probable American use of the atom bomb, Martin counsels caution: it would be divisive to the Allies; it would upset the delicate relationship between America and England. But the actual American use of the bomb on Hiroshima becomes the catalyst that changes Martin, and he writes a strong letter of protest to be sent to the press. Eliot, though agreeing with Martin's horror at the Hiroshima holocaust, now urges caution: the letter would end Martin's career in government. Only the greatest persuasion by Eliot convinces Martin that he should not send the letter. But Eliot is accused by Martin's wife, Irene, of preventing Martin from being the man he would like to be, and when she says she wonders whether Eliot understands Martin at all, Eliot thinks, "I meant to tell her my real motive for influencing him, but I was inhibited" (206–7).

These thoughts of Eliot's in reaction to Irene's charge are somewhat cryptic, perhaps meaning that his real motive is his possessive desire to preserve Martin's career, or perhaps something else. This tangled skein of family relationships, in any case, now blossoms into a new element in the sequence, and in no other book is the possibility of Eliot's inability to exert personal influence more revealed, though we indeed did have glimmerings of it before: his essential mismanagement of the people he has set his heart upon. He seems to be adept in dealing with strangers but sadly lacking in dealing with brothers and with the very close friends who are like brothers. (Wives, of course, are in a special category: his record in this regard is, or seems to be, 50-50.)

The parallel between Lewis Eliot and Leonard March is quite pronounced. When Martin finally throws away his very promising prospects for governmental advancement to go back to his ordinary teaching post in Cambridge, the parallel is even more delineated; he is doing to Eliot what Charles March did to his father. Martin's act is fairly convincing within the context, but it is not so meaningful and powerful as Charles March's in *The Conscience of the Rich,* because in that book the act is central; in *The New Men,* it is peripheral. Further, the intense reaction of Charles March against his father, plus the father's counterreaction, has more mythological-psychological justification, being one of the central, built-in patterns of human relationships established through the ages— an archetypal relationship. The relationship between brothers, though undoubtedly important in the same mythological-psychological way, is of markedly less importance, if Freud and most other psychoanalysts are to be believed. Moreover, Eliot as a father substitute to Martin does not come off at all well, and in this respect, the reader may well wonder about their real father, who has been left hanging in limbo somewhere back in their hometown (in *Time of Hope*), apparently still living, though neither brother ever mentions him or shows signs of his existence. Like Martin in this book, Mr. Eliot reappears suddenly and surprisingly in *The Sleep of Reason.*

The Affair

The Affair (1960) begins in the autumn of 1953 and concludes in the summer of 1954. Eliot is now 48 and Martin is 40; the setting for the third and last time is in Cambridge; and the ingredients are extensions of material found in some of the earlier novels. The basic situation in the book's structure is, as one critic has pointed out, similar to that of *The Masters:* it is a novel about a group rather than about an individual, and its plot depends on the group's decision as to whether or not the college will reverse its dismissal of a former fellow rather than, as in the earlier novel, about who will be the next Master.[21] The last situation, however, is a secondary theme, for since Crawford is now almost at the end of his time as master, candidates to be his successor are starting to come forward: Martin, Francis Getliffe, and Arthur Brown.

The story mainly concerns a fraud in the publication of scientific research, an ingredient taken from *The Search*. The offending fellow, Donald Howard, is cut from exactly the same cloth as Sawbridge in *The New Men:* thoroughly and aggressively unpleasant, he is a militant Marxist who despises everyone with whom he works in the bourgeois world. Though Howard, since his case is central to the plot, is treated at greater length than Sawbridge, there is no more depth in his depiction, and there is actually no more than an iota of difference between the two young scientists. In the earlier book, however, Martin was the chief opponent of Sawbridge; here Martin is one of the chief defenders of Howard.

Nightingale reappears in this novel as the closest approach to a villain, even though he is made to appear somewhat mellower because he has married and is much more content with his position in the college: he has been a very efficient bursar during Crawford's administration. (Incidentally, Eliot's belief in *The Masters* that Crawford will never give Nightingale a position of power for being a turncoat can be seen to have been wrong.) As in *Strangers and Brothers,* Snow again returns to the lengthy details of a trial, though the trial in this case is before not a civil court but one of senior college fellows.

The old ingredients, however, are mixed skillfully with a sufficient injection of new material so that *The Affair* emerges as a highly credible, dramatic portrayal of the clash of diverse personalities. The element of "How will the story turn out in the end?" is much more paramount here than even in *The Masters,* though we can say that it is a generally weaker novel than the latter because, with few exceptions, the characters are thinner in substance and certainly do not command the same fascinated attention of the narrator.

The story is in its essentials more momentous, more far-reaching than that of *The Masters* because the question of justice for a person one dislikes personally and politically is, except possibly to a limited few, more important than the mere selection of a college head. In the earlier novel Eliot was personally more directly involved, still on his way up in the world of power, both in the college and outside it, still not very sure of himself or of those he touched in his daily life. But now he is an established senior citizen, reasonably secure everywhere, much admired and trusted by the Establishment (that word is used in this novel) in the academic ranks, in the legal profession, and in the corridors of the government. It is from an entirely different viewpoint that Eliot presents this story: he is no longer an insecure insider of the college but a secure outsider brought back by Howard's supporters to help them because of his growing reputation and because he is now considered one of the Establishment. Though as always we see things through his eyes, these eyes are now older and apparently more tired (some have said more smug), even more given than before to abstract generalizations and moralizations (and surely this trait has always been quite marked in him, even from the first).

It is probably because of Eliot's older vision that Arthur Brown and old Gay, the now-decrepit (he is in his nineties) authority on Old Norse sagas, emerge as the most vividly delineated of the characters. The one is the very personification of a shrewd academic administrative functionary; the other, a comic character who insists on all of his rights as the most senior fellow, much to the consternation of the younger and more vigorous fellows. The younger dons are, in the main, not a very impressive group, though we are probably intended to find a few of them admirable.

The Affair gets its name from its supposed similarity to the famous Dreyfus affair, which shook France in the 1890s. In a prefatory note, Snow says that the Dreyfus affair was the starting point of this book. It is Tom Orbell, a young history fellow, whose overheated imagination seizes upon the comparison.[22] This comparison is not very apt, but there are several points of similarity: the anti-Semitism that motivated the French army officers to engage in the conspiracy against Dreyfus and to charge him with treason is here transmuted into merely a dislike of Howard by some of the dons because of his left-wing views; the conspiracy itself is changed into no more than the possibility that someone (and the finger of suspicion eventually points to Nightingale) may have altered a scientific photograph and pinned the charge of fraud on Howard.

Though the comparison is slight, the question of justice is essentially the same in principle: in a democratic society justice should be meted out equally to friend and foe alike. Tyranny begins when one makes the distinction. Surely Eliot is correct in condemning the testimony of G. S. Clark that character and opinion go hand in hand, for Eliot maintains that this view is dangerous nonsense. This clash of views is the crux of the novel. To Clark, Howard ultimately stands condemned because of his social convictions. "I'm never quite happy at judging character outside the Christian framework," he insists, by which he means that if one is not a Christian but a Communist—or for that matter a Jew, an atheist, a

Moslem, or a Hottentot—he does not deserve justice, or at least not so much justice as should be given a Christian. If one does not believe as Clark does, he stands condemned even before he starts. Eliot, however, argues, "Could the Court really give the faintest encouragement to the view that character and opinion went hand in hand? Wasn't this nonsense, and dangerous nonsense? . . . Wasn't it the chronic danger of our time, not only practical but intellectual, to let the world get divided into halves? Hadn't this fog of prejudice—so thick that people on the two sides were ceasing to think of each other as belonging to the same species—obscured this case from the beginning?" (328–29).

The critic who rebukes Snow on the grounds that he simplifies human nature and is illogical in having Eliot make this argument—in short, the critic who seems to be agreeing with Clark on this point—is himself more than a little illogical when he says, "Of course, character and opinion go together, as much as form and content of a poem are inseparable."[23] Literary criticism should be more sensible and responsible, though one must admit that the subject is a slippery one. We cannot separate Hitler, for example, from his political and social views, because these views ultimately led to a world war and the holocaust of Europe, and it would be nonsense to say that the man who was responsible for sending millions of people to their death because he disliked their race was really a man of good character. Yet even Hitler, had he lived, would have deserved his day in court before the Nuremberg tribunal and a fair and equitable trial, in order to be judged by his deeds alone and not by his supposed character and opinions. What Eliot is saying is therefore the cornerstone of justice in any decent society. If we cannot see this simple point; if we confuse it by illogically making a supposed similarity between the character and the opinion of a human being and the form and content of a poem, which is an artifact made by human beings; and if we cannot subscribe to this point with our whole hearts and minds, then what are we but prejudiced beings who are in danger of inflicting injustice on human beings outside our own inner circle? Clark *is* uttering dangerous nonsense, and it is pathetic that a prominent literary critic and teacher could not perceive its enormity.

Justice is not entirely served at the conclusion of *The Affair;* the case ends in a compromise that is not entirely satisfactory to anyone, neither to the defendant and his supporters nor to his antagonists: Howard will not be dismissed, but his fellowship will not be renewed at the expiration of its term. On the other hand, a rank injustice has not been perpetrated; in an imperfect world, at least this is something. The conclusion will not satisfy violent partisans, but it may not be inimical to the majority, who will feel that this is the way things usually happen in life.

Corridors of Power

Corridors of Power (1964) begins in March 1955, when Eliot is 50 and at the high point of his career in government; it ends on a summer night about four and a half years later. Snow says in his Author's Note that the action is set in 1955–58.[24] This work is Snow's one parliamentary novel, or rather it is his novel dealing with high political power in England in which governmental and parliamentary figures are the chief characters. The title is taken from a phrase in *Homecomings* that had become widely circulated by the press until Snow appropriated for his own use what he calls his own cliché. Novels about Parliament and the corridors of political power are not new in English fiction: Disraeli, Anthony Trollope, and more recently Maurice Edelman have worked in this field, and the latter, himself a member of Parliament, gave Snow some help in preparing this novel.[25]

Like *The New Men* and *The Affair, Corridors of Power* deals with a subject of extreme importance to the destinies of humanity. In a sense, it can be said to be a continuation of *The New Men* on a new plane: what shall be the future of the most modern weapons of war—nuclear power, atomic warheads, and guided missiles? Shall we continue to build them and escalate the arms race, or has the time come to call a halt to armed power for the good of humanity? Unfortunately, *Corridors of Power* is a weaker novel than *The New Men,* though it is moderately dramatic. In fact, the basic faults of most of the novels in the sequence are more apparent here than in the other novels that preceded it. Snow has written that Upton Sinclair's Lanny Budd had a "preposterous intimacy with the great" but that nevertheless, he, like all Lanny Budd addicts, had a secret wish to have been that character. To this statement a critic has remarked dryly, "Being Lewis Eliot is next best."[26]

The wonder of it is that Snow, having perceived Sinclair's ineptness, should have himself repeated it. In *Corridors of Power* we are often surprised at Eliot's ability to be almost everywhere at the right time and place; to be present at almost every conceivable conference called by those who are concerned with England's political policies; to be the singled-out confidant of the political greats, the industrial tycoons, the leading scientists, and the social leaders of the nation.

Eliot, a professed socialist, is a follower of the Labour party policies, if not actually a member of the party (it is never made clear whether or not he is a member). Nonetheless, a Conservative minister, Roger Quaife, chooses him from among the lesser government functionaries as his chief confidant and as his political associate who is to take care of most of his investigative needs, including what amounts to hatchet-work in undermining his opponents. This position within the inner circles of Quaife's political group enables Eliot to be privy to much that would be denied the ordinary observer. Eliot is also strongly opposed to the views of the right-wing Conservative Basset group of Diana Skidmore (rather obviously patterned after Lady Astor's Cliveden set), especially to their support of the disastrous Suez campaign in 1956, which forced Anthony Eden out of power, but he is invited time after time in the course of the novel to Basset, where he hobnobs in the chummiest manner with shallow socialites and tough-minded politicians whom he professes to despise, or at least to be uneasy about. An American finds this extremely peculiar, but he thinks that maybe the English do behave this way in politics.

The Basset set's extreme confidence in themselves irks Eliot, and he rebukes his American scientist friend, David Rubin, for supposedly judging England by this group. But Rubin replies, "No. You're a far-sighted man, I know it, Lewis. But you're just as confident in yourself as these characters are. . . . You don't believe a single thing that they believe, but you've borrowed more from them than you know" (162). Rubin's insight into Eliot's nature helps explain Eliot's ready acceptance by the Establishment, and it certainly makes more plausible what at first seems to stretch our sense of credulity. Eliot is a chameleonlike creature: he is both at home and at odds with the power structure of society; in it, yet apart from it, he changes shape and hue to fit the needs of the moment.

Another apparent fault in Snow's novel is that once again an important subject, the struggle to control the arms race, which was already growing to alarming proportions in the 1950s, is weakened by an undue amount of attention to relatively trivial subjects, particularly to an adulterous affair by Quaife with Ellen Smith, the wife of another member of Parliament. This mixture of ingredients, as has been stated before, is a mark of Snow's kind of realism, which has as its objective the immersion of the reader into the entire milieu of the characters' lives so that he will know just what motivates their behavior in the minor as well as in the major affairs of their lives.

If done with finesse, as in at least several of the earlier novels in the sequence, this technique is often effective. But it is not done so effectively in this book: the theme of Quaife's downfall as a minister for the sake of his idealistic belief that the arms race must be stopped has to share too much attention with his love affair with Ellen Smith. At the end of the book we are left by the author with the distinct impression that this adulterous affair probably had nothing to do with the defeat of Quaife's plans but that there is a slight possibility it may have. Whether or not either case is true, the attention paid the affair dilutes the impact of Snow's aim to exhibit the supposedly obscene or ridiculous spectacle of a nation's arriving so haphazardly at a decision that might determine its fate for many years to come.

The older Eliot becomes, the greater his tendency is to reminisce, to make references to how he felt in the past toward some person or event; he also seems as eager to seize on every available opportunity to talk about a person from his past as from his present life. For the reader who has read the whole series, this trait provides an interesting ambience—a pervading, continuing atmosphere—by means of which not only can one measure the present against the past but also the reader can learn more about the narrator himself and especially see where the narrator has been right and where he has been wrong. The influence of Proust on Snow is great in this respect; quite obviously he is trying to do something similar to Proust in linking the past and present together. The difference, however, between the two authors is marked: Proust did not try to write a unique story with an entirely different plot and with almost always a new set of major characters in every part of *Remembrance of Things Past,* as Snow tried to do in every novel.

In reading *Corridors of Power,* we realize most sharply that the Proustian presentation of the past meeting the present may at times be artificial in a Snow novel; at any rate, in this particular novel it slows the telling of the main story, and more important, brings into the story confusing digressions. A new reader would certainly find that this ambience makes some of what happens inexplicable or tiresome; even the noted historian A. J. P. Taylor, who had previously read *The Masters,* has complained that too many allusions to the past made *Corridors of Power* very difficult.[27] When Snow takes a chapter to show us Ronald Porson, who was fairly prominent in an earlier novel (but not so prominent or so vivid that we easily recall him), as living in poverty but as nonetheless rather happy, and then later shows us Eliot learning by telephone that Porson has been arrested for homosexual pandering, we wonder what the point is. The upshot of this digression is that Eliot reveals that he might once have taken an active defense of Porson, but now, somewhat weary of his active work in aid of Quaife, all he can do for Porson is pay his legal fees.

Surely this revelation is not psychologically of much weight, especially since we recall that Porson was never one of Eliot's special friends or even one that he had liked very much. Most people would have acted similarly to Eliot, except that they would not have felt obligated to contribute much, if anything, to Porson's fees. Is the purpose to show Eliot's broad-mindedness, or his generosity, or possibly his weakness—the latter two, perhaps, indicating a masochistic trait in that he is unable to refuse some help to anyone?—or what? With such episodes as this one, we are tempted to suspect that the author is not so much completely recalling the past for us as exhibiting an inability to select the important and revealing from the trivial and unrevealing. If we are to believe that Snow's conscious design is to exhibit Eliot anew (whatever the exhibition may be), there may be some point to many of the digressive episodes. But if they lack some such sort of conscious intent or design, then we are merely left wondering: conscious cleverness or unconscious unselection of material? In a Snow novel, we sometimes find it extremely hard to tell, and in *Corridors of Power* hardest of all. This much we should say: the later novels in the sequence can be more fully appreciated by those who have read most of the earlier ones.

On the positive side, one of Snow's strong points—his ability to depict skillfully, often in just a few pages, the eccentric or unusual qualities of persons who in the eyes of most people are merely ordinary—is again in evidence. Sharply etched is Mrs. Henneker, who bothers Eliot into reading excerpts from her uncritical biography of her idolized, dead husband, an admiral, whom she regards as an heroic personage. At the height of Eliot's distress over the major crisis in Quaife's career, while Parliament is debating the white paper advocating curtailment of England's nuclear weapons, she cannot understand why Eliot seems unwilling to consider a more important happening—the rejection of her manuscript by a publisher. The depiction of minor monomaniacs Snow does extremely well.

Even more skillfully depicted is Lord Gilbey, the old and infirm minister whom Quaife, his parliamentary secretary, undermines so that he may step into Gilbey's post. Gilbey, an ex–military hero, is a Colonel Blimp type of elderly, pompous, unimaginative official who is unwilling to face the realities of Britain's diminished military and political position in the nuclear age; to him, any talk of the curtailment of arms is unpatriotic and tantamount to treason. Within a small compass, Gilbey is conveyed to us as more than a flat character, which he might have been in the hands of many writers, who would be tempted to show him as merely the personification of Blimp.

Eliot's well-known tolerance brings him to reveal other facets of Gilbey's character, such as the unhappiness of the old man when he is dismissed impersonally by the prime minister by means of a letter. "He ought to have come himself. He *ought* to have!" Gilbey cries out, pointing in the direction of Downing Street. "It's not very far. . . . It's not *very* far." Later, in the debate over Quaife's white paper, old Gilbey stirs the House of Lords by his impassioned condemnation of those who would leave England defenseless in a world at arms. But Eliot, listening to him and being at least a bit moved in spite of his opposition to the old man's position, is not altogether sure whether Gilbey's motive is pure patriotism or satisfaction at getting revenge against Quaife; there are indications that his reaction is probably a mixture of both. Gilbey emerges finally as an honest but badly flawed patriot of a bygone age, as a remnant of an England that time is sweeping away but one that is still capable of exuding an aura of past glories.

There are a few other reasonably effective portraits of minor characters: Ellen Smith, Quaife's mistress, whom he finally marries after his downfall; Sammikins, the wastrel, effeminate brother of Quaife's wife, Caro; and once again Hector Rose, the consummate and Machiavellian civil servant in whose department Eliot has served as second man for years. Rose and Eliot function together as always as an efficient team, but they lack any ground of mutual sympathy, since Rose is an arch Conservative whose outlook and ways sometimes grate on Eliot's nerves.

Unfortunately, the leading character, Quaife, and his main political henchmen are colorless and lifeless despite valiant attempts to build the plot around them. The real drawback of the book is that the dark "corridors of power" through which they walk are not illuminated by their presence. Fascinated as Eliot is by political activities and caught up personally as he is in them, he cannot make these politicians come fully alive. It would take a rare reader to believe in Quaife or to feel that he is really what he is probably supposed to represent—a strong-minded, farseeing leader with broad human sympathies whose political destruction has retarded the cause of peace. We are told much about Quaife's activities, both in and out of the corridors of power, but the generally low-key writing does not help to make us feel their import. For once, Snow's fine sense of economy and understatement has failed him; it is the wrong approach for such a man and so momentous a subject. Quaife is like an interesting character study in an essay on political behavior, but an essay is not a novel.

The Sleep of Reason

The Sleep of Reason (1968)[28] begins in April 1963 and concludes just about a year later, and most of the action takes place in the Eliots' native town. The title, from one of Goya's etchings, *The Sleep of Reason Brings Forth Monsters,* is very appropriate, but a subtitle could well have been "Fathers and Children." No other novel of the sequence deals so much with the relationship between the generations, except possibly *Last Things;* moreover, Eliot, now in his fifty-eighth year, returns to the place of his beginnings and confronts his own past and that of his early friends, and he finds much that needs deep contemplation and possibly revision. Throughout the book, he is measuring the present against the past, and he comes in this novel to see that despite the superficialities of progress, there is no real advance in what counts. Man's old nature is still what it always was–capable of evoking monsters in unsuspected and devious ways when reason is allowed to sleep. If any reader has ever suspected that Eliot has been dominated by a fatuous sense of optimism, this novel perhaps shows him otherwise.

We cannot say, however, that this novel is one of despair, for a few hopeful notes exist in the human condition as Eliot presents it. The book is thus not overwhelmingly gloomy; Snow's realistic and pragmatic attitude forestalls such an extremist point of view. But certainly not even in *The Light and the Dark,* the gloomiest of the preceding books, are we given such a harsh appraisal of the human condition: Eliot finds little cause for rejoicing as he makes what is presumably a final exit from his birthplace.

This novel is a marked improvement over *The Corridors of Power,* and one reason is that though Eliot is telling the story of others, he is also, in a greater sense than in any of the other novels of observed experience, telling his own story; there is also a greater amount of personal soul-searching than in any of the novels except the three of direct experience—*Time of Hope, Homecomings, Last Things*—and *The Light and the Dark.*

The plot of *The Sleep of Reason* has two main strands. The first—the story of a university educator—occupies most of the first half of the book; at the same time, a slow progression occurs toward the second, the account of a murder trial. Throughout the novel the relationship of various fathers and children is explored and becomes a counterpoint to the two strands of the plot. The plot is remarkably integrated (though it may not be readily apparent to the casual eye), even for Snow, one of whose fortes, at least in his better books, is good plotting. The reminiscences of Eliot—the injections of people and events from the past into the narrative, which in the more recent novels in the sequence seemed to be sometimes artificial and terribly digressive—become for the most part very appropriate and meaningful, for they are closely related to the theme of a man who is measuring the past and the present.

In April 1962 Snow was installed for a term as rector of the University of St. Andrews in Scotland; in the same time of the following year, 1963, Eliot returns to his native town to attend a meeting of the governing body—the executive Court—of a new university that has grown out of the old College of Arts and Technology where he had many years before attended the law lectures of George Passant. Eliot, the elected representative of the students, is now a full-fledged writer, very successful, and now wholly freed from the official business that had kept him occupied for much of his life. He describes himself as now "happy really because I had reached a stage when the springs of my life were making their own resonances clear, which I could hear, sometimes insistently, not only with my family but with people I had known" (14). But bothersome problems await him just at the time of life when he would prefer not to have them, and the first is that of Arnold Shaw, the vice-chancellor since the inception of the new university.

Shaw, an extremely conscientious administrator and also a genuine scholar of chemistry, has recruited to the faculty a group of excellent young scholars, including a physicist of international recognition, Leonard Getliffe, the son of Eliot's old friend Francis. But Shaw has made many enemies among the members of the Court and the faculty who are now trying to ease him out of his position. The argument between himself and his opponents is basically a difference in educational views. Shaw's trouble is that he is an extreme conservative in education, and he insists on parading his views at every opportunity and without compromise: "A university was a place of learning. No more, no less. The senior members existed to add knowledge. If they couldn't do that, they shouldn't be there. Some of them had to teach. The students existed only to be taught. They came to learn. They weren't there for social therapy. They weren't there to be made useful to the state: that was someone else's job. Very few people could either add to knowledge, or even acquire it. If they couldn't, get rid of them. He wanted fewer university students, not more. Fewer and better. This university ought to be half its present size" (21).

When Eliot arrives for the meeting of the Court, he learns that the university is torn with strife—the students are also in opposition to Shaw's authoritarianism. In comparison with the violent student uprisings in America and parts of Europe during the 1960s, this opposition is mild, but it is symptomatic of a new spirit in education. The basic source of immediate contention is Shaw's insistence that four students, who have been caught having sexual relations in a student hostel, be dismissed from the university. Their appeal to the Court means that Eliot, as the students' representative, must be directly concerned. When he argues with Shaw that "most of the people we knew—probably most people in the whole society—didn't really regard fornication as a serious offence," Shaw answers, "So much the worse for them." But, Shaw adds, they are not talking about his moral sanctions, or about fornication in general: "We're talking about a university which I'm in charge of. While I'm in charge of it, I'm not going to allow promiscuous fornication. I don't see that needs explaining. It gets in the way of everything a university stands for. Once you turn a blind eye, you'd make nonsense of the place before you could look round" (23).

Eliot and most of the executive Court are not in sympathy with Shaw's hard line; suggestions are made that differentiation be the principle by which justice should be dispensed—that two of the students with great academic ability be given lighter penalties than the others. To this argument Shaw is scornful: "It would be wrong to distinguish between the four. Morally wrong. . . . We are judging a matter of university discipline and moral behaviour. No one wants to deprive the university of able students; we haven't got enough. But you can't make a special dispensation for the able when they've committed exactly the same offence. . . . I'm surprised that anyone could find it morally defensible (36).

Because of a decided clash of views, the Court decides to postpone a decision until its next meeting in two months. This decision is unsatisfactory to Shaw. Eliot's reactions are interesting, and in evaluating them a knowledge of a few past events in his life is needed. The compromise is not rational, he thinks, and reflects back to the events in *The Affair* when "I had twice heard an elder statesman of science [Crawford, the master of his college] announce, with the crystalline satisfaction of someone producing a self-evident truth, that sensible men usually reach sensible conclusions. I had seen my brother cock an eyebrow, in recognition of that astonishing remark. I had myself reported it, dead pan, to others—who promptly came to the conclusion that I believed it myself (40).

The reference is to the dispensation of the case of Donald Howard. The reader will also remember that in *The Corridors of Power* a brief mention is made of the fact that neither Martin Eliot nor Francis Getliffe nor Walter Brown had been elected to succeed Crawford, as the reader expected at the conclusion of *The Affair*. Instead, the successor was Clark, whose remark at the trial of Howard—that character and opinion must go together and that he (Clark) differentiated Christian from non-Christian justice— aroused a strong reaction in Eliot. As *The Sleep of Reason* progresses, we find additional references to "the affair": Howard, despite the blot on his record, has been hired by Leonard Getliffe for his department in the new university and is becoming an excellent scientist. Moreover, the dons who elected Clark realize their mistake at last, for he has made a very poor master, and they are counting the days until his retirement.

Sensible men reach sensible conclusions! The irony is inescapable. This is one time when we can be sure Snow uses irony—and to good effect. The great difference between Clark's point of view and Shaw's should not escape us, and we feel that Snow fully intends us to see all the implications. Shaw's argument against the differentiation between students is the exact antithesis of Clark's. As soon as a person makes distinctions between people and judges from emotional biases, whether on the ground of academic ability or that of religious beliefs, justice is being perverted. When emotion is allowed to overbalance reason, even in otherwise sensible men, reason can indeed be said to be asleep—and monsters spring forth. Though Eliot does deplore Shaw's authoritarianism and may not agree with many of his other views, he seems on this point to be at one with him.

Shaw is a vivid creation, one comparable to Leonard March in *The Conscience of the Rich;* they are, though quite different in other respects, the two principal older men who are attempting to resist the changes in time by standing for the old verities that youth is thrusting aside. (In a lesser sense, because he is given less attention and space, Lord Gilbey in *Corridors of Power* belongs with them.) Shaw is a man of firm principles, a loving father who has a beautiful relationship with his daughter, and a devoted, kind friend. Shaw's significance in the context of the total narrative is great; we do not lose sight of him entirely, though his story becomes obscured by the more dominant and sensational part of the plot.

The principles of education he represents are no less at stake than those by which society as a whole is able to function day by day. In any examination of our civilization—which is ultimately what this novel is about—education is one of the most vital parts in civilization's total organism.

The second strand to the plot deals with a frightening subject, murder. It is undoubtedly based to a large extent on Snow's personal knowledge of the Moors murder trial held in Chester in April 1966, an event Snow and his wife, Pamela Hansford Johnson, attended; the latter wrote a book, *On Iniquity* (1967), dealing with her personal reflections on the case. The defendants were Ian Brady and Myra Hindley, both of Manchester, who in a peculiarly horrible manner had murdered at least three children and possibly several more. This case attracted the horrified attention of the whole civilized world, for few murders so revolting are recorded in the annals of crime.

Eliot is drawn closely into the murder case dealt with in *The Sleep of Reason* through his association with the family of one of the students involved in the university's sexual episode in the first half of the book—the Patemans—and through his old association with George Passant. Cora Ross, George's niece, and Katharine (Kitty) Pateman are convicted of the murder of an eight-year-old boy and are sentenced to life imprisonment (as were Brady and Hindley; the death penalty had been eliminated in England). As in the Moors case, there are implications of sexual abuse of the murdered child and also of sexual deviation on the part of the defendants, but these details are greatly toned down from the original ones. Cora and Kitty, a pair of lesbians, have murdered the young boy ostensibly, as they finally admit, to "punish" him, to "teach him to behave," and like Brady and Hindley, they have disposed of the body by burial.

In a desire to help anyone connected with Passant, Eliot agrees to attend the entire trial and to be available for advice. But the trial proves to be more shattering to both than they had ever suspected, particularly for George, who now is faced with no less than the final result of the fondest thinking and behavior of his whole life. As the copy on the book jacket says, George watches "his most passionately-held libertarian principles come sickenly home to roost." We cannot be sure whether Snow intended to bring about this conclusion when he wrote the earlier books dealing with Passant, but it is probably safe to say that he did not, because surely he could not have known, years before, about anything comparable to the Moors case and his own and his wife's fascinated interest in it. This fact is just one among many clues to the suspicion (mentioned before) that the whole sequence of novels was planned in a most haphazard and vague manner, that much of it came about as a direct reflection on the events during his own life as they unfurled.

Though Snow probably did not plan it exactly in this way, the conclusion of Passant's career, so far as it relates to Eliot's life, has an inevitability about it that was unavoidable, for surely, given Eliot's nature, we could not expect that he would ever place a final approval on Passant's life. His unwavering loyalty to Passant is always marked, but there are many signs in the earlier books, even in *Strangers and Brothers*, that Passant's ways are not in accord with Eliot's. Fate brought this diverse pair together, and fate finally separates them. The second hand of fate is the murder trial of George's niece and her companion.

Just as Lady Snow attempts to demonstrate in her book that the Moors' pair were dominated in their thinking, and probably ultimately in their crime, by the reading of Sade and other writers, including Hitler, who stressed either the erotic or the savage undercurrent of human nature, so Snow in his novel is showing that Cora and Kitty may have behaved as they did because they believed in Passant's libertarian principle of enjoying one's instinctual desires without reference to the restraints of society. To George, the conventional life has always been the great barrier to happiness, which is the achievement of the satisfaction of the physical. The early trial, from which he barely escaped imprisonment, and the other rebuffs of life that he endured have not deterred him from carrying on not only his old ways but also his desire to put an impress on others. Cora and Kitty are among his later disciples.

Now we see Passant in his sixties as a broken-down old man, still fulminating against the restraints of the community and still scorning the stultified thinking of the middle class. Despite his ill health, he is still sure of the rightness of his views, which have driven him to bodily extremes: Eliot tells us that Passant is now lecherously pursuing very young girls to satisfy his strong physical drives; we are told that all the details of George's licentiousness, however, do not come to him until after Passant's death. Passant is a partial, latter-day Marquis de Sade—partial in that there is no hint of abusiveness toward his victims. Or perhaps a better analogy can be found in Proust, since the French writer's influence on Snow is great: Passant is a lesser English version of the Baron de Charlus, though the latter is a homosexual and the former is very much a heterosexual. Though a diminished Charlus, Passant is Snow's most outstanding character; a complex human being, he ultimately stands as the symbol for modern society's inclination to strip away the civilized covering that hides a person from his instinctual nature. The trial, which has such memorable consequences for Passant and for Eliot, is dealt with in a restrained fashion; in this restraint, it follows the Moors' trial, for as reported by Lady Snow and others, the judge, the lawyers, and almost everyone else connected with the Moors' trial behaved with an admirable decorum. Otherwise, the harrowing subject matter might have been unbearable. In the trial of Cora and Kitty, we constantly expect horrifying revelations and dramatic outbursts, but they do not appear; however, the hints as to what happened are horrifying enough. The ultimate depths of our common human nature are unavoidably made clear.

Kitty and Cora, two seemingly ordinary young women, have kidnapped and systematically tortured for several days their young victim until his death brings him relief. Like the Moors' murderers, they show no remorse for him, only for themselves. When finally imprisoned, Cora is shown daydreaming about her possible release in 10 years, when she will be able to resume her life with Kitty. She tells Eliot, who visits her in prison, that everyone can be sure she will not be repeating the crime—not because it in itself was wrong but because she does not want to have to endure imprisonment and separation from Kitty all her life.

The only ultimate explanation for such atrocious cold-bloodedness in human beings, Eliot believes, is the religious explanation, original sin—depravity as the basic nature of a person fallen from divine grace—though belief in this doctrine in his case is without benefit of religious faith. Eliot had said once years before, when confronted with the plight of Roy Calvert, that he believed in original sin; now he reiterates his conviction. Passant had believed and taught: "Let the winds of life blow through you. Live by the flow of your instincts. Salvation through freedom. George, like many radicals of his time, believed, passionately believed, in the perfectability of man. That I could never do, from the time that I first met him, in my teens. Without possessing a religious faith, I nevertheless—perhaps because I wasn't good myself—couldn't help believing in something like original sin" (276–77).

If something like original sin must be invoked to explain Cora and Kitty (the latter is described by a journalist as like a creature out of hell), then what about Kitty's father, upon whom Eliot directs much attention? Mr. Pateman is a "paranoid" who howls for his "rights" every time he meets Eliot or telephones him (and makes Eliot pay for all the charges); Eliot is bothered even late at night by his pleas for assistance, understanding, or even just a hearing. Pateman is one of the little men who make up the bulk of the world's population; he has been unable to get far in acquiring society's rewards and is miserable because of his failure. He insists that his failure is society's, not his own, and that society must help him achieve what is rightfully his own.

Mr. Pateman, though a minor character, is a vivid appendage, or perhaps a link, to the trial and the educational aspects of this novel. Does society owe an obligation to its little people crying out for their "rights," even if they exhibit a "paranoid" manner? (Snow's excessive use of the word *paranoid* to apply to Mr. Pateman may be revealing to some; in any case, it certainly is what the logicians would term "loaded" because it implies delusions when he cries out for his "rights.") If original sin is the basic explanation for people's inhumanity, then is society excused from responsibility? When a journalist, Edgar Hankins (who appeared also in several other books), suggests everyone's responsibility for the murders, Martin Eliot rejects this view as a convenient excuse for freeing the individual from responsibility for his own mistakes.

The jury's decision, which Eliot seems to find reasonable, tends to back up Martin's belief: that "diminished responsibility" cannot be allowed in the case of Cora and Kitty as an escape from punishment—that is, that these women may not elude it on the ground that when committing the crime, they were of abnormal mind. But as Eliot listens to Martin reject Hankins's belief, he remembers the films he had seen of Auschwitz and of the almost-corrupt fascination with which he had beheld the horrors there. The "horror came before our eyes like a primal, an original, an Adamic fact" (276), and he realizes that the horror is built into the very nature of people, not a few. The question, then, of basic responsibility— society's or the individual's—is never answered: opposing views seem to cancel each other out.

An added statement by Martin offers a way out of the dilemma of decision making on this complex subject: "What people feel doesn't matter very much. It's what they do, we've got to think about" (276). This pragmatic view apparently seems reasonable to Eliot, and in his novel at least, it puts a finishing touch to much further speculation. It's what we do that we must think about; never mind fixing responsibility. We have seen the ultimate depths of our common nature; we have looked into the volcanic depths of humanity; and we must recoil from it. We must never again let another Auschwitz come into being. We must never again let reason sleep.

At the conclusion of the novel, a reader may wonder if he is supposed to believe that Arnold Shaw's version of education is the right one after all, even though he may have some of the same doubts about parts of it that Eliot had. Shaw's insistence that education, especially higher education, is for the development of the mind and not for any other purpose seems to fit snugly into the general tenor of the book that reason must prevail. How can reason prevail if the mind does not see and understand the fallacies of poor logic, such as the insistence on instinct's rights? But no, our own reason also tells us that if only the few are taught to use reason properly, one is left prey to the unreasonable many. Perhaps Shaw's type of higher education for the talented few is wrong; enough doubts have been cast upon it here and there in the book to help justify this view. The author is not saying so: he is objective enough to leave it up to us to choose. This book raises more questions than it resolves—or than Eliot can resolve.

This penultimate book of the sequence leaves the strongest impression of any volume in the series that Eliot has all along been doing little more than reflecting over his life in order to explore the problem of his (and the author's) bewilderment in the face of both human and societal complexity, and finally exhibiting his inability to reach many definite conclusions. Life and human beings are too bewilderingly complex for certainties, but people can behave, he is saying, as if human beings are creatures of reason and can keep their savage instincts under control. Perhaps some will find this view a little amusing for one of the chief complaints of reviewers has been that Eliot and his wife Margaret are a nice, contentedly uxorious couple with too much of the traditional British sangfroid.[29] An answer to this charge may be found in this statement by Margaret, near the conclusion of *The Sleep of Reason:* "Margaret said, she had been brought up among people who believed it was easy to be civilized and rational. But she had hated it. It made life too hygienic and too thin. But still, she had come to think even that was better than glorifying unreason" (375). George Passant is a warning on how not to live.

Even George himself, by the time of his niece's trial, is shaken by the implications of his own life, and he leaves England because he cannot face his past, though his ostensible reason is that he is leaving for the good of his young disciples (371). George's extreme permissiveness may bring temporary satisfaction to a few individuals, but it ultimately leads to debauchery and the undermining of that delicate structure of order by which the civilized can prevent another holocaust. Our acts determine finally what we are. Even if we are not inwardly perfectible, we can try to make society perfect and bring about a better life for all. This is all we can do; this is what we must do. If we do not, we are headed possibly for extermination, or at least chaos, anarchy, and curtailment of personal liberty.

Perhaps the hand of a Dostoyevski was needed to show adequately the depths of the volcanic undergrowth of human nature against which reason is supposed to prevail. The influence of Proust once again can be finally and clearly discerned, however, in Snow's shaping of the next-to-last movement of his novels. Snow is presenting his own unique version of *The Past Recaptured,* the final volume of Proust's long novel, when he shows us so many of the younger generation in contrast to the older generations in *The Sleep of Reason.* Eliot's father, whose funeral brings the book to a close, contrasts to Eliot himself and to the grandson Charles; Arnold Shaw and his daughter; Mr. Pateman and his children; Martin Eliot and his son; Francis Getliffe and his son Leonard; Eliot and Margaret and her father, whose urge to suicide is thwarted; even Roy Calvert's daughter is brought into the book, and surprisingly, she marries Martin's son, and is to bear a child.

The past is also being recaptured and the devastations or changes that time makes are being shown in the presentation of so many figures from out of Eliot's own past—not only Passant, but also Jack Cotery, who has become a religious fanatic and who attempts to convert Eliot to Christianity, and Olive, who is now a dowager of extreme conservative views who denounces Eliot for his liberalism. We hear faint echoes of how many others have turned out, such as Martineau, who has been converted from religious wanderings to the life of a contented and settled married man. All these changes that time makes indicates the inexplicable and often-surprising quality that seems to be built into human affairs.

Finally, the light and the dark imagery, which has run as a leitmotiv throughout the series of novels and which has even given a title to one of them, is a strong element in *The Sleep of Reason,* and the imagery reinforces this view of inexplicable time and human behavior. Eliot, like Snow, has an eye defect that is remedied by an operation. In the chapter entitled "The Dark and the Light," he lies in the hospital, eyes bandaged, in "the claustrophobic dark." His mind swirls about as he thinks of the present and the past. He is troubled by the light and the dark things that have taken place in his life, and he can't seem to make much sense of the meaning of anything. "Ageing men went in for rhetorical flourishes: but were they real? One didn't live in terms of history, but in existential moments. One woke up as one had done thirty years before. Certainly that was true of me" (149). Each novel in the sequence has been the record of an existential moment, a fluctuation between the light and the dark.

Chapter Seven

"Strangers and Brothers": The Last Novel of Direct Experience

Last Things

The aptly titled *Last Things* (1970), the third and last novel of direct experience and the concluding novel of the series, begins only a few months after the ending of the murder trial in *The Sleep of Reason* in 1964 and terminates in the late summer of 1968. The purpose of *Last Things* is undoubtedly to establish a coda to the whole series and, in doing so, to give Eliot the chance to examine his own mind at a time of life when he is ready to say farewell to his readers. If we expected, however, a more intense and profound philosophical unification of the main themes, especially the strangers-and-brothers one, we can see now that it was really in *The Sleep of Reason* that this was done, even if only partially (see my comments in chapter 6). *Last Things* is really a book-length appendage to that novel, for it presents very little that is new or ideologically substantial. The change of title from *The Devoted,* which Snow had announced for so long, may have some significance; it may indicate that he had given the last book a title before he actually knew what its contents would be.

The avid readers of the previous novels should welcome *Last Things* for its final glimpses of Eliot and of some of the other, older leading characters in the series. Those who read Snow for the first time will probably be frustrated or bewildered by the absence of a strong plot that can intrigue them without benefit of what has preceded it; in fact, this novel depends more than any of the others upon a knowledge of Eliot's past. *Last Things* has almost no plot at all in the sense that all the others had: a crisis or trial, a central controlling and unifying story, either for Eliot or for some other character, around which most of what happened in the novel revolved, even though there were often innumerable subplots.[1]

The only semblance of such a central situation in *Last Things* is aborted. A few Cambridge students of the New Left persuasion (Charles, Eliot's son, is one of them) attempt to purloin an official document proving the university's collaboration with the military in research for germ warfare. But this affair is dropped by the authorities after a brief, vague investigation, presumably because the son of a prominent Tory politician is involved and because not much damage to national security has been accomplished. This whole affair is dealt with in only a few chapters. The rest of the book is mainly concerned with three other matters: whether Eliot should accept the offer of a position in the new Labour government (he, unlike his creator, Snow, turns it down); Eliot's eye disorder, a continuation of his physical troubles in *The Sleep of Reason;* and Eliot's relationship with his son. All are of interest to Snow's devotees, but they do not form a very compelling central plot; moreover, each of them occupies only a fraction of the book. As a result, *Last Things* is built around subplots only.

Eliot's bad eye—a displaced retina—requires a second operation, and the chapters dealing with it in the short central section are certainly the high point of this novel. As an added filip, which a similar episode in *The Sleep of Reason* lacked, Eliot's heart stops beating for a few minutes, and he is, in a strained sense, a man who has returned from the dead. This dramatic recovery, which might have been used with an intensity of effect to plumb the relationship between human nature and that of the cosmos, stimulates Eliot to indulge in a mild, semiruthless self-examination of his past life that extends through several chapters while he is lying quietly in the hospital bed with both eyes bandaged.

Eliot realizes now, if he had not before, that he has not always been at his best in personal relationships; that he has sometimes been a bad husband, son, and friend; that he regrets much he has done. He does not conduct an intense exploration of any one of the episodes of his past life; concrete details are lacking; and vague generalities abound. Since the discerning reader of the whole series always recognized Eliot's faults, he does not find Eliot's own recognition of them startlingly revealing; in fact, Eliot's obtuseness in failing to understand the implications of the clumsiness of his personal relationships is something he himself has either indicated or implied from time to time. It is therefore somewhat anticlimactic to be told about it now. Stated in other terms, the resonance between what Eliot sees, does, and feels, which was announced as one of the controlling themes of the series, is not so acute in *Last Things* as it ought to be, because since we have already seen it in action, it is repetitious to be merely reminded of it.

Eliot in his sixties is a man of greater humility and of chastened mood; he is seemingly content to take his place on the sidelines of life and to write about life's experiences rather than live them; he is no longer dominated by the urge to succeed in government, love, or any other area to which his past, somewhat inordinate, desire for power extended. He is now more like his brother Martin, who had renounced power early in life at the very moment he had power in his grasp. The difference is great, however: with Martin, such renunciation was a tremendous act of will; with Eliot, it is more the inertia of age.

A restrained mood permeates almost the entire book, especially after Eliot's illness, for he is now able to look with greater equanimity on the things he encounters. He is chagrined, of course, when he realizes that some of his hopes are dashed, such as his desire to have Charles keep free from erotic turmoil and to have his son follow in his footsteps by becoming a Cambridge fellow upon taking his degree, but he accepts Charles's decisions without much arousal of emotion. Near the end, when Charles decides to leave his mistress and depart for the Middle East as a would-be journalist, Eliot tells Margaret that he will always be unable to sleep well until he knows his son has returned home safely. But after Charles has departed and the book nears its close, Eliot walks home thinking, "I didn't feel any of the anxiety that had afflicted Margaret and me at other homecomings. . . . For that evening, all was peace." He is certain that in "days soon to come" he will be troubled again, but "There would be other nights when I should go to sleep, looking forward to tomorrow."[2]

That final sentence of the series indicates that Eliot has regained a modicum of the optimism he had lost during the period of *The Sleep of Reason*. The knowledge that many of those he had been associated with through the years, such as Francis Getliffe and George Passant, had died and that others would soon be passing on, leaving the younger generation struggling for power, makes him slightly apprehensive for the future— but little more than slightly. He resorts once again to his previous thinking that original sin helps explain inhuman behavior and most of the other irrationalities in society, but he feels, after having taken a look at Charles and his friends, that though he cannot always understand what the younger people are doing, they will ultimately behave more responsibly when they achieve power.

Implicit in Eliot's thinking is the fairly confident belief that the young men in Charles's circle—and their counterparts in the other leading universities, mostly sons of the wealthy and powerful—will gain power in the future. That power may pass them by and that more irrational, less learned people—those who may arise from outside the charmed circle of the established ruling class—may supersede them pass through his mind only tangentially. Yet the events of *The Sleep of Reason* and in fact of his whole life should have made him more sensitively aware of the whole problem of power in the modern world and especially of the volcanic depths that lie underneath the surface of society. The penultimate sentence of the book and entire sequence, however, is just as revealing as the last sentence: "Who would dare to look in the mirror of his future?"

This tone of inconclusiveness concludes the series—an impressive, somewhat uniquely organized, though uneven group of novels, in which Eliot experiences a variety of moods, from deep depression and gloom to measured optimism and hope, from moments of tragedy to comic relief. These novels are the record of the unusual life of a person who has experienced much and has received rewards beyond those attained by the majority. In the end, he is a man not sure of the meaning of it all and of its portent. Indefiniteness is the fitting note for Eliot to use in finishing his long series of tales. Anything else would have been contrary to his creator's own view of human existence in our time.

Though undoubtedly Eliot is far different in some aspects from Snow, they were similar in some ways; many of Snow's utterances for many years showed the same kind of measured optimism, the refusal to surrender to abject pessimism, and the inconclusive pragmatism in the face of possible future horrors that seems to be the final viewpoint of the narrator of the series of novels. We should remark, however, that though in this respect Snow and Eliot were basically similar, Snow was a bit more forceful and more aware of the potentialities of the future than Eliot seems to be. In 1958, Snow warned against "the characteristic intellectual treachery" of our day, which is "to take refuge in facile despair."[3] In 1962, he called for the assertion of the virtue of magnanimity in our Western world, for, if we did not exercise it, "this world is going to be hell." In the same speech, he attacked the expression of that kind of "nihilism which fills the vacuum created by the withdrawal of positive directives for living, whether religious or humanist."[4] In 1968, at Westminster College, he confessed that "I have been nearer to despair this year, 1968, than ever in my life."

Although the objective conditions in the world had led Snow to such a state of despair, he felt that the chances of immediate catastrophe in the form of nuclear warfare were not very great. To avoid the more probable future catastrophes of famine, overpopulation, and the increasing gap between rich and poor nations, he called upon all of us, and especially upon the young, to stop being trivial and to take up the great cause of working for collaboration between the powers "on the curve of population and the curve of food supply." "I should be less than honest," he concluded, "if I told you that I thought it was likely to succeed. Yet we should be less than human if we did not try to make it."[5] This desire to achieve a balanced attitude, one somewhere in the middle between extremes of easy optimism and easy pessimism, is a civilized and rational attitude, but it is probably not pleasing to those who are "hot for certainties" immediately.

Chapter Eight
Last Novels

The intriguing title *Last Things* had helped to delude those who thought Snow had put a finis to his fictional writing. Snow surprised some by publishing a new novel in 1972, and perhaps to literary critics surprising also was his reversion to the third-person-omniscient narration that he had used only once before (in his anonymous novel, *New Lives for Old,* 1933). In 1972 he was 66 years of age, and he had been, as one critic stated, elevated from a phenomenon to an institution.[1] It was strange, however, that an "institution's" new novel should have received such sparse reviews. Moreover, most of the few reviews were either unfavorable or lukewarm. The consensus was that Snow had tried hard to catch the flavor of the youth culture as it existed in the first year of the 1970s but that he had failed to portray that culture convincingly. The reviewer in *Time* observed, "On the evidence of *The Malcontents,* C. P. Snow seems to have heard about youth from a distance and caught only a faint echo."[2]

The Malcontents

The reader of *The Sleep of Reason* remembers that the relationship of children and parents was obviously of great concern to Snow and that Lewis Eliot's son, Charles, appeared in it as a teenager. In *Last Things* Charles was still more prominent, becoming a dominant character in the novel, for the aborted central situation concerned Charles and several other Cambridge students who attempted to steal an official document about germ warfare. The situation in *The Malcontents* (1972) is, in essence, similar, but the third-person narrator focuses attention almost entirely on the behavior of eight young people who are in their late teens or early twenties. It ought to be noted that Snow's son, Philip, was approximately the same age as several of the youths in the story (he was born in 1952), a fact that probably indicates Snow was basing his characters and his incidents on at least a measure of personal observation and experience with his son and his companions.

The Malcontents takes place in January 1970, shortly after seven youths (two of whom are girls), who call themselves the "core," have engaged in a conspiracy to expose a slum landlord who is a prominent Tory politician. They are motivated by their hatred of the deplorable conditions in which the West Indian inhabitants of these slums live; they also believe they are striking a blow against not only racism but the older generation who stand in the way of a better society. The book opens after the conspiracy of these malcontents is under way, and we do not know what has preceded it. They discover, in the early chapters, that one of them is a turncoat who has disclosed their plan to the Establishment. The question during the first half of the book is, Who is the informer? This part of the novel is like a detective story.

The informer is revealed to be Bernard Kelshall, a brilliant Jewish student in economics; he has been, in the tradition of the detective story, the least suspected by the others. Soon after, having been given a few drops of a drug (LSD) in his drink, Bernard dies by falling out a window. Two members of the core are arrested and tried for possession of drugs, though only one actually used hard drugs and never resorted to selling them; the other used only marijuana. The authorities decide to make an example of them by giving them prison sentences, and there is reason to believe that this treatment has been instigated by a Tory politician and his friends in the Establishment. The other five, all of reasonably prominent and respectable families, are allowed their freedom.

The chief protagonist of the core is Stephen Freer, a Cambridge student in physics. His surname is appropriate, for he is probably the one member of the core who is the least bound to hold personal animosity against the older generation, the least tied to intellectual or emotional stereotypes in his views. We do not imply, however, that he is completely free, but he is freer than the others.

One of the things Snow tries to suggest is that the youths of our time, in their urge to destroy, may be motivated by the best of intentions, but they have lost sight of the fact that a better society is not necessarily brought into being by this means. Moreover, the ends do not justify the means that have been used, for these particular youths have engaged in bribery to obtain the information they intended to use against the Tory politician. The second half of the novel concerns the disintegration of the core under the onslaught of the Establishment, whose members, it is evident, will strike back savagely at any threat to its power. The novel ultimately becomes once again a study in the uses and abuses of power, which is, of all the subjects Snow deals with in his novels, the most dominant one.

Most of the reviewers of *The Malcontents* found it extremely slow moving, especially in the first half: there was too much talk and not enough action. They also thought there was too much moralizing and intellectualizing, and they noted that almost all of the young people were indistinguishable from one another despite surface differences. Several thought Snow's core members sounded like replicas of the older committees portrayed in previous novels. Several found the conclusion particularly disturbing because it indicated complacent optimism: Stephen Freer is preparing to marry Tess Boltwood, another core member and the daughter of the bishop of the local Anglican diocese; he will return to Cambridge and take an academic position; the two families, relieved that their names have not been publicized in any scandal, welcome Stephen and Tess back into the conventional fold. If these young people are ever again to fight for a more decent society, they realize they will have to burrow from within rather than from without. "They were all, except Sylvia, talking with a kind of comfort, like passengers having got over mountains in an aircraft, the air still turbulent, but with the assurance that the worst of it was over."[3] (Sylvia is the one young person not a member of the core, whose lover, Mark Robinson, has decided to go to India and work with the downtrodden of that country; Mark is the one who had given Bernard the drug, but he confesses his guilt only to Stephen.)

We find in this novel several new departures for Snow. One is that he has abandoned the chapter titles and uses only numbers. Perhaps he did so because so many of his critics in the past had mentioned that chapter titles were old-fashioned, but no advantage is to be found in the new method. The second minor development is Snow's use for the first time of four-letter words. Several of these words, used five or six times during the novel, are spoken by core members. Obviously an attempt to make the youths' language seem authentic, the innovation is of doubtful value. Had Snow not used these words, however, he would have been charged with timidity by some critics.

Though this novel is not one of Snow's better ones, it is not without interest to his avid readers. Probably the most enthusiastic reviewer, Brom Weber, presented the intriguing view that Snow had finally shown just how "contemporary science can be incorporated into literature with enriching results." Weber reminded us that Snow insisted during the Two Cultures controversy that the "general culture must begin knowledgeably to absorb arcane specifics of its scientific subculture" and that Snow "evoked incomprehension and negation when he insisted that up-to-date

understanding of the Second Law of Thermodynamics was as humanistically essential and vitalizing as a reading of Shakespeare." *The
Malcontents,* Weber stated, "is an exciting novel, displaying not only the
ripening of Snow's literary art but also a model for those still doubtful
that science and art can be harmoniously combined."[4]

Weber's point is that Stephen Freer, a student of physics, is applying to
what has happened Werner Heisenberg's principle of indeterminacy,
which is undoubtedly one of the great theories of the twentieth century
about the physical nature of the universe. Heisenberg, a Nobel Prize
winner, asserted that fixed limits exist to our knowledge of nature, that
we cannot make infinitely accurate microphysical measurements or
predictions. According to Weber, "The principle has often been extended
into the assumption that man's ability to know any part of the world
outside himself is similarly limited."[5] Stephen Freer, thinking about the
disintegration of the core and about the individual fates of the members,
enunciates on the last page of the book, "Indeterminacy. The word from
his own trade chased through his mind. One couldn't foretell their fate,
except the fate that must happen to everybody."

We find it difficult to agree that Stephen's brief expression of
indeterminacy, or anything else to be found in this novel, represents a
thoroughgoing assimilation of science and literature; nor can we see
anything proving that a knowledge of science is as humanistically
essential and vitalizing as a reading of Shakespeare. Moreover, we can find
throughout Snow's novels the same or similar assertions or implications of
indeterminacy: the view that no one can foretell with certainty any aspects
of one's fate except the common fate—the death of all. Snow expressed
this view many times, having assimilated it into his own outlook, and
since Stephen is apparently the nearest to being his spokesman in the
novel, he is to some extent expressing Snow's almost habitual attitude.

A knowledge of this fact, however, would perhaps counteract the view
that Snow's ending of *The Malcontents* is complacent optimism. All of
Snow's novels, including this one, conclude in a similar manner: after the
conflicts have occurred, the protagonists assess in a moment of calm what
is left of the wreckage and have a sense that the worst, for the time being,
is over. This final mood is Snow's approximation to the classical trait of
reconciliation with fate that often marks so much of Greek and Roman
literature. If we believe firmly in the scientific principle of indeterminacy,
then how can we be complacently optimistic? Perhaps we may be mildly
optimistic, but we certainly cannot be complacent about very much of

anything in life. Everything is indeterminate in human affairs; all we can do is our best and hope that it is adequate.

In Their Wisdom

Snow dedicates *In Their Wisdom* (1974) to a famous American neurosurgeon, Irving S. Cooper. "Without him and his own writings, one theme in this book would not have been written," Snow says in his expression of indebtedness in the front of the book. One of the characters in this novel, Lord Sedgwick, an elderly member of the House of Lords, has Parkinson's disease, and near the end of the book is operated on by an English disciple of Dr. Cooper, using a technique perfected by Cooper that greatly improves his condition. Nevertheless, it is apparent that his improvement is only a stopgap and that in a few years the passage of time will do to him and his other elderly friends in the House what time always does to all of us. We know that in the few years preceding the publication of this novel, Snow had undergone a serious eye operation very much like that of Lewis Eliot in *The Sleep of Reason* and *Last Things*. Upon his elevation to the peerage in 1964, Snow entered the House of Lords and there became acquainted closely with some of the other members. The conjunction, therefore, of elderly lords and illness, which he had known firsthand, gave Snow one of the book's themes: these elderly lords, facing the imminence of decay and ultimate death, are a paradigm of what had happened to England in recent years since World War II. The nation that built the largest and perhaps greatest empire in the history of humankind had suddenly, in the past forty years, become a shadow of its former self; in fact, England had become relegated in modern times to the status of a second-rate nation so far as international power was concerned. This gloomy theme underlies the behavior of the many characters in *In Their Wisdom*.

The main plot of this novel concerns the settlement of a contested will. But interspersed throughout are chapters dealing with a few elderly lords who only indirectly had anything to do with the law case. These old men meet in the Bishops' Bar of the House of Lords or in some other drinking establishment nearby and discuss their problems, commiserating with one another on how difficult life has become for them. The first time we meet them, in chapter 2, part 1, we learn that Lord Lorimer puts in a fair amount of time in attendance in the House because he needs the £6.10. It is 1970, and Snow writes: "The point was, members of the House were

paid £6.10s by way of expenses for a day's attendance. There were a
number of penurious peers and some derelict ones. Of the latter, a few
appeared in the Chamber for half an hour, maybe just for the length of
question time, got ticked off on the attendance sheet, and duly claimed
their pay. Which was noticed, and not approved of, by conscientious
men." And in a footnote on the same page, Snow states that this
conversation happened some months before the introduction of decimal
coinage: later the Lords' allowance was raised to £8.50.[6]

According to Snow's brother, *In Their Wisdom* was first called *The
Onlookers*. In several ways this seems to be a better title because the
members of the House of Lords that we meet in so many chapters appear
to be nothing more than onlookers to what is supposed to be the main
plot, the contested will; they are also onlookers to what has happened to
Britain in the years after World War II, namely, its severe decline
economically and politically. Philip Snow also states that Lord Ryle, one
of the three lords whom we meet in chapter 2 and often later, is based on
his brother.[7] For many years Lord Ryle had been a historian in one of the
universities, but now, having been elevated to the ranks of nobility, he is
spending his declining years in Parliament. Lord Ryle's specialty in
history had been the industrial revolution, and he had written a number
of books on the subject. It was during the industrial revolution that
Britain had reached its heights; now that his nation was no longer at its
peak, it was somehow fitting that the historian of the revolution that had
helped make it great should be mourning what he saw during the decline.
Another member of the upper house whom we meet early in the book is
Lord Hillmorton, who tells his fellow lords in the Bishops' Bar that his
daughter Elizabeth has been wondering whether she should marry a man
called Julian Underwood. In the first chapter the reader is introduced to
Julian. An attorney, a Mr. Skelding, had been reading the will of a Mr.
Massie, who had left his entire estate, worth somewhere between
£200,000 and £400,000, to the son of his housekeeper and secretary,
Mrs. Underwood. Why Massie had left his entire estate to Julian and not
to Julian's mother, who had devoted many years to her employer, is a
mystery, though the common assumption is that Julian's mother had so
arranged it. Another mystery is why Massie had cut his own daughter,
Mrs. Jenny Rastall, off from his estate. In chapter 3 we meet not only Mrs.
Rastall but also another leading character, Reginal Swaffield, who tells her
he is determined to fight in the courts for her rights; being very wealthy,
he assures her he will bear all the costs of the fight. His motive is that
some years before he had imagined that Mrs. Underwood had snubbed

him at a dinner party given by a Lord Schiff. "Mrs. Underwood, in Swaffield's view, behaved as though she were conferring a favour on the Schiffs, by eating their dinner. Much worse, he, Swaffield, was becoming eminent as a tycoon—and she asked him what he did" (26–27).

Another important figure is Dr. Thomas Pemberton, the heir of Lord Hillmorton's title. They had seen each other only twice before the period of the book in the 1970s and had developed a mutual dislike of each other. Twenty years before, when Pemberton was in his early years as a physician, he decided to approach Hillmorton, who was then in the cabinet, in the hope that he could get some financial assistance. He was met with a stubborn resistance on the part of Hillmorton. He tried to interview Hillmorton again but could get only letters of refusal. It took some years before Pemberton accepted that he would not be able to extract one penny from his relative. "Rage smoldered. He regarded his relation, his very distant relation, with angry loathing." He couldn't understand why Hillmorton was behaving so. "The answer was simple. He was Hillmorton's heir but not his son. Hillmorton hated him, or at least was affronted by his existence—because of that. It wasn't subtle: it was instinctive: it was primitive, irrational, atavistic" (79).

Much of the concluding chapters of part one (there are three parts) is taken up with the law trial to determine whether Massie's will should be maintained or thrown out by the court, as Swaffield, more than anyone else, seems to want. It is brought out by Mrs. Rastall's lawyer, Lander, that over many years her father had made will after will leaving at least half of his estate to his daughter—until the last will. An allusion to King Lear by Lander had provoked a headline in a newspaper: "Cordelia Cut Out by King Lear." Until his last will also, Massie had left bequests to a number of people. But after Mrs. Underwood took charge of the household, all these bequests were dropped in the final will, along with that to his daughter, his only child. In 1966, four years before he died, and after Mrs. Underwood took charge of his household, his physician was changed, as was his legal adviser, who had served him for most of his lifetime. There are many pages of the events of the trial; finally, Mr. Justice Bosanquet declares the will invalid. When the trial is over, Elizabeth (called Liz most of the time), who is in love with Julian Underwood, goes to her father to beg him to give her some money, since she doubts Julian will go through with the proposed marriage without the money he had expected from the will. The most that Lord Hillmorton will give her is a promise to consult his lawyers and his accountants. It is obvious to Liz that the reason her father will not commit himself is that he is eluding her attempts to marry Julian, whom he, and almost everyone else, dislikes and distrusts.

During the course of the story, Jenny Rastall becomes acquainted with Lord Lorimer and they develop a love affair. While the trial is on she often waits for him, at his suggestion, three or four nights a week while the lords are debating a bill, "that is if she wouldn't be too bored." She sometimes sits through several hours of debate, "her English soul enjoying the flummery, her debunking mind telling her that the first necessity of the Parliamentary life must be an inordinate capacity to put up with boredom, with sheer jaw-aching boredom. Lorimer had spoken truer than he knew, but it would have upset him if she told him so" (127–28). Now and then, Snow mentions the sheer boredom of parliamentary life. It is unwittingly ironic, therefore, for him to spend so much time going into the details of a life that is tedious. If there is a fault in this book that we do not find in any of the other novels, it is this. There are just too many sheer details of parliamentary life to awaken much interest in anyone unlike Jenny whose English soul enjoyed the flummery. On the other hand, perhaps this novel is unique in the history of the English novel and may therefore have a special place all its own, for it is difficult to remember any other novel ever written that presents so much of the life of the upper house of Parliament.

In part 2, which takes place during the summer after the trial's end, Liz, in her despair, visits Lord Ryle and seeks advice as to her chances of getting money from her father so that she can marry Julian. He "seemed warmer and more forthcoming than most of her father's friends." She had imagined that she was going to ask him businesslike questions about her father's money. She does that, but the main point of her talk with Ryle, much to her astonishment, is her affair with Julian. She finds herself pouring out to him more than she had intended about Julian because somehow she feels that Ryle is "a man of feeling who cared what a man and woman felt for each other, as she felt for this one." She "found words for a cold view of Julian, not only cold but disparaging. Of course he wasn't to be trusted. Of course he was mercenary beyond any limit. . . . And yet . . . she added that he was also strictly honest with money, never borrowed from anyone and hadn't taken a penny from her, except perhaps by letting her pay for a taxi or a meal." But Ryle realizes that was what she thought she felt; he knew she feels something nearer the complete opposite. "What she most deeply felt for Julian—against most of her own utterances, and, it is true, against most of the objective evidence— was close to passionate respect." Ryle comes to realize as she talks to him that there is a fissure in her: "She was born to be a pushover for a man like Julian, and no doubt that was why he had selected her at sight." Ryle realizes as he had many times before that "repetitive patterns tell their own story. . . . What you want is what happens to you" (143–44).

Julian Underwood, the object of Liz's "passionate respect," is probably the dominant character in *In Their Wisdom,* despite the fact that there are several other strongly developed characters. In part 1, Lander, the attorney on the side of Julian, tells another attorney, " 'I take it he's a pansy.' In which Lander, like a good many others, was possibly in theory correct, in practice remarkably wrong" (108). This statement seems somewhat ambiguous and is never explained. What it probably means is that though in reality Julian is homosexually oriented, he exhibits himself outwardly to the world as a heterosexual. Though it is not Snow's method to present much of the sex life of his characters, being in this more like a Victorian than a twentieth-century novelist, we do learn here and there a few things about Julian's sex life. Liz never knew when Julian wanted to go to bed with her. "Among his charms . . . was a mildly luxurious hypochondria. He had told her recently that an orgasm spent as much energy as a three mile run" (45). One of his superstitions is attached to sex. At the beginning of their relationship she had thought this was a part of his sadistic play. "Later she believed it, or wasn't certain when to disbelieve. . . . Open-eyed, solemnly, fluently, absurdly (was he jeering at her, provoking her, making fun of her?), he had lectured her. Copulation on a Tuesday meant bad luck the following day. Or even milder sexual pleasures. It had happened to him more than once. It had become an absolute tabu" (111).

The main theme of part 2, despite a medley of minor themes, is the appeal to the legal decision. This appeal threatens to hold up the final dispensation of Massie's estate for many years; however, the two sides are finally brought together and the settlement terms announced. Mrs. Rastall will collect 55 percent of the proceeds, amounting to about £70,000, after the state gets its share; Julian will collect 45 percent, amounting to about £60,000. This settlement represents a compromise for Swaffield, who for much of part 2 had determined that he would fight on until the case could be settled in court once and for all. But just when it looked as if everybody would compromise, Julian pulls his surprise: he will not compromise for a lesser share than the other side even though he had lost the initial round. He throws everyone in a state of consternation by his decision to go ahead with his appeal.

When part 3 opens, it is the summer of 1972. Lord Ryle admits to himself that London is the most comfortable capital in the world to live in. "Ryle, whom foreigners sometimes considered very English, liked it as it was. Manners, in shops, in the streets, were less gentle than they used to be: among his own acquaintances, rather more so." When he went out to dinner, he noticed that food was much better than in his youth and that more wine was drunk and far more spirits.[8] Yet despite these matters, which were minor, there were plenty of objective reasons, he thinks, for worry: the world was really in a mess. "He didn't anticipate anything dramatic. The nation-states wouldn't suddenly collapse, certainly not in the United States; it had proved remarkably resilient, and would stay so for a foreseeable time. So incidentally, would the collectivist world" (236–38). Ryle didn't envisage any cataclysmic change in his sons' time. Quite probably, however, England would become a poor relation on the Western side. The trouble with England now, he thinks, is that the governing class is thoughtless, shortsighted, and uniformed. It is in this mood that he telephones his son Francis, who works for the Treasury, and asks him to drop in one evening after his work at the office.

When his son comes to see him, they start talking about the state of the nation, but suddenly Francis warns his father that people are talking about him and Liz, that Ryle is making a fool of himself over her, for they've been seen together a few times. Ryle becomes angry and shouts that if Liz would care to have him, which she doesn't, he would marry her tomorrow.

The scene then turns to Swaffield, who decides he will give a large party as a gesture of goodwill to each side in the dispute over legalities. He decides to invite all the principals on each side. He does this so that he can demonstrate to the leaders of the Tory party, and especially one with the most unlikely English name of Meinertzhagen, who had been seen in a number of earlier scenes, that he is a man of goodwill; this should, he thinks, help him in his future political and social ambitions. When Meinertzhagen arrives, Swaffield shows him Liz and her party and then Jenny Rastall and her party. He boasts that he has managed to get them all together in one house. "Swaffield said this with the modest satisfaction of a junior diplomat who, no credit to himself, had been able to persuade Arab and Jewish delegates to sit at a conference table" (250).

In October Lord Hillmorton dies. Dr. Pemberton becomes the first person, apart from the hospital staff, to learn of his death. He immediately sends a formal letter to the lord chancellor making known his claim to the title. Snow spends several pages describing the valedictory speeches about Hillmorton in the House of Lords and several more on the views of his friends who meet in the Bishops' Bar. One of those in the bar is Lord Sedgwick, who confides to Ryle that his disease has become worse and that in a few weeks he is to undergo the type of operation invented by the American surgeon Cooper.

As an aftermath of Hillmorton's death, Liz learns that her father had left her £20,000 but that after the death taxes are paid, she will receive next to nothing. Her fears that because she has little money, Julian will not marry her are increased. When his mother interrogates Julian about his intentions, his replies are extremely ambiguous. About the same time, Jenny Rastall moves in with Lord Lorimer as they announce their engagement. A few months later their marriage takes place; Swaffield insists on taking charge of the matter. Several pages are taken up with a description of the wedding. Shortly thereafter, Pemberton becomes Lord Hillmorton and enters the House of Lords. He had always prided himself on his abilities in medicine, but when he hears the Lords debate, he realizes that he is deficient in the art of speaking.

Shortly thereafter, as the book nears its close, the appeal court gives its decision on the case. Two of the three lord justices voted for the appeal; one voted against it. This meant that Julian's side won and Jenny Rastall's side lost. In giving his decision, one of the justices supported Justice Bosanquet in stating that the parties concerned should have reached an amicable agreement as soon as the will was disclosed, for in his opinion, going against Justice Bosanquet, there was really no basis for anything other than an agreement. On the question of costs, it was decided that half the costs should be paid from the estate, the other half by the unsuccessful party. Swaffield promises Jenny that he will give her a job that will bring in an income sufficient to live on and to help her and Lorimer to buy a house. This was a little better than Jenny expected and considerably better than she had feared, for Swaffield "had a curious reason for a little benevolence. If he had been compelled to pay the whole costs, he wouldn't have felt it. Still, like other rich men, he enjoyed saving money, and the Appeal Court order had saved him a good many thousand pounds" (314). On Julian's side, his mother had asked him what was the first thing he would do with his money. He answers that he would buy a ham. Liz is astonished. "She gazed at the babyish face on the sofa, and felt all the yearning craving love—and another kind of hate . . . she looked at him with hating love" (316).

The next-to-last bit of action in the book is mainly about the operation of Sedgwick according to the method of the American Cooper. Pemberton visits Sedgwick in the hospital and praises Cooper to him, saying that his work is so impressive he ought to be an Englishman. Pemberton, being a physician, is allowed to witness the operation, which is described in some detail. The date is 2 January 1973.

The day after the operation, Swaffield summons Pemberton to visit him; it is about a financial matter, but not at all what Pemberton expects. Swaffield tells him that his niece, Liz, is running around with "that bleeding gigolo Underwood, and he's run away with the cash. Well, you'll have to make her do the decent thing." But Pemberton insists that he has nothing to do with that side of their family. A violent argument ensues. Swaffield also thinks Julian and Liz should be made to arrange a settlement for Jenny. Pemberton says he wouldn't do it even if he could. Swaffield warns him that "Reg Swaffield isn't a good man to tangle with." But when Pemberton leaves, he tells Swaffield that, speaking as a medical man, he ought to ask his doctor to have a good look at him. "I'm not sure I like that tremor in your hand" (338–39). They both end up miserable and lonely.

The last chapter tells the course of the year 1973. Sedgwick was now walking around like a fit man, for the operation had been a success. Julian had become worried about how to safeguard his money. He bought a small house and there allowed Liz to live with him. They entertained very little, since he decided it was a waste of money. To Liz, Julian pointed out that an argument for marriage no longer existed, since her younger sister had given birth to a boy, and so the child would ultimately inherit the Hillmorton estate. In May Swaffield received a letter from the prime minister saying that he would be recommended for a knighthood, nothing more. The last page finds Ryle in the Bishops' Bar. It occurs to him to wonder how historians of the future would judge the society he had lived in. "It was possible, it was more than possible, that historians of the future wouldn't be much fascinated. It might seem a period of confusion between great epochs, and those didn't shine very bright in history." Moreover, it "seemed equally certain, from what Ryle knew of history, that the future couldn't live again the existence of any present." Was this a consolation? No, it was humbling. "Not that anyone should require humbling, Ryle thought, if he had lived in our time" (345).

On this very prosaic, undramatic note, the book ends. On the whole one can say that *In Their Wisdom* is that kind of novel: prosaic, undramatic, possibly more so than any other of Snow's novels, except perhaps the last. It has all the evidence, especially in the concluding words, of an elderly sick man's summing up of the society he had been living in, a sort of swan song. But this novel would not be the end of Snow's endeavors in that field of writing.

A Coat of Varnish

Snow's first published novel, *Death under Sail,* and his last novel were both of the detective/murder mystery genre; in the 46 year interim he wrote novels of quite a different type. Yet in some ways this last novel was not so much a detective/murder mystery tale as a novel very much like most of the others.

A Coat of Varnish (1978) is divided into four parts, and at the end of the first part, which happens to be the shortest of the four, the murder occurs. The book has to do with a group of people in the summer of 1976 who live in or near Belgravia, a section of London where Snow lived for a number of years. "At this time, Belgravia remained the most homogeneous residential district in any capital city in the world, and in a quiet and seemly fashion the most soothing to the eye."[9] At the mention of Belgravia, Snow embarks on two solid pages of what one of the book's reviewers called "a socio-economic essay on the origins of an upper-class 19th century housing development."[10]

The main character is a 60-year old retired member of the British secret service named Humphrey Leigh; there are very few scenes without Humphrey, as he is called throughout, and we are led to see almost everything through his eyes, though the book is narrated not in the first-person mode but in the third person. From beginning to end, Humphrey's observations, as well as those of many of the other characters, plus the authorial commentary, have to do with death, not only the death of human beings but also the decline of society and humankind. When one remembers that during this latter period of Snow's life he was writing amid his own personal physical decline and also that of his wife, then perhaps one can see the reason for this morbidity of viewpoint. In the second chapter, after Humphrey calls on Lady Ashbrook, the person who will shortly be found murdered, we are shown Humphrey observing and talking to two characters in their late twenties, Paul Mason and Celia Hawthorne. We are told that Humphrey "knew that he wasn't likely to live, by chronological time, more than another twenty years at most." And "he had observed in others of his own age" the same attitude. No one, however, young or old, paid much attention to the years and the passage of time and what it would bring. "Everyone, including the young, lived with the certain prospect of death, and no one believed it" (17).

Although Humphrey has these innumerable observations on the frailty of human life and human aspirations, they do not stop him from having one of the most improbable love affairs in the history of the English novel. Kate Lefroy is a beautiful woman in her late thirties or early forties; she is married but is no longer in love with her husband. She is in love with Humphrey. He is a widower, and when he sees Kate he hopes he will be able to help her free herself from the bonds of what seems to be an intolerable matrimony. Monty Lefroy is 15 years her senior; he has a high reputation as a researcher in mathematical logic: he "had an ambition to lay down the foundations of mathematics from the inside, proving them to be a man-made construction" (29). Kate had married him at a time when she was impressed with what she thought was his genius. He had retired from his academic post a short while after their marriage in order to have time to think, and Kate had spent the rest of her married life, 15 years in all, supporting Monty. Now she is disillusioned and seemingly wants to throw Monty overboard for Humphrey. Or so Humphrey thinks. However, every time Humphrey wants Kate to take some action in freeing herself, she demurs, claiming that she feels sorry for Monty, for how would Monty survive without her? And so throughout the novel Humphrey and Kate sleep together at intervals, and Humphrey feels that something should be done to enable Kate to free herself. But by the book's end, Kate is still suffering in matrimony and Humphrey is filled with desires that will not be satisfied. Apparently Monty, so Kate tells Humphrey, doesn't seem to care whether Kate is sleeping with another man. This situation enables Humphrey and Kate to give some dinner parties together and to invite some of their friends and acquaintances to talk over their problems. To the observant reader it seems apparent by the end of the book that Kate is little more than a device by which Humphrey, who appears to be helping the police in their search for the killer of Lady Ashbrook, can meet and bring together some of the suspects. In the upper-class society of London whose members live in or around Belgravia, it probably would be difficult for a man like Humphrey to give dinner parties by himself, and Kate Lefroy seems to have access to some people whom a man like Humphrey wouldn't have much to do with under ordinary circumstances. Monty Lefroy has so little to do in the book, having absolutely nothing to do with the mystery, that one wonders why Snow felt he had to give Humphrey such a love affair. Why couldn't Humphrey and Kate (or any woman, for that matter) be happily married and still perform the function for which the story needs them? But one never knows what possesses an author to do a lot of things in his book.

There are a number of characters in the novel, but by the middle of the book the police seem to have narrowed the suspects down to the murdered woman's physician, Ralph Perryman. Until the police fasten their interest on Dr. Perryman, the chief suspect had been Lady Ashbrook's grandson, Loseby, who is stationed in the British military at a base on the Continent. Humphrey and the police suspect him for the murder of his grandmother because he seems to need money often and because he has done some peculiar things in his love life, both with women and with men. He is so openly carrying on affairs with other men that to an American it seems odd that the British military would tolerate it. Whether Snow is accurate about this matter is difficult to ascertain; perhaps this is one of many aspects of life in which the Americans and the British have different attitudes. One of the peculiar things Loseby has done to make the police place him high on their list of suspects is this: during the weekend in which his grandmother was brutally murdered, he was supposed to be abroad with his military outfit but is found to have secretly come back to London, having told his superior officers a story about being seriously needed back home. He tells the police at first that he had really been carrying on with a young woman, Susan Thirkill, the daughter of a prominent member of Parliament. Then it is discovered that Loseby had actually been in a love nest with a man but had prevailed upon Susan to lie in his behalf. Amazingly, Loseby and Susan get married, much to the dismay of her father, the politician.

What leads the police to Dr. Perryman is the discovery that Lady Ashbrook had been arranging to smuggle money from America to an unknown Englishman who in turn smuggled money to her. This arrangement had been going on for several years and explained why Lady Ashbrook, who had appeared to be almost penniless, could nevertheless carry on a fairly expensive life-style. The purpose of the smuggling was to escape paying British income taxes. Probably the best part of the novel is the chapters that concern the confrontation between Perryman and Detective Chief Superintendent Frank Briers and the latter's cohorts; Humphrey can be counted among the latter, though in an unofficial capacity, despite the fact that he too could be counted among the suspects. Occasionally Briers reminds Humphrey that he is a suspect, but for the most part neither one pays any heed to this idea and Humphrey is allowed to sit in on almost every undertaking in which Briers and his crew engage, including the interviews with Perryman. It is in part 4, near the end of the year, some six months after the murder, that this interrogation takes place. Perryman at first denies being the one through whom the American conspirator funneled money to Lady Ashbrook; later he admits his complicity but denies vehemently that he had anything to do with the murder. Finally, in January 1977 Briers calls up Humphrey and arranges to meet him in the murdered woman's house; he confesses to Humphrey that even though all those in the police force engaged in the undertaking are positive Perryman is the murderer, they cannot get him to confess and there is not enough evidence to prove the case. Humphrey agrees. Briers admits his defeat and the case ends in this manner. Despite this defeat, a short time later Briers is promoted to head up an antiterrorist group in the British secret service and invites Humphrey to be an unofficial member of the group. Humphrey accepts.

The title of this novel comes from a remark by Alex Luria, a prominent American psychologist who is a good friend of Humphrey and who appears every now and then during the book's time span, which is a little over six months. The two had been in a pub and a commotion occurred by a gang of young ruffians. After the ruckus is over, Luria and Humphrey confess to each other how frightened they were. "It wasn't pretty tonight," Luria says. "Civilization is hideously fragile. You know that. There's not much between us and the horrors underneath. Just about a coat of varnish, wouldn't you say? . . . There's not much between us and our beastly selves. Human beings aren't nice, are they?" (39–40). A coat of varnish: this expression seems to fit into the mood of the whole book, and it is apparent by the book's end that the murder mystery is somewhat extraneous from the central theme. If it is a murder mystery, it is unlike any other in the entire history of the genre.

The final chapter, which is an account of the funeral of Lady Ashbrook, seems more central to the book's core than the attempt to discover who her murderer was. After the funeral is over and Humphrey is walking home, he thinks, "It was a quiet end, quieter than her life, and like the rest of us . . . she would soon be forgotten. A life, any one of our lives, was disagreeably like that day's weather, a spasm of light between the dark before and after" (328).

Perhaps when one understands that the book's true subject matter is that our lives are only a coat of varnish and that the murder mystery is somewhat secondary, then any criticism stating that it is a very peculiar murder mystery is not to be taken seriously. Of course, it *is* that, but did Snow ever intend it not be? One of his reviewers asks, "Is Snow pulling an Agatha Christie trick on us"? He is referring to a trick in one of Christie's novels, *The Murder of Roger Ackroyd,* in which at the book's end the narrator reveals himself as the murderer. This reviewer speculates that perhaps Humphrey is really the murderer, and that the book as it exists was written by him a long time later from Brazil, where he had gone to hide away from the authorities.[11] Though amusing, this type of observation is not to be taken seriously. My belief is that *A Coat of Varnish* shows every evidence of being Snow's fictional swan song, that it fits into the mood of his last few years, that he ended his life on a note of great pessimism, having been convinced that our society is so terribly fragile that perhaps it could not ever be saved. This attitude meshes with the description of his brother's account of Snow's final years, which he refers to as Snow's prevailing final pessimism.[12]

Chapter Nine
Later Nonfiction
Variety of Men

A book of biographical essays like this was, according to Snow's brother Philip, the type of writing Snow enjoyed doing and did easily. Some of these essays had originally been published in periodicals. At first the book was to be called *Men Who Have Changed the World; or, Nine Originals.*[1] That title certainly applied to several of the men, but it would have seemed to most people a farfetched title when applied to the rest; the final title chosen was surely a better one, though not so flamboyant or eye-catching.

In his preface Snow writes, "I should like the book to be read as a set of personal impressions, and no more than that." Each essay, with the exception of that on Stalin, is a biographical sketch of a person whom Snow had met. None of the sketches is a complete biography, and Snow's personal tastes dominate his impressions. It is readily apparent that he was most impressed during his life by scientific figures like Rutherford, G. H. Hardy, and Einstein. It is therefore not surprising that his sketches of these three should stand out or that his sketch of Robert Frost should be the weakest. In fact, so unsatisfactory is the piece on Frost that one is led to wonder why Snow includes it in the book. In Snow's defense, however, one can perhaps cite his remark in the preface that had he known Frost when he (Snow) was younger, he might have been tempted to use him as a character in one of his novels. Snow's remark is curious, however, because though Frost was near his life's end, Snow's still had about 15 years to go and a number of novels—about five—yet to write.

It is fitting that the sketch of Rutherford should start the volume. The great physicist represented the magical center of Snow's youthful days as scientist (see my remarks in chapter 1). From the first time he met Rutherford, early in 1930, until the physicist's death seven years later, Snow had some opportunities to watch Rutherford at close quarters and to hold serious conversations with him. In his essay Snow makes a number of sweeping statements about Rutherford and his work: "No scientist has made fewer mistakes. In the corpus of his published work, one of the largest in scientific history, there was nothing he had to correct afterwards. . . . He was as original as Einstein, but unlike Einstein he did not revolt against formal instruction. . . . [He was in his lifetime] the greatest of living experimental scientists."[2] It is clear on reading *Variety of Men* (1966) that Rutherford and Einstein represent the pinnacle of science for Snow. Of course, there can be little doubt that he was eminently correct about the worth of these two men.

One of the things that drew Snow to Rutherford was the latter's deep sympathy with the creative arts, particularly literature, which was undoubtedly unusual in a scientist. Snow describes a meeting with Rutherford shortly after his novel *The Search* was published in 1934. "He hoped that I was not going to write all my novels about scientists." Rutherford praised the novel, much to Snow's gratification. One reaction is certainly astonishing and makes a person wonder about Rutherford's knowledge of literature; he told Snow, "I didn't like the erotic bits. I suppose it's because we belong to different generations" (13). This is the one and only time, to my knowledge, that any of Snow's novels has been accused of being erotic; his work is about as erotic as that of Trollope, whom he so much admired.

The second essay in the book is probably the best, for reasons not difficult to see. Snow said his friendship with G. H. Hardy "was intellectually the most valuable of my life." This essay later appeared as the foreword to a book by Hardy.[3] They first met at Cambridge and were drawn together by their mutual love for cricket. "That night in the combination-room, it was necessary to discover whether I should be tolerable as a cricket companion. Nothing else mattered. . . . I owed my friendship with Hardy to having wasted a disproportionate amount of my youth on cricket" (23).

Among the many traits of Hardy's character that Snow writes about, several stand out. One, which was a "curious tic in his behavior," was that he was the "classical anti-narcissist" in that he "would not have any looking-glass in his rooms, not even a shaving mirror. When he went to a hotel, his first action was to cover all the looking-glasses with towels" (26–27). Another curiosity is that he never used a watch.

The research of Hardy with another mathematician, Littlewood, which produced nearly 100 papers, began in 1911 and lasted for 35 years; it dominated the world of pure mathematics for all that time, says Snow. In 1919 Hardy left Cambridge for Oxford, but in 1931 he returned to Cambridge. Otherwise Snow would probably never have met Hardy. One reason he returned to Cambridge is that at Oxford professors were turned out of their rooms when they retired at 65, whereas at Cambridge they could stay there until they died.

Another trait of Hardy's was that early he had decided not to believe in God; in fact, "God was his personal enemy" (30–31). But when he went to the cricket ground at Cambridge to watch the games, in order "to deceive the sun into shining, he brought with him, even on a fine May afternoon, what he called his 'anti-God battery.' This consisted of three or four sweaters, an umbrella . . . , and a large envelope containing mathematical manuscripts. . . . He would explain . . . that God, believing that Hardy expected the weather to change and give him a chance to work, counter-suggestibly arranged that the sky would remain cloudless" (50–51).

Snow dedicated *The Masters* to Hardy's memory "in love and reverence" (as stated in a note to that novel).

The third and last scientific figure in *Variety of Men* is Einstein. Snow begins his sketch by quoting G. H. Hardy, who said that only two men in all fields of human achievement in his lifetime qualified for the highest kind of excellence—Lenin and Einstein. Snow writes: "I wasn't quarreling with that. It was clear, all the theoretical physicists told us so, that if Einstein had not existed, twentieth century physics would itself have been different: this one could say of no one else, not even Rutherford or Bohr" (87). He does not mention why Lenin was picked as the other superexcellent being of our time. But both Snow and Hardy "took it for granted that . . . [Einstein] was the noblest man we had met" (88).

Of the many paradoxes in Einstein's career, Snow defends him on the most famous one: that he was credited or blamed for the atomic bomb, "that he, the prophet of human brotherhood, had to take on his conscience the slaughter of Hiroshima and Nagasaki, and the possibility of genocide to come. It would have been an irony, but it was not true. In practice, the discovery of nuclear fission owed nothing to his work; and his part in sending the famous letter to Roosevelt in 1939 was not significant" (90). Snow tells the story that ought to be well known. A group of refugee scientists in America (Szilard, Wigner, Teller, Fermi), having no direct channels of communication with the White House, very sensibly explained their position to Einstein. They wrote a letter, which was then signed by Einstein and sent on to Roosevelt. Einstein said he served only as a "pillar box." In 1939 there was—"unless one was an unqualified pacifist—no moral dilemma. Everyone was afraid that the Nazis would get the bomb first. If so, they would rule the world. It was as

simple as that. It was as simple to Einstein as to the crudest of men"
(120).

According to Snow, at age 12 Einstein emerged into "the kind of
cosmic religious non-belief which lasted him a lifetime. He used the word
'God' so often that people were often deceived. From his boyhood he
possessed deep religious *feeling:* but when he spoke of God he did not
mean what a religious believer means. . . . As he said himself in
middle-age: 'I believe in Spinoza's God who reveals himself in the
harmony of all being, not in a God who concerns himself with the fate
and actions of men'" (93).

Einstein was a man of powerful sensuality—that was one of the
impressions he gave to Snow when they first met. But "it is entirely
possible, and perhaps more probable than possible, that he, like Tolstoi
and Gandhi, both of whom he revered, felt that his sensuality was one of
the chains of personality that ought to be slipped off" (100).

Much as Snow admired Rutherford, it is possible that he admired
Einstein more. The portrait he paints of Einstein is of a man who had
qualities that were overwhelmingly admirable and eminently sensible.
Americans in the later period of Einstein's life often called him naive.
"This made me cross: he was not at all naive: what they meant was that
he didn't think that the United States was always 100 percent right, and
the Soviet Union 100 percent wrong" (107).

No more profound intellectual debate has ever been conducted, Snow
asserts, than Bohr's in *Epistemological Problems* and Einstein's *Reply;* this
ought to be a part of everyone's education, but unfortunately, says Snow,
it cannot be followed without some background in physics.

Snow met Einstein in his Long Island home in the summer of 1937.
They discussed politics in some detail. Snow asserts that about politics in
the wider sense there has been no wiser world figure in our time than
Einstein. His "major insights into the world situation, and his major
prophecies, have proved more truthful than those of anyone else" (114).
They discussed the coming conflict. "Einstein thought that we should be
lucky if the human race was going to stand a chance; but nevertheless, as
an absolute moral imperative, we had to do what little we could until we
dropped" (115).

Snow concludes his essay on Einstein with the assertion that of all those
he'd ever heard of, "this one was—in any sense I can imagine,
intellectual, emotional, spiritual—the most unbudgeable" (122). Unfortunately, he doesn't describe what he means by "unbudgeable," but one
takes it to mean, in light of his descriptions of Einstein's qualities, that in

the three categories of personality mentioned, the person who was least corrupted by the demands of the things and persons of this world was Einstein, the man of the highest integrity Snow had ever encountered.

In *Variety of Men* are two essays on English political leaders—Lloyd George and Winston Churchill. Snow met Lloyd George by sheer accident. He had gone to Antibes to spend the Christmas season of 1937. The former British prime minister was also there with his family; seeing Snow alone, he asked the young man to join his party. When Snow got to know Lloyd George better, he asked him why of all the guests at the hotel he had picked out Snow. "I thought you had an interesting head." Lloyd George had a passion for phrenology. "I had been selected as a subject for cranial investigation" (123–25).

The only contemporary of Lloyd George, says Snow, with greater political gifts was Lenin. From the time Lloyd George entered Parliament in 1890, he was the effective spokesman of England's Left. The greatest feat of statecraft was the founding of the welfare state (132). Because of this, for many years he was the most hated man in England in conservative circles, "much as in similar American circles Franklin Roosevelt was the most hated man in the United States" (135).

There were a number of differences Snow writes of between Lloyd George and Winston Churchill. Lloyd George was fond of women and throughout his career was known as an extravagant womanizer. Tories often called him the Goat. Churchill, on the other hand, had no use for women's company. "For me at least," Snow observes, "this softened him [Lloyd George], made him more complicated and more likeable" (137).

Watching Lloyd George during the last years of the 1930s, Snow thought that "the pursuit of power could be a passion more preoccupying and more irresistible than passions of the flesh. . . . This passion, at its most grandiose, got linked more closely than the sexual passions to a kind of supreme vanity. That was true of L.G. For he, the most subtle and proficient of flatterers, himself constantly required flattery." Lloyd George had met Hitler at Berchtesgaden in 1936; the German "out-charmed and out-flattered" the Englishman, and there was no doubt that the latter came away "admiring and bemused." And the "saddening result was that he felt ambivalent about Germany until the war began, and for some time afterwards" (144–46). In comparing Lloyd George with Churchill, Snow says that the country was lucky to have Churchill.

In the essay on Churchill, Snow asserts that oddly enough, in the early days of the war—in the early 1940s—"most of us were very happy. . . . There was a kind of collective euphoria over the whole country. I don't know what we were thinking about. We were very busy. We had a purpose." The English people "were sustained by a surge of national emotion, of which Churchill was both symbol and essence, evocator and voice" (150). During that period, until about the spring of 1941, "Churchill spoke for a nation undivided and curiously happy, as it has never been in my lifetime, before or since" (151). A curious paradox was that Churchill got little applause from his own party in those days; his real support, Snow insists, came from Snow's party, the Laborites. And another twist: after five years, when the war was won, Churchill was "promptly thrown out of office . . . by a gigantic labor majority, in the biggest political turnover in English history" (153).

It is interesting to note that the two politicians Snow wrote about in this book were the two most hated politicians in the country and both became wartime leaders. Despite Churchill's leadership during the war, Snow asserts that "anyone used to drinking in London pubs and talking to service men before the 1945 election could not be surprised when he was thrown out of office." (This writer, who was in England for only a brief time during the war—i.e., for about five months of 1944 before the invasion of France—can testify to the truth of Snow's assertion; much to my surprise, in the pubs of Britain, outside and within London, many of those who frequented the pubs spoke of throwing Churchill and his party out of power, when the war was over.) "The mass of the population wanted sweeping social reforms, and, with a surge of feeling, decided that the conservative party could not make them" (165).

One reason Churchill was distrusted was that there was no "burking the fact that Churchill's judgment was, on a great many occasions in his life, seriously defective." Compared with George Marshall, the American chief of staff who worked with Churchill during the war years, the general was dull alongside the prime minister. Yet Marshall's judgment was "usually by long odds the better" (166—67).

Snow ends his essay on Churchill by stating, "Whatever could be said against him, he had virtues, graces, style. Courage, magnanimity, loyalty, wit, gallantry. . . . He really had them." Despite his faults, "his existence had after all sweetened English life" (172). These remarks echo a passage at the opening of the same essay, wherein Snow describes listening with a friend to one of the "grand Churchillian speeches" during the desperate summer of 1940. When the speech was over, his friend said, "We must never deny our gratitude. Don't forget. We must *never* deny our gratitude" (150).

The first of two essays on contemporary writers in the book is the one on H. G. Wells. At Cambridge during the 1930s Snow said that he never exchanged a word with G. E. Moore or A. E. Housman, probably the two best-known literary people who were there during that period. But he met Wells under odd circumstances. Snow's novel *The Search* came out in September 1934 and had a good reception. Later that autumn a letter came from Wells telling Snow that he had read the book and inviting him to London for lunch.

Wells at first talked to Snow of nothing but the fact that someone called Moura would not marry him. Only occasionally did Wells get off the subject of marriage. "He was taking my novel as though it were straight, factual autobiography. . . . He assumed that I had had a disappointment in research, and so wanted to give it up. He didn't want me to. He had always wished that he had stayed a scientist" (65). What Wells wanted to talk to Snow about was "marriage, Moura, and the scientific life."

Then Moura herself entered. She was then a woman in her early middle age, "handsome, dashing, strong as Mother Russia." Wells looked at her with love and irritation. His irritation grew when Moura talked to Snow. He was not invited there again, though he and Wells met many times away from the latter's home. Snow writes that he became fond of Wells, "though I doubt whether I picked up very much that I could not have divined from his books" (66). Snow relates that he had never seen anyone more upset by bad reviews than Wells. "He suspected conspiracies. He wanted to murder literary editors and critics. He didn't think his friends were protecting him. More likely, he hinted darkly, he hadn't any friends. Then in a few days it all blew over, and he seemed to have forgotten that the book had been published at all" (66–67).

Snow compares Wells with Dickens in being a man of strong sexuality. "Like Dickens, in his early manhood he was a bad picker" (77). Had Wells gone into university life, as he often wished he had, Snow believed he would have gotten into trouble because of his sexual exploits. Though he was not much to look at, being short and tubby, he was "a wonderful talker, he wanted women—it did not take long for women to want him." He "chose for his major loves (or they chose him) some of the most remarkable women of his time" (79).

The only poet in the book—and the only American—is Robert Frost. Of all the poets of our time, why was it Frost, one wonders, to whom Snow was attracted? And why, as Snow speculates, had the Russians so embraced Frost? It was in Moscow several months after Frost's death that Snow attended a memorial lecture on the American poet.

Analyzing Frost, Snow says of him that he was not an especially good man by the standards of Einstein or Hardy. He was capable of acting. He spared nobody in getting anything he wanted. "He was sometimes a bit of a fraud. His character was altogether more variegated, more heterogeneous in its structure, than that of any of the others in this book" (176). Snow admits that much of what he came to know of Frost was from the letters the poet wrote for nearly 50 years to Louis Untermeyer, "a literary record that is one of the great documents of self-revelation" (178). In fact, much of what we read in Snow's essay can be found by any good reader of Untermeyer. It is only a good digest of what can be found there; missing is any analysis of Frost's poetry. Indeed, one wonders whether Snow had read much of Frost's poetry—the assumption is Snow had done so, but there is little evidence of it.

One interesting note is that Frost received more honorary degrees than any writer—around 50, according to Snow. Do we detect a wistful note in Snow? Not really, for Snow didn't do badly himself—31 honorary degrees in addition to a number of other awards.[4]

Despite the honors Frost accrued, he was envious of the honors given to T. S. Eliot, especially the Nobel Prize. "Of all the passions, envy . . . is the least agreeable to contemplate. It is the passion most of us detest bitterly in ourselves. But unluckily it is the occupational disease of much professional life, particularly of the artistic life." Comparing writers and scientists, Snow writes: "Scientists are no more angels than writers, but they haven't the same temptations. . . . Of all professionals, I thought, seeing Frost in great age, still not serene, writers have the hardest job to make themselves good men" (194–95). This said, Snow states that of all the people in this book, he would have chosen Frost, after Hardy, for sheer company. (Lloyd George would have been his third choice.)

The last two essays in the book are on Dag Hammarskjöld and Stalin. Snow was uncertain when he first met the secretary general of the United Nations; it was in either 1959 or 1960. Incredibly to Snow, he was reminded of G. H. Hardy, which he admits was absurd. Hardy was the most extreme of antinarcissists, whereas Hammarskjöld was the most extreme of narcissists. But despite their surface contradictions, they would have understood each other. Of the nine men covered in this book, Snow says Hammarskjöld was unlike all the rest in two particulars. First, he was the only one of them who was a religious believer: "Einstein was a man of strong religious *feeling,* but no belief, and that is quite a different thing." Second was Hammarskjöld's heritage: "He was the only one of them, with the exception of Churchill, to be born in the upper-class" (207).

Snow quotes a great deal from W. H. Auden's preface to Hammarskjöld's book *Markings,* his introspective diary. The single point on which he disagrees with Auden is the remark that for a man of his temperament, political life was not Hammarskjöld's natural milieu, that he was a man whose job was to carry out a policy, not to decide one. Auden, says Snow, was misreading Hammarskjöld's history: from the time he was 30 he had been making major decisions in Swedish public policy. The evidence is conclusive that he was impelled into the life of action at its most exposed (213).

There is one very startling remark in this essay: "If the UN had never existed, the world today would be exactly the same place." Since 1945 the world has been governed by power politics. The United Nations has been nothing more than a debating society (216). Hammarskjöld exaggerated the importance of the United Nations, an outlook that was, of course, natural to him. He "was one of the heroic failures." But that should not make us despair too much, for "without heroic failures, we shouldn't have many hopes at all" (217).

The last essay, on Stalin, is the longest one. Stalin is the only one of these persons Snow had never met. He begins with a frightening anecdote related to him by the Russian novelist Leonov. When a young man, Leonov had been invited to meet Stalin. A number of writers were at the party, including Maxim Gorky. The subject of Dostoyevski came up, and Leonov observed that though Dostoyevski was a reactionary, Russian writers always needed him. Stalin barked out in almost a fit of frenzy, *"What right had he to say that?"* Leonov told Snow that if Gorky, the patron and benefactor of many Russian writers of his generation, had not intervened and told Stalin that one must respect what Leonov said, he was sure his life would not have been saved, "for he belonged to a literary generation, the first after the revolution, that suffered many deaths in the coming purges. . . . No, said Leonov, he had no reason to love Stalin" (227–29).

One of the singular features of this story is that Stalin "was much more deeply educated in a literary sense than any contemporary western statesman. By his side, Lloyd George and Churchill were abnormally ill-read, and so was Roosevelt. . . . It is difficult for westerners to realize that in meeting Soviet politicians and scientists they are entering a society better educated in literary (not visual) terms than their own" (229–30).

Snow insists that had he met Stalin, he would have been more disinterested than most of Stalin's interviewers whom he had read. Why? "I love Russia. I have done so since, as a boy, I became fascinated by

Russian literature. . . . I couldn't resist the mixture of broadnatured realism with the subliminal desire for salvation. . . . When I was still a boy, I learned a simple fact that seemed to escape some of my acquaintances: it was just that Russia didn't begin in 1937. I think that bit of sense has made me keep a fairly level attitude to the Soviet system'' (237).

In assessing Stalin, Snow points out that only Lenin before the revolution was shrewd enough to see that Stalin had important abilities; all the other Bolsheviks around him, like Trotsky, despised Stalin because he didn't have the oratorical and writing talents they felt a leader should have. Lenin, however, "wanted a practical man: and he had discovered one of the most effective practical men of all time" (245). In later years Trotsky was still expressing incredulity at Stalin's rise, and Western intellectuals have wondered how Stalin ever got there next to Lenin and later succeeded him as head of the party and government. "The question doesn't need answering. The government was faced with civil war: the economy was wrecked. . . . Stalin was a first-rate administrator, the only one Lenin could rely on." In return, in Stalin's whole life "Lenin was the only man for whom he felt absolute respect and loyalty" (246–49).

In just a few pages Snow traces the power struggle between Stalin and Trotsky following Lenin's death. During Lenin's lifetime Stalin played it cool. Unobtrusively he got the party apparatus into his hands, and he got hold of the party's personnel machine. Trotsky didn't have much of a chance. He was an intellectual's politician; he was arrogant; his judgment tended to be brilliantly wrong. He didn't have the animal instincts a politician needs. Stalin did.

In discussing Stalin's later actions, Snow says there can be little doubt that he was a paranoid. "It is true that western observers in the Hitler war meeting Stalin for the first time, found an impassive harsh, magisterial statesman. But one ought to remember two things. First, paranoia can and does co-exist with complete rationality at other levels, in fact at all levels when the root of persecution is not touched. Stalin could remain a masterly strategist and administrator on all subjects which didn't impinge on the delusional system" (264–65). Despite Stalin, many Russians, contemporaries of Snow, "warm one with the illimitable Russian hope" (270). The essay ends on this note of hope for the future. When Snow wrote this essay there were few others in the West, in Britain and America particularly, who felt this glow of hope and understanding of the Russian people; most were, and still are, highly suspicious of things Russian.

Trollope: His Life and Art

Throughout the last decade of his life Snow gave much of his time to thinking and writing about those novelists of the nineteenth and twentieth centuries who were closest to his literary tastes—the realists of novelistic fiction. Two books were the result of this work. The first (1975) is on Anthony Trollope, the novelist of the past toward whom Snow seems to have felt the closest affinity, despite the statement made in his brother's book that Trollope had been "far less" of an influence than "Tolstoi, Dostoevski, Balzac, Stendhal, Proust, Turgenev," and "perhaps R. M. du Gard."[5] (Du Gard, incidentally, is a surprise, because if Snow ever mentioned him elsewhere, one is not aware of it.) But if we read Snow's critical writings on his own novelistic influences, there can be little doubt as to Trollope's stature in Snow's mind, despite occasional remarks like the one in his brother's book and perhaps elsewhere.[6] In his book about Trollope, Snow's affinity with and tremendous regard for the nineteenth-century English realist is discernible.

The book on Trollope is handsome, containing many black-and-white illustrations and photographs in addition to 22 extremely attractive color plates. The book is subtitled "His Life and Art," but of the 19 chapters in its fewer than 200 pages, only 2 are on his art—about 23 pages in all. Now and then, however, in the chapters on Trollope's life, Snow makes a comment on artistic matters.[7]

Much of the book's first part deals with Trollope's childhood and youth—a period Snow describes as extremely miserable. "It is hard to think of any good writer who had as wretched a time and had to endure it for so long. By comparison, Dickens's experience in the blacking factory was an episode, and Dostoevsky, shut up in the claustrophobic apartment of a Moscow hospital doctor, had a relatively ebullient boyhood." The young Trollope "was weighed down by twenty years of neglect and humiliation" (9–11). When one thinks of how much some human beings suffer during their youthful years, it is difficult to believe that Trollope's suffering is the worst that any "good writer" has ever suffered; however, one would not want to argue with Snow about the two examples he gives of "good writers" who suffered less than Trollope. What was the type of suffering Trollope endured? He was a day boy at Harrow, for example, which meant that the young boys who were not day boys, who lived at Harrow, jeered at Trollope's type "as an inferior pauperized breed." His father was responsible for this treatment because he spent hundreds of pounds on their house and farm but allowed his sons to wear shabby clothes. "Patches, their sleeves too short, footwear out at heel—it was a sight to arouse moral derision to any right-minded schoolfellow." Of course, the Trollope boys "felt wounded, ashamed—and these shames in youth were never quite forgotten" (21–22).

Snow's greatest scorn for Trollope's harsh treatment during his childhood is reserved mainly for his mother, the noted writer Frances Trollope. She neglected Anthony and invested great hopes on her son Tom, "who actually had good sound second-rate ability." And she spent considerable efforts to find something for her other son Henry to do. "The most preposterous exhibition of this neglect occurred when he [Anthony] was twelve." The Trollope family, she decided, was to move to America, and she would restore their fortunes by opening an emporium in Cincinnati. Mrs. Trollope lost all her money in this crazy venture, but the most curious feature of all was that she took her other children with her to America but left Anthony behind. He didn't see his mother for three years. "There weren't even rudimentary provisions for his holidays. . . . It isn't even clear where he managed to go or how he managed to feed himself, in what must have been intolerably long and lonely summer vacations. There was one which he spent, quite alone, in his father's deserted chambers in Lincoln's Inn. There Trollope read an old edition of the plays of Shakespeare, because he could find nothing else to read" (25). The young Trollope, says Snow, was weighed down by 20 years of parental neglect and humiliation. When he was left behind in England, he contemplated suicide.

The book that made Frances Trollope famous was *Domestic Manners of the Americans*. Although she expected to make a fortune from it, she made only £900 in the first year of publication. The book still reads "fresh, snobbish, malicious, irrepressible, often funny, curiously enough more sympathetic than the total flavour of her personality. It has something of the impact of Malcolm Muggeridge writing about the Soviet Union. In modern times, she would have been a first-rate descriptive journalist" (33).

His mother, despite her neglect of Trollope, did occasionally do something for him, Snow admits. She moved the whole family to Bruges; this time she took all her children with her. Then, when he was 19, she managed to procure a position for Trollope in the post office, where he would stay for most of his life. But at the end of the same year his brother Henry died. His older brother, Tom, was summoned to the funeral; Trollope was not. Two months later, their father died; again Tom was called, but Trollope was not. "No wonder, he cried out in old age that, at nineteen, he often cursed the hour he had been born. Even in his sixties that wretchedness was unassuaged" (38).

In 1843 Trollope started writing. He had been sent to Ireland by the post office. The Irish countryside and the life there set his imagination going. "Like all realistic novelists—like Tolstoi, Dostoevsky, Proust, Galdós—Trollope needed the reassurance of something he knew at first-hand to set his imagination going" (64). His first novel, *The Macdermots of Ballycloran*, is, according to Snow, an exceptionally good novel. But "[o]wing to the crass misjudgment of Michael Sadleir, it has continued to be under-rated in England, and it has taken the fresh eyes of young American critics to see just how good it is" (65). It ought to rank, Snow declares, not too far below his five or six masterworks.

From 1857 onward, Trollope was a very successful professional writer. That was the year of the publication of *Barchester Towers,* one of his best novels and one of the best in the whole Victorian age. That was also the year of Dickens's *Little Dorrit* and the year Matthew Arnold gave his famous inaugural lecture at Oxford, in which he regretted how low was the present state of English creative writing. "When Arnold published it (in 1865), he could have read, say, *Little Dorrit, Adam Bede, Great Expectations, The Last Chronicle of Barset.* Who believes that he had done so?" (79).

As to Trollope's art, Snow points out that Tolstoi, among others, admired Trollope's novels. "It is a nice irony of literary history that when English critics were being scornful about *The Prime Minister* (the entire press the worst he ever had for a serious novel, while modern opinion would rank it among his best) Tolstoi was overcome with enthusiasm for precisely the same book. 'Trollope kills me, kills me with his excellence.' Tolstoi was at that time writing *Anna Karenina*" (106–7). It is evident that to Snow, as expressed in this book and elsewhere, Tolstoi is just about the highest judge of literary excellence. If he could admire Trollope tremendously, then why could others not do so? Snow rushes to defend Trollope from his detractors, even those of the past. Trollope was to many critics of his time little more than "a photographer. It was a worthy thing to be, but not the highest. He could be respected for giving an exact replica of various sections of mid-century society" (108). Trollope, however, did not mind this type of criticism. He was both a modest and a realistic man. "If people in his own time knew him as a social photographer, that was better than nothing. A writer like himself was lucky to be known for a tiny part of his intention. He would probably have been overjoyed and astonished if he could have known that a hundred years later he was still known as a social photographer. For that does remain . . . until readers acquire extra intuition—a major part of his reputation" (109–10).

It was Henry James who understood the depth of Trollope's art more than any other, and it is this aspect of Trollope that Snow champions also. "There is no simple term for Trollope's greatest gift—without which he would be an entertaining minor novelist." For want of a better shorthand expression, Snow comes up with the term *percipience*. "He possessed it to an abnormal degree, perhaps as high as any on record." The quality may be more common in women than in men, Snow states, "and it may not be an accident that women often seem to understand Trollope's novels more naturally and deeply than men." Trollope had this percipience. Tolstoi understood it. Henry James wrote about it in the middle of a long essay that expresses his anxiety to discover why he found Trollope's work so good; Snow quotes James at length from this essay, written in 1883 for a review and published again in a revised version in *Partial Portraits* in 1888. According to James, "If he was in any degree a man of genius (and I hold that he was) it was in virtue of this happy, instinctive perception of human varieties. . . . Trollope will remain one of the most trustworthy, though not one of the most eloquent, of the writers who have helped the heart of man to know himself." Snow says nothing of the derogatory clause about Trollope's eloquence but merely adds, "There aren't many better statements about Trollope's percipience or the meaning of the realistic novel" (114–15).

Trollope's percipience, his attitude toward other human beings, can be ranked, says Snow, with that of Tolstoi, "the greatest of all." Among his abilities, he possessed "the most useful piece of technical equipment a novelist can possess"—his ear—"his ability to suggest in his dialogue the tone of spoken speech, and of each different person's spoken speech." Trollope was one of the masters of such dialogue. "When Henry James said that Trollope had a good ear, he was using that as a metaphor for Trollope's general sensitivity" (153–56).

Snow concludes his very readable account of Trollope's life by saying, "For some of us, he will remain one of the most admirable characters in literary history, where experience shows it isn't easy to be such a character. The reason for this is simple. A writer, particularly an exploratory psychological writer such as Trollope, has to live on close terms with the blacker—including the worse—side of his own nature. . . . It takes unusual moral fibre for a writer to make himself into a decent man. Trollope did it" (175).

The Realists

Three years after the book on Trollope was published, *The Realists* (1978) came out. It comprises eight portraits of realistic novelists, a short preface (6 pp.), and an even shorter epilogue (3 pp.). All the portraits are approximately the same length, with the single exception of the one on Dostoyevski, which is much longer than any of the others. (To be exact, here are the lengths of all the portraits: Stendhal, 34 pp.; Balzac, 36 pp.; Dickens, 29 pp.; Dostoyevski, 75 pp.; Tolstoy, 38 pp.; Galdós, 38 pp.; Henry James, 40 pp.; Proust, 36 pp.)

In his preface Snow attempts to define realistic novels. The following statement is clear and fairly definitive of Snow's view of what he is attempting to show: "In the great realistic novels, there is a presiding, unconcealed, interpreting intelligence. They are all of them concerned with the actual social setting in which their personages exist. The concrete world, the world of physical fact, the shapes of society are essential to the art. The people have to be not only projected, as novelists, major and minor, have tried to project them, but also examined with the writer's psychological resources and with cognitive intelligence. Both these components are features of realism" (iii).

The first novelist dealt with in the book may offer some problems for the readers, if not for Snow. The inclusion of Stendhal among the realistic novelists was remarked on by several of the first reviewers of the book. As one reviewer stated, Stendhal seems out of place in a book titled *The Realists* because he is usually considered a transitional figure and not a pure realist, and Snow unwittingly seems to imply as much when he states that Octave in *Armance* is the first romantic antihero, that the plot of *La Chartreuse de Parme* is "romantic in the extreme," that Stendhal remained a romantic, and so on, continuing with a number of similar statements.[8] One of the most surprising statements, which follows Snow's explanation of Stendhal's outlook on life, is that "he loved to hear people call *le beylisme*." This was in reference to Stendhal's real name, Marie-Henri Beyle, which he wasn't overfond of, preferring his assumed name. "*Beylisme* was, of course, the expression of his romantic dreams, though it was half mocked by his classical and disgruntled mind. Often his cynicism and outbursts of sarcasm tell their own story. They were the protests of the unworldly. Worldly men don't talk or even think like that. To operate in the practical world you have to feel as others do, and take it on trust" (11–12). One might also look at the following paragraph about the political passages in Stendhal's novels. They might have been written, says Snow, "by an intelligent stranger—or by a Martian." Mosca in *La Chartreuse de Parme* as a politician "is something constructed by an alien." Certainly these aspects of Snow's treatment of Stendhal seem to be running counter to his definition of realistic novels in the preface.

If the reader can digest Snow's inclusion of Stendhal among the greatest realistic novelists without any severe internal discord, then the rest of his portrait will go down easily. (Lest the reader misunderstand my attitude, the argument is not with Stendhal, who is undoubtedly among the greatest of all novelists, but with Snow, who includes Stendhal among the realists.) Snow traces Stendhal's life from childhood to his death and paints an interesting portrait, managing now and then to bring in several of Stendhal's outstanding novels, though focusing primarily in this and all the other portraits on Stendhal's biography. Snow makes no claim to present a solid, lengthy discussion of a work of art; it is the portrait of the artist rather than his art with which he is mainly concerned.

He begins his portrayal of Stendhal by asserting that the proper age to begin reading him is 20: he has a "special fascination or poignancy for young readers." This is because he "preserved a young man's hopes, restlessness, discontent, romantic dreams, isolation" (2). As a young man and even later as an older writer, according to Snow, Stendhal sought self-knowledge unsparingly. This search did not give him any of the empathy with other human beings that came so naturally to other writers, such as Chekhov or Trollope. "In fact, Stendhal showed little insight and foresight about other human beings, especially women, all his life. . . . He wasn't a psychologist in the sense of understanding others' makeup or having perception about their purposes and their fates. He hadn't any such kind of detached curiosity. His intense curiosity about himself was for his own benefit" (5).

Snow next asserts that Stendhal showed unusual mathematical insight. Snow then makes the first of many statements in which he compares a facet of one writer with aspects of some or all of the other writers dealt with in the book or even with facets of a writer not treated in this book. He says that "[l]anguages apart, [Stendhal] probably had the best academic mind (in the technical sense) of any eminent novelist, except maybe George Eliot." He never defines what is meant by "technical sense," but since he is speaking about Stendhal in the context of his mathematical abilities, one supposes that is what is meant by "technical." Because of his mathematical ability, Stendhal was sent at 17 to Paris to study, but he deceived his father and didn't sit for the entrance examination into the École Polytechnique. Instead, he decided to obtain literary glory.

It took him until he was 43 to write his first novel, *Armance*. The stimulus, says Snow, always came from outside. There had been published several novels in Paris on the theme of impotence. Stendhal thought he could do better, and so he wrote *Armance* very fast, as he did all his other novels. This leads Snow to assert: "Most, though not quite all, of the world's great novels have been written fast. . . . Flaubert's example to the contrary for a long time interfered with the true record of literary history" (25). We are not told how quickly Stendhal wrote *Le Rouge et le noir,* perhaps his greatest novel, but that he wrote his second greatest novel, *La Chartreuse de Parme,* in five weeks in November and December 1838. It runs to 300,000 words. "It was written at the rate of eight thousand to ten thousand words a day, which is the all-time speed record for a major novel" (30–31).

The next writer Snow turns to is Balzac, whose miserable childhood Snow describes as such: "There are plenty of accounts of the wretched school days of illustrious writers, but for neglect his ranks high, at least as high as Trollope's, which is saying a good deal" (38).

Balzac's family wanted him to study law, but at 18 he decided he would be a writer; his mother agreed to pay for an attic apartment in Paris and to give him just enough money to keep him alive for two years. Let us have a look at him at 19, says Snow. He was very short. "The average height has gone up by inches in the past 150 years, and nearly all writers in this book were short by our standards. Balzac wasn't much above five feet." Owing to lack of food, he was very thin. But he didn't stay thin. "As soon as he could get his hands on any money, he became remarkably fat." Snow pictures him walking down a street with Stendhal. "It is a nice picture . . . both little, both fat, two of the finest writers on earth" (41–42).

In 1833, at age 34, Balzac wrote the first of his great novels, *Eugénie Grandet.* It was a success, and that was the arrival of the legendary Balzac. "Commercial success didn't reduce his debts but increased them." He couldn't resist the lure of furniture, objets d'art, all sorts of things. "Like Stendhal he had great faith in dazzling clothes, and went to an expensive tailor. The minor fact that a tiny little man, ludicrously fat, with very short legs, wasn't really equipped for the fashionable costume of the 1830s didn't strike him. . . . He was ridiculous. He was Balzac. He had proved that he was a great genius. He was" (50).

Snow seems very much concerned with the work habits of the writers.

He spends much space on Balzac's. He got three or four hours of sleep between dinner and midnight. Then he put on a white robe and sat at his desk for six hours. He kept himself alert by drinking coffee. "He may have notched a world record in cups of coffee consumed per year." From nine in the morning until one, he corrected proofs. For many of his novels there were six drafts. He had an egg for lunch, then more hours of proofreading. This meant a working day of about 13 hours. "No modern professional could endure anything like such labor, and it wouldn't be good for anyone to try. Of course, it wasn't good for Balzac. It may have shortened his life" (52–53).

Snow wonders how Balzac found time for his love affairs. One affair in particular, however, Snow spends much time discussing near the end of his portrait: Balzac's 18-year wooing of one Madame Hanska. With the exception of his telling the story of *Le Père Goriot,* which Snow and almost everyone else consider Balzac's greatest novel and one of *the* greatest novels, Snow spends more time discussing this affair than he does discussing any of Balzac's novels. Though the episode is amusing, one wonders why Snow devotes so much space to it. Balzac genuinely felt he loved Madame Hanska, but his love was buoyed by her money; for a writer in much debt, this was something very important. He visited her several times in her home in Poland. Finally, he had a heart seizure. The czar, Nicholas I, had prevented the other attempts to woo Madame Hanska. But now, with Balzac dying, the czar, who admired his books, gave his consent. Balzac survived three months. Victor Hugo, "the other monstrous genius of contemporary France," delivered a funeral oration.

Charles Dickens is one of the two English writers dealt with in this book, and Snow states in his first paragraph on Dickens that it is possible to argue that in the English language he is "the most marvelous writer after Shakespeare" (72). Snow looks into Dickens's life and points out, first of all, that he was "more profoundly wounded by class than any other major English writer. No one wrote with more passion, indignation, and concern about the sufferings of the poor; but the last thing he wanted was to be identified with them" (74). In fact, Dickens so overcame any sense of inferiority the wound may have given him that he went to the extreme of considering himself "the Inimitable" (note the capital *I* used by Snow): most great writers are not lacking in self-confidence, "but Dickens lacked it less than any other" (75).

After reading the first two portraits we are not surprised that Snow early in his portrait of Dickens points out Dickens's relationships with women. Like Stendhal and Balzac, Dickens seemed to be a physically passionate man. Unfortunately, "he had remarkably little intuition about women. This is evident in his novels, and in that respect they don't stand the remotest comparison with Balzac's." Poor Dickens: he had everything in his favor—attractiveness, glamour, early and continuing fame, plenty of money from 25 onward, "everything that the other great novelists might have envied," but "he was a worse chooser of women than any of them." The women he was associated with in his life "were all disasters" (77).

Snow's penchant for making sweeping statements comparing writers comes out again when he turns to Dickens's specific literary works. He became a national figure at 25 when *Pickwick Papers* was published. "No first novel in any language has made such a stir" (77). Five years later he wrote *Martin Chuzzlewit,* "which has strong claims to be the best sustained comic novel in English" (81). Writing then of Dickens's comedy, Snow declares that little of Dickens's humor is gentle, less perhaps than "that of any other of the novelists, though he was more exuberantly funny than all the rest put together, if we forget about Proust" (82). This is a surprising statement, for though few can deny that comic moments do occur in Proust's works on occasion, who except for Snow has ever considered Proust as outstanding as Dickens was in his comedy? This one statement does a great deal to whet our appetites for the portrait of Proust later in the book. We look forward to Snow's proofs for the preeminent comic genius of Proust.

Snow indicates that Dickens from age 25 until his death was a powerful man of business. "The moment he had his first intimation of moneymaking success, he was determined to get what he wanted. Nothing should stop him" (84). This leads to a lengthy paragraph on the differences between the fortunes of major Victorian writers and those of their contemporaries elsewhere: "The English were all competent at literary business and effective with their money—Dickens, Trollope (straightforward, but driving hard bargains), Thackeray (after youthful extravagances, just as prudent), George Eliot (with Lewes beside her, the sharpest operator of the lot), Hardy (careful to the point of miserliness). Their French colleagues, Hugo apart, were usually in financial trouble, and Stendhal and Balzac never got out of it. The Russians were either well-to-do landowners (Tolstoy, Turgenev) who made unnecessary fortunes out of books, or penurious men (Dostoevsky) who made much less" (85).

Despite being a tremendous success as a writer, Dickens found himself under an increasing strain as the years went on. An answer, which he came increasingly to accept, was his unhappy marriage. His wife, Kate, had borne 10 children in 15 years, along with several miscarriages. "But he had been bored and irritated by her very early—and Dickens wasn't the man to accept that some of the trouble was on his side. . . . Poor dear Mrs. Dickens, said the benevolent millionairess Angela Burdett Coutts. At the heart of the domestic life of the greatest apostle of glowing family well-being there was a falsity and a fraud" (89). Dickens "had little insight about women, and less about what a woman could give him. . . . The description of David's utter abandonment to Dora [in *David Copperfield*] is one of the best descriptions of young love in any literature—but it is all on David's side." Again we are brought back to a sweeping comparison: "All the English Victorian novelists were handicapped by comparison with their European colleagues, he more than any. The English shone in their business deals—but, when one thinks of them alongside Balzac, Stendhal, Hugo, Tolstoy, Dostoevsky, they hadn't much knowledge of adult women in their flesh and bone" (90).

Much of the last pages of the portrait of Dickens is spent on the unhappy love affair with a girl of 18, Ellen Ternan. Poor Dickens: "The detail of his life in its last years is harrowing even to imagine" (98). It is not a pleasing portrait of the novelist whom Snow considered his greatest predecessor and second only to Shakespeare in the pantheon of English writers.

He next turns to Dostoyevski, and his portrait of the Russian novelist is almost twice as long as any of the others. Snow spends the first five pages on Dostoyevski's childhood, after which he states: "Whether those years of childhood left much of a mark on him is doubtful." The reader may wonder why, then, so much space is given to the subject, but Snow never gives an answer. All he goes on to say is that "underneath all the forces that struggled unresolved in his nature, he had astonishing resilience, as much as any man" (106). Perhaps, then, this is why the Russian novelist is given twice as much space as any of the other writers, even the other Russian, Tolstoy. In the others, the forces that struggled within were resolved, but in Dostoyevski alone the internal forces were unresolved. This is, of course, sheer speculation; Snow never tells us. But it can be seen that Dostoyevski's life was more eventful than the others and also perhaps more enigmatic.

Take the case of the Petrashevsky Group and its aftermath. It is safe to say that no other major novelist was ever faced with such an ordeal. The group was liberal; in a society like that of America, Britain, France, it would have encountered no great opposition from the government. But

Russia was then, as it has been in our time, an authoritarian society. The czarist government had a remarkably efficient secret service. The Petrashevsky Group was arrested, and all of them, including Dostoyevski, were in prison for months. And then the czar played his famous trick on them. They were sentenced to death, but at the last moment, when they were expecting to be shot, the czar commuted the sentences. Instead of being executed, the prisoners were sent to spend years in Siberian prisons. If this was not excellent material for biographical exposition, nothing was. And Snow gives up another five or six pages telling this familiar story. The episode also provokes Snow to some interesting speculation:

It has been thought that this exercise of the Tsar's humor was the cause or trigger of Dostoevsky's epilepsy. That isn't true. It had started years before. In a life so ravaged by drama, and so full of what appeared like mental changes, it is a temptation to pick on simple causes. Why did he become devoted to the Tsarist regime? Why did he become the most fervent of Christian spokesmen? . . . [T]he short answer . . . is that Dostoevsky had a mentality, as well as a temperament, of wonderful ambiguousness. It would be possible, if one selected quotations from his work or letters, to prove that he believed almost anything, or alternatively nothing. (122)

Is it any wonder that to portray Dostoyevski, Snow felt he had to write more pages than for any of the other novelists? And after being sentenced there were the four years spent in prison in Siberia. "Those convict years were an experience that no other great writer had to endure. Later he wrote an account of it, only slightly transmuted, in *The House of the Dead,* clear-eyed, utterly without rancor, as though this had been a singular act of God that had happened to someone else. Tolstoy thought that it was one of the most truthful studies of human suffering ever written, unsentimental in its fellow feeling, which is true. It was the only book of Dostoevsky's for which Tolstoy expressed any praise" (124).

Out of prison, Dostoyevski was sent to serve as a private soldier. He was not allowed back in Petersburg for 10 years after he had been sentenced. He kept on writing and became a success. With his brother he started a new magazine. Unlike Tolstoy, he supported the emancipation of women. Meanwhile, he had married, but the marriage had gone wrong from the beginning. Then he had a disastrous love affair with a girl 20 years his junior. He began to gamble. Debts piled up and threatened to overwhelm him. Throughout all these and more vicissitudes he kept on writing. And Snow has what amounts to a field day telling of all the troubles and turmoils of this great novelist who, along with Tolstoy and Turgenev, was famous not only in his native land but elsewhere, as in England. Snow devotes many of his pages to an account of another love affair with a 20-year-old woman, Anna Snitkina. His first wife having died, Dostoyevski married Anna; they had 14 years together before he died. Through Anna he was able to let his instinctive realism guide or even control his imagination, according to Snow. "That is why the major novels of those last fourteen years are sensually much richer, and much more balanced between mind and body, than anything he had written before. There is nothing disembodied about the women in *The Idiot, The Possessed, The Brothers Karamazov.*" Anna saved him "from his own imagination" (148).

The marriage between Dostoyevski and Anna was a supremely happy marriage, Snow declares, "one of the very few enjoyed by major figures in literature." And it was one that no one who knew Dostoyevski "could have conceivably predicted. Who would have given him chance of happiness—compared with the glamorous Dickens, and the massively prepotent Tolstoy? But it was Dostoevsky, not they, who became happy" (150).

It was not, however, a marriage without difficulties. Snow spends a number of pages on the hardships the husband and wife endured while abroad for four years. He had epileptic fits, and she had to look after him. He gambled, and she had to endure that; very few wives would have coped with his gambling mania and all the other strains of their marital difficulties. "Visits to pawnshops became part of their way of life." And in Florence, "where they had run out of money altogether, Anna pawned some of her underclothes" (154). Anna had to fit herself into another of his routines. Like Balzac, Dostoyevski wrote at night. "Anna went to bed while he wrote for five or six hours. . . . Then he woke Anna, at four or five in the morning and gave her . . . a long and lingering good night" (155).

Not only does Snow give more space to Dostoyevski's life than to the lives of any of the other novelists in the book, but he also discusses the novels themselves at greater length than he does the novels of the other writers. Dostoyevski, says Snow, accused himself of never carrying his conceptions to their proper fulfillment. He thought he often lacked the technical power to do so. "He wasn't specially interested in finding a mode to express the movements of the inner consciousness." Dostoyevski really had only one resource that he used for every effect in his novels: a dramatic dialogue "heightened beyond the limits of any dialogue that could be spoken, yet miraculously suggesting not only actual emotion but also the intermittencies and purposes of the mind and soul" (157). Using this single technique he created the great character of Prince Myshkin in *The Idiot*. And for Snow that novel ranks at the peak of Dostoyevski's art, second only to *The Brothers Karamazov*. A feat without parallel, Snow declares, is using Myshkin to suggest goodness. No other major writer has been able to equal that.

As Snow nears the end of his portrait of Dostoyevski, it is fitting that he discusses *The Brothers Karamazov*, which he, and almost every other literary critic, thinks is not only Dostoyevski's greatest work but also one of the greatest of all works of fiction. The principal triumph in that novel, Snow declares, is the dramatic conversation between Ivan and Alyosha in a saloon. "Few people who have read that conversation . . . can forget it. It is one of the most memorable scenes in all literature. To some it seems above and beyond literature, and the impact has been so shattering that they can remember the precise place and time where they first read it" (172).

That was the greatest triumph of Dostoyevski's career, and it came near the end of his life. The book was serialized in a periodical during 1879 and 1880. In his sixtieth year, Dostoyevski died peacefully, on 9 February 1881. "It is estimated that twenty thousand people joined the funeral procession. Nothing like that had happened for a writer anywhere, though four years later as large a crowd in Paris followed Victor Hugo's coffin to the grave" (176). In Russia, the climate for Dostoyevski's writings has changed several times, according to Snow. In the hard climate of the 1930s, his books were disapproved of. Though Stalin thought he was one of the most marvelous of all writers, he also thought he was a dangerous influence. But in recent years the attitude has softened: new editions have been printed, works of scholarship have appeared, and the public appetite for Dostoyevski has become much hungrier than in his lifetime.

The next novelist Snow discusses is Tolstoy; this portrait is half the size of the other, but Snow's admiration for Tolstoy is just as pronounced. The question is, he says, whether *War and Peace* or *The Brothers Karamazov* is "the ultimate height of all novel writing." But neither Tolstoy nor Dostoyevski would have considered any comparison reasonable. Dostoyevski couldn't understand why all the fuss about Tolstoy. Tolstoy had even less use for "the one contemporary of his own stature." He thought Dostoyevski's work "*superficial.*" In any case, according to Snow, there is no question about Tolstoy as a writer, but there is considerably more question about him as a man. He quotes several writers' views of Tolstoy. The one by Gorky, who knew Tolstoy, is one of the more interesting: "Count Leo Tolstoy is an artist of genius, perhaps our Shakespeare. But although I admire him, I do not like him. He is not a sincere person; he is exaggeratedly self-preoccupied; he sees nothing and knows nothing outside himself. His humility is hypocritical and his desire to suffer repugnant" (180).

According to Snow, there are no factual uncertainties about Tolstoy's life, as there are about so many writers; this is so because of his own diaries, the diaries of his wife, and "the hypnotized attentions of contemporaries. . . . Very few lives, maybe none, are better documented day by day." The difficulties rest entirely on how to "interpret a personality at the same time so overwhelming and so inconsistent." Tolstoy was inconsistent, rather than, like Dostoyevski, "multifariously complex." His personality mystified the "most acute psychological observers in Russia, including at times himself" (181).

Tolstoy's childhood was exceptionally happy and exceptionally privileged; accordingly, the time spent looking at his childhood and youthful years cannot give us much of a clue to the Tolstoy of later years. He spent a few terms at a university but soon decided he could educate himself better than his instructors could. When he was 19 he inherited a large estate of many acres and more than 300 serfs. He began living the life of his peers, which consisted of gambling, drinking, and womanizing. "The last occupied more part in Tolstoy's existence than even in that of most men, and it was a determining, dark, and, in the end, disastrous part. He had immense appetite for the natural world, and more immense still for women. His sexual passions were imperative. But he doesn't seem to have had much affection for women. That may be a strange or foolish thing to say about one who has produced some of the most delectable pictures of women in all literature. It has to be said with all kinds of qualifications. Yet, with reserves, it contains a truth" (187).

The trouble with Tolstoy, says Snow, is that he suffered from an extreme form of sexual guilt. "After each copulation—and there were very many—he went through agonies of self-reproach." *The Kreutzer Sonata* is "the fiercest expression of sexual guilt that most of us have ever read. Women were the temptation and the enemy, exactly as they were to Christian saints like St. Anthony." Tolstoy was in this respect a great contrast to Dostoyevski, who was capable of being guilty about many things, but not of sex and women. Tolstoy would today be considered a male chauvinist: "Women were made for bed, in lawful marriage, for breeding children, since copulation, even in marriage, was utterly unjustifiable without the object of reproduction; for suckling children . . . ; for the kitchen" (188).

Snow discusses Tolstoy's marriage with his wife, Sonya Behr, at some length and compares it with that of Dickens. Tolstoy's marriage was one of the most famous and written-about in literary history. Both he and Dickens had "egos of adamant impregnability. Both lacked, to an extent astonishing in great writers, passive sensibility. Both had a simple and absolute belief in God, and in no other religious formulation whatever." Unlike Dickens, Tolstoy was not bored with his marriage, because Sonya was a "far more intelligent and spirited woman than Dickens's Kate. . . . But it would have taken an ego as powerful as Tolstoy's own to give her a chance of winning through to a tolerable life." Both men were inconsiderate with their wives, and neither wife enjoyed her marriage. There are several other resemblances between their marriages, but one of the most unusual is that "both of them developed something more than an affection for their wife's younger sister." Dickens made a "mawkish cult of Mary Hogarth, and idolized her in his half-childish characters such as Little Nell. Tanya Behr was the original of Natasha Rostova, one of the most truthfully drawn and endearing women characters in all fiction" (199–201).

In writing about *War and Peace,* Tolstoy's greatest novel, Snow again comes back to comparing Tolstoy with Dostoyevski, who had written the only other novel, Snow had said previously, that is comparable to Tolstoy's great epic. Dostoyevski's insight and imagination were unmatchably different from those of other men. But "Tolstoy's weren't." He dispensed with imagination in the conventional sense when he looked at human beings. "Dostoevsky revealed human beings, with his complicated vision, from the inside out. Tolstoy revealed them from the outside in. That is, of course, how most people try to understand others." In most of his art, "Tolstoy was as direct and as near ordinary mortals as a great writer can be. That is one of the reasons why the personages in *War and Peace* seem immediately people we know, and don't need interpretative effort on our part." After 100 years there has not been a novel that gives us such an assurance of truth with such finality (203–5).

Seven years later Tolstoy wrote *Anna Karenina.* He wrote *War and Peace* in cheerfulness, but not so for the later novel. And after it was finished, he came more and more to lose his respect for art. He became almost like a world evangelist, "to many the symbol of moral hope and redemption.

His voice reached beyond Russia all over the world, to an Indian lawyer in South Africa by the name of Gandhi. To those longing for a secular religion, or a practical ethical rule to live by, Tolstoy became a leader and something like a saint." Tolstoy attained his position by the written word because he was no good at speaking. He wrote of the moral life; that one should have faith in God; that one should live like Jesus; that one should turn the other cheek, never offer violence; that killing was absolute evil, and so was war; that punishment was a crime; that one should possess nothing and live like the poor; that the flesh was sinful and by chastity one could avoid sin (208–9).

The last pages of Snow's portrait of Tolstoy show that despite the picture that appeared to the world of Tolstoy as the peasant prophet saint the reality was that his home was "riven and seared by the bitterest family hatred." He wanted to give away all he possessed, which meant giving away all his wife and children possessed. They finally settled on a compromise by which the earnings on his books written before 1881, which included his two greatest successes, *War and Peace* and *Anna Karenina,* remained in the family estate. "So the family lived like richer people than Tolstoy's ancestors. And he was living with them, even if he did dress like a *muzhik* and eat nothing but vegetables and eggs" (210). But the battle within the family, led by his wife, went on. Snow recounts the famous end of Tolstoy's life, but a few pages before that he compares Tolstoy's attempt to live the moral life and to exhort others to do the same with Balzac's nonattempt. "No one ever tried less strenuously than Balzac in those directions. All the evidence tells us that everyone who was close to Balzac, including women who were simultaneously his mistresses, felt that he had brought them happiness. To all those close to Tolstoy, his children, most of all his wife, he brought misery" (212). Snow draws no moral from this comparison; nevertheless, the implication is strong that there was something hollow at the core of Tolstoy's life, however one admires his great art.

From the two great Russians, Snow's next portrait is of an artist almost entirely unknown outside Spain. But Snow insists that Galdós "was a great novelist, of the same kind, and of the same stature, as others in this collection." He goes on to compare him with Balzac, and Galdós is "not . . . diminished by the comparison." His masterwork, *Fortunata y Jacinta,* "is one of the finest of all novels, and no more profound studies of women's personalities (the two women of the title) have been written" (217).

Snow paints a portrait of Galdós as a man almost cocksure of himself as a future great writer. When he was in school he won awards for his oil paintings, and later in life he often ornamented the margins of his manuscripts with drawings. His mother insisted that he go off to Madrid from their household in the Canary Islands to study law, but the young man knew he would be a great writer: "he didn't really doubt that he would make it." That was his state at 19; that was still his state "when he was old, blind, after he had fulfilled his vocation," and when he was "nearly as poor as when he had started" (200–1).

He began by writing plays in the manner of Schiller; they are said to be dreadful and have never been performed. "Determining whether they are more dreadful than the other plays executed by the greatest nineteenth-century novelists and poets would be a nice exercise in comparative literature" (223).

Galdós was a liberal all his life, and fought for liberal ideas: He wanted a national rebirth for Spain, but, like Dostoyevski, he was skeptical of any political solution; like the great Russian he thought that rebirth could come only from inside the individual. He believed that this rebirth could start with his own novels. One of the ways he felt he could lead his fellow Spaniards was to attack the church. "It was the Church, untouched in its medieval power and in blank ignorance, that kept Spain primitive. Galdós was immovably anticlerical" (226). But he was a man of strong religious feeling, and in some of his later novels this religious feeling is intense.

According to Snow, Galdós was the most disciplined of professional writers because he had to be: he wrote more than 80 novels and more than 20 plays. Some of his novels are of immense length. He had to sit down to his work and to do it methodically. He got up at dawn, and with sips of coffee he started in writing till one o'clock in the afternoon, day after day. Snow goes on to compare Galdós with Balzac in his knowledge of his subject matter: Balzac knew Paris with almost complete familiarity, but Galdós knew Madrid in a way that Balzac did not know Paris: he knew the lower depths; he knew Madrid from the aristocracy down to the seething slums. "James Joyce proclaimed that, if Dublin were destroyed, that wouldn't matter. It could be reconstructed from the text of *Ulysses*. It wasn't in Galdós's style to make that kind of boast, but he could have done so about Madrid, and with more justification" (232).

La desheradada (The Disinherited) is the right introduction to Galdós for English-speaking readers. There is an effective translation by Lester Clark, says Snow. *Fortunata y Jacinta* is deeper and richer, however. It was written when Galdós was between 42 and 44 and was published in four parts, each of them more substantial than the standard twentieth-century novel. Snow gives a short summary of it and several other novels.

Galdós had a singular life. He never married, but no one knew how many children he had: he spent much of his life among prostitutes and his children. "It isn't easy to think of anything much like it among major writers." Maupassant picked up many women "with an addiction as compulsive as Galdós's. . . . As a footnote, Maupassant acquired syphilis, and died in his early forties. Galdós didn't acquire syphilis, and lived to be seventy-seven" (245–46).

Galdós became the grand old man of Spanish literature in his later years, not only for his novels but also for his plays. Despite the fact that he had some enormous successes in his novels and in the theater, he spent his later years in poverty. There is some mystery about that, but he was an incompetent where money was concerned, being a spendthrift. His friends rallied around him and tried to obtain the Nobel Prize for him. But the conservatives refused to cooperate; the Catholic press became violent. Galdós never got the prize and never became much known outside Spain. But near the end of his life the government saw to it that Galdós did not die in poverty. When he died of uremia, he was given a funeral procession such as no writer had ever had in Spain; some 20,000 people were in it, and it was comparable to the processions for Dostoyevski in Russia and Hugo in France.

The second English novelist in the book is Henry James, who was born an American and didn't become an English citizen until World War I. Snow starts off his portrait by stating something that is undoubtedly true, but to someone like me—a person more familiar with James's writings than with those of any of the other writers in the book, with the exception of Dickens—it seems most unusual and particularly indicative of Snow's own interests: "It is difficult in the records to discover anyone who knew Henry James and didn't like him. He was the most decorous and responsible of great writers. He was polite beyond the limits of politeness, and he was also very kind" (256). In the back of one's mind one knew this, but certainly few of those who have written of James ever stressed it, and a teacher dealing with James's works almost invariably ignored it. But Snow puts it at the outset of his essay and goes on to show how James was sent floods of manuscripts from fellow writers; he read them all and wrote letters of immense length trying to find some good in all of them. In England he attracted more respect from his contemporaries than any other writer then or since. "He was the literary pundit of his time." In the midst of all the veneration given to him, he didn't have much personal happiness outside of his literary work. He never achieved great popular success. "More than with any other major novelist, except maybe Galdós, . . . his life consisted of being a professional writer, and nothing else" (265).

In America in the 1860s James was encouraged by literary friends like James Russell Lowell, Charles Eliot Norton, and William Dean Howells to write not only stories but also literary criticism. He started his career "with a very long, pontifical, intricately worked-out essay on the Art of Fiction." He had "conceived most of his theory of fiction before he wrote fiction himself." He could say as a young man that Dickens was "the greatest of the superficial novelists," which, says Snow, "was not sensible." And it was also not sensible to remark "that the novels of Tolstoy and Dostoevsky were loose, baggy monsters, which meant that he didn't understand their art at all." But at the same time he could believe, and did so all his life, that Balzac was the greatest of all novelists. Curiously, says Snow, "there isn't any doubt that of the great novelists, Balzac is about the last to be fitted inside the Jamesian confines" (266). A few pages later, Snow observes that James's only genuine admirations in literature were for Flaubert and Turgenev, especially the latter. Their feelings about novel writing were similar, and James's novels "can stand beside Turgenev's, as they cannot, in spite of his attempts at critical demotion, beside those of Dostoevsky and Tolstoy" (268–69).

The only novel of James's that Snow discusses at any length—and that only superficially, for three or four pages—is *The Portrait of a Lady.* "People can and do disagree about other works of Henry James; this novel is, however, recognized as one of the best ever written in English" (274). But his novels in the 1880s were not as well received. *"The Bostonians, The Princess Casamassima, The Tragic Muse* had the virtues of his gift, but didn't strike his admirers as utterly right. Nor were they. He wasn't the most adroit of theoreticians for nothing, and he could put up elaborate defenses, but he may have known that there was something faulty at their roots" (278).

What was wrong? It is not altogether clear as presented by Snow. But apparently it was something sexual. There was developing a deep disquiet. James was shaken by meeting and reading Maupassant. "That hard and explicit sexuality couldn't be the way to understand people, Henry reflected on paper. It was the enemy of all psychological explanations. . . . No one can be sure. What is established is that Henry was walking, half blindly, into a tenuous relation with a woman. Nothing happened. It would have been better if it had, for through his negligence the woman suffered great harm" (279).

The reference is, of course, to the tragic affair with Fenimore Woolson, a novelist who had achieved more popular success than James. She admired his works and apparently came to love him. He gave her some encouragement. "He was obtuse and, if you like, egocentric not to realize that to her he was the one home for her emotions. . . . At last, alone in Venice one winter, she threw herself out of a window" (280).

The next sentence reads: "We had better think for a moment of Henry's sexual temperament." Then: "It is now the conventional wisdom to regard him as a homosexual in the Proustian mode." Snow continues: "Proust probably was a genuine homosexual. He also was not timid about sex, very likely not timid with women, and quite surely not with men. Henry was abnormally timid about it, so timid that it wouldn't be unreasonable to guess that he never tried. Instead of thinking of him as a homosexual, we may be nearer the truth to change the term. He was more like a crippled, profoundly inhibited, frustrated male" (280–81). And Snow quotes at length a paragraph by a psychologist, Edgar Friedenberg (but, unfortunately, does not tell us the name of the essay or book that the quotation is from), who writes that there are men who have great anxiety about heterosexual relations and who therefore retain the erotic attitudes of preadolescence. Presumably, therefore, Henry James could be put into this category.

Snow goes on to portray James as discontented with his novels because he never achieved the popularity he thought he deserved. He turned to the theater, hoping that through the drama he would be able to achieve some great popularity. He was deceived, or rather, he deceived himself, because "Henry wasn't made to write plays." Besides, "he had another deficiency that was fatal. He despised the drama as an art form." One cannot, Snow declares, write anything valuable "if one despises what one is doing." James may have thought "that no plays, except maybe Shakespeare's, could compare, in depth and richness of effect, with the best novels, including his own." What he failed to realize was "that good plays are more difficult, perhaps more chancy, to write than good novels" (285–86).

Snow turns from the theater to James's writings on the art of fiction and again finds James deficient. "He is the only major novelist who has developed a defined ideological theory of the art. . . . On the whole, it is perhaps fair to say that the James theory did harm rather than good.

It was made too restrictive. His insistence on the point of view would have made the whole of Dostoevsky, Tolstoy, Dickens impossible to write. . . . Above all, the theory couldn't have accommodated Balzac— to whom . . . Henry with generous inconsistency produced the most passionate of all tributes" (287). His theory did, however, serve a more direct purpose:

It should be said that what follows is a minority view. By late middle life, Henry's art was tending to run thin in substance. He wanted to say some difficult, or certainly complicated things, but there were not so many of them as appears. When a fine and conscientious writer runs thin in substance, he falls back on his technical virtuosity. . . . Henry had great technical virtuosity, which was more than reinforced by an ideology of technique. He had been allured by Ibsen's symbolism, and used it, as in *The Wings of the Dove* and *The Golden Bowl.* It didn't really suit him. It did, however, help out a substance wearing thin. Similarly with the language of the later novels. Often it did not say more than he had said already, though not in such Alexandrian profusion. (288)

One wishes Snow had gone into this diatribe against James a little deeper. For example, what is that Ibsen symbolism that allured him and wore thin the substance of his novels? But one supposes that Snow is not writing a critique of novel writing but is painting a portrait and can therefore possibly be excused for his lack of positive information to substantiate a charge.

The best of the later James, according to Snow, is *The Ambassadors.* It would have been better for the reader had Snow gone into his choice of this novel a bit more, but after stating this choice, he said only that it is a book in which there is a reworking of earlier themes.

The essay on Henry James is undoubtedly the most unsatisfactory of all the eight in the book. The reason is simple: of all the novelists dealt with, the work of James, especially the later James, was to Snow too "Alexandrian." The reader senses that in dealing with James, Snow felt he was again coming very close to his differences with the literary intellectuals, such as F. R. Leavis.[9] And it was not only the Alexandrianism of James's later works that Snow disliked—it was also James's literary theory, especially his condemnation of those writers who departed somewhat from the strict point of view. James's advocacy of the strict point of view undoubtedly hit home against Snow's own writings, which occasionally departed from it, as some critics, including myself, had pointed out. A big question mark remains: If James was not in harmony with Snow's beliefs, why did Snow include James in his book and omit, glaringly for some people, Flaubert, whom so many critics have believed to be one of the greatest of the realistic novelists? There is apparently no answer to the exclusion of Flaubert. But could it be that by putting James into *The Realists,* Snow was able to have someone he could use as a literary punching bag?

The final novelist dealt with is Marcel Proust. Several pages into the portrait, Snow makes a surprising statement about Proust, very similar to an earlier one made in his portrait of Dickens—that "Proust is the funniest of the supreme novelists, if we except Dickens." By "supreme novelists" one can only suppose Snow meant the eight discussed in this book. The reason the remark is surprising is, as mentioned earlier, that even though most readers of Proust are aware of the writer's sense of humor, it has never been viewed by critics as one of his leading qualities. No one can deny that Proust's humor is probably equal to that of the other writers addressed in this book, excluding Dickens, but no one would choose any of the others as particularly distinguished by their humor. It is perhaps revealing that after mentioning Proust's great use of humor, Snow drops the subject for the rest of the portrait.

Snow presents Proust's life as biographers have come to know it, spending several pages on Proust's homosexuality, on his relationship with the Jewish community—especially the fact that his mother, Jeanne Weil, came from a prominent Jewish family and that most of Proust's money came from her side of the family—and on his schooling and other such things. Among other matters, Snow notes that Proust was a snob of the most determined type. In his novel *Jean Santeuil,* published after his death, Proust is "completely candid. He wanted to climb. He was beglamored by the aristocracy." But "[t]here are worse vices than snobbery. One has to be pretty self-bound when young not to imagine that there must be some life more glamorous than one's own." Still, "[i]t didn't take Proust long . . . to conclude that the very rich and very lofty were no more admirable than those he had known elsewhere" (312).

After about five years of the beau monde, "the highest society that he could reach in Paris," Proust discovered that it was no good. "It wasn't always stupid, but it often was. It was heartless. It was empty. It had no reason to exist, except to preserve its existence. He would have reached that verdict anyway, for none of his romantic dreams could survive his honest and relentless mind; but his disenchantment was quickened by the Dreyfus case." Most of the French society was anti-Semitic. Proust "behaved with absolute guts. . . . If that was society . . . he wanted no part of it." He took part, with his brother Robert, in pro-Dreyfus campaigns from the start (314–15).

After the turn of the century, Proust began writing in earnest. He wrote first a long novel, *Jean Santeuil,* and it is puzzling that he would not allow it to be published. It is in the same class, according to Snow, as an English novel published not long after Proust put his manuscript away—Maugham's *Of Human Bondage,* "which is at present undervalued." The reason may be personal: some of the things in it would have pained his mother. But there is another reason that "may cut nearer Proust's artistic core. People may differ about some of his gifts, but it is difficult to differ about his insight as a critic." He knew that *Jean Santeuil* was a good work, but "emphatically not a great one" (316–17). He had to write a great work.

Several years later, he wrote *Contre Sainte-Beuve.* It was an attack on the most famous of the nineteenth-century French literary critics who represented most of what Proust considered destructive, since he was setting down his own theory of the novel. "It is a masterly treatment of novel writing. By his side Henry James as a theoretician seems to be trying altogether too hard. In *Contre Sainte-Beuve* Proust is writing like a supreme novelist, and with intellectual dexterity that no critic has surpassed" (320).

Contre Sainte-Beuve is undoubtedly an interesting and good piece of literary criticism. But one wonders why Snow felt that in exalting Proust as a critic he had to downgrade Henry James, especially in light of the fact, admitted by him in his essay on James, that the majority of the critics did not agree with his views on James as a critic. (I myself admit to being on the side of the other critics.) Undoubtedly, however, Snow was expressing his own long-held view and that of his wife on Proust and on James.

In 1909, at age 38, Proust began writing his masterpiece, *A la recherche du temps perdu (Remembrance of Things Past).* The first volume was published in 1913. He took resolute steps to see that it was promoted properly. Money did not pass hands, wrote Snow, in Proust's attempts to court the critics. But "[n]early everything else did," for Proust wanted fame, recognition, prizes. Not surprisingly, the book, titled *Swann's Way,* had a good press. News of the book reached England soon. "If the war hadn't intervened, Proust would have had international fame within two or three years" (325). As it was, he did achieve international fame before his death in 1922.

The portrait Snow paints of Proust is by no means entirely praiseworthy, despite his great regard for Proust as a writer. Snow seems to have followed Proust's biographer, George Painter, whom he quotes (328). Painter "tells us . . . with passionate and poetic regret" of Proust "climbing to the loftiest level of his art and also . . . descending to the pit of Sodom." Snow mentions the scene of M de Charlus being whipped in Jupien's homosexual brothel. It wasn't invented; it was something he had watched. "It is now known that he had financed that brothel, and got a spectator's interest out of it."

Snow says that *A la recherche* has a young man's wisdom. As with Stendhal, the book is best read in one's early twenties. That book was Proust's life. Snow stated that we wouldn't be much interested in Proust had he not written that work. "We should have been interested in some writers if they had not produced their major works or (as with Dickens, Dostoevsky, Tolstoy) any literary works at all" (330). One is incredulous at that remark; except for Snow, who would be interested in Dickens, Dostoyevski, and Tolstoy had they not produced their literary works? How could one have known about them?

Snow concludes his portrait of Proust by saying that if he were asked to select one Western work of literature written in the twentieth century, Proust's *A la recherche* "would be the one" (333).

In the short epilogue, the question is asked, "Would it be possible to write such realistic novels today? Will it be possible again?" As a provisional guess, Snow says that the social conditions in the advanced societies of the West are not at all suitable for the writings of great realistic novels. "From what we can deduce of the past and from the writers in this book, the best conditions appear to be an untidy but energetic social life around one; a public that may be quite small but is ready to respond, appreciate, and believe that such novels are really worth studying and cherishing; and above all, hope, social and individual, somewhere in the future" (335–36). Snow says that some of the Western societies possess the first of those conditions, but not the other two.

The Physicists

This book is a first draft, completed just before Snow's death on 1 July 1980. An introduction, written by his friend William Cooper, states that Snow intended to write the book at greater length. Cooper relates that when Snow first told him about the book, he asked, "Good God, you'll have to do some research for that, won't you?" To which Snow replied,

"I'm writing it largely from memory."[10] It is an amazing piece of work to have written it largely from memory, and one can forgive Snow's errors that some of the reviewers have mentioned. As one reviewer states, the expert can quarrel with Snow's book as being peppered with small errors, but these imperfections should charitably be blamed on the fact that the author died when the book was only in its first draft.[11] The layperson in physics, like myself, has no idea what the errors were exactly, and since the reviewers mention that the errors were small and trivial, one can assume that on the major matters Snow was generally accurate.

It is a handsome book. Its 192 pages have a large number of drawings and photographs, such as a full-page photograph of the Curies and of such eminent physicists as Edward Teller, Enrico Fermi, and Niels Bohr, as well as of places, such as one of Times Square, New York, with a view of the large crowds that celebrated America's victory over Japan in World War II.

Among the statements made by Cooper in the introduction, this one stands out: "He was one of the most magnanimous of men, in all senses, public and private, I've ever known. I venture to suggest that the dark view, the hope, and the magnanimity all shine through *The Physicists*" (10). The dark view of the work of the physicists and the hope are dealt with at the very beginning of the book and at the conclusion, because Snow wanted his readers not to forget that there were two sides of the immense labors of the great physicists. That is what he meant by calling his final chapter "The Double Legacy." His very first paragraph in the book in the first chapter sets the tone for the whole work: "In not much over a generation, physicists have changed our world. That applies to the most elemental of situations, life and death. Nuclear weapons are an achievement of applied physics. To many people they have brought a new kind of fear. It is hard to be cool-headed about this, in the atmosphere of our times. . . . [I]t isn't comfortable to live with the thought that it is within human power to exterminate a sizeable fraction of the world population within a matter of hours" (16).

Snow's book traces the history of modern physics, which began in the last years of the nineteenth century. "Modern physics began with the discovery of the particles of which atoms are made: first electrons, then protons and neutrons" (21). The 40 years to the outbreak of World War II "were a wonderful time for the physicists to be alive." There were many important discoveries, but in 1938 came "the most fateful experiment of all, the splitting of some uranium atoms with an emission of particles which could lead to further splitting, with the possibility of a chain reaction and the release of huge amounts of energy" (35). Throughout this period, the dominant figure was Ernest Rutherford, who ranks with Faraday as the greatest of British experimental physicists. As Snow had stated before, Rutherford occupied a large place in Snow's own life. It is interesting to note that though Rutherford is usually associated with Cambridge and the Cavendish laboratory, which under his guidance became the world center of physics, his major individual work was done at Manchester before he came to Cambridge. There is a rare photograph in the chapter called "Founding Fathers" showing Rutherford in the Cavendish laboratory and above him a sign stating TALK SOFTLY PLEASE. The notice was aimed at Rutherford, whose booming voice upset the apparatus.

Snow emphasizes how little money was spent on the great scientific researches. Rutherford's experiments were built with the help of one laboratory technician; everything was homemade. "The Cavendish was a great experimental laboratory, but it would look like a badly equipped high school compared with the big physics institutions of today." Until World War II there was little industrial support for physicists. Young physicists in the 1930s considered themselves lucky to get decent jobs in schools. "A few years later, in the war, they were being snatched up as the rarest and most valuable of human commodities." Rutherford and his colleagues had little to do with money. It bored Rutherford. "He was a remarkable unmercenary man." When he died he left almost exactly the amount of his Nobel Prize, which at the time was something like £7,000 (42).

After discussing Rutherford, Snow spends some pages on an even rarer character leaving his mark on world physics, Albert Einstein. Ironically, Einstein was not awarded the Nobel Prize for his major theory, relativity, but for some early work on the effect of light on metal surfaces. Though his work was so important, he was not at all portentous. "He was the best company of all the great physicists." He was often "more than a bit of a deliberate clown." But when he felt deeply, "he was rather like an Old Testament prophet" (43–50).

In the center of the book is a long chapter entitled "The Golden Age" (62–75). This was the period after 1919 when Rutherford started firing alpha particles at nitrogen atoms. "By knocking out a hydrogen nucleus (later called a proton) from the nucleus of nitrogen he had converted it into another element, oxygen." That work led to the great experimental work on the atom at Copenhagen, under Niels Bohr, and at Göttingen, under Max Born. Among their disciples were Paul Dirac and Werner

Heisenberg. They were all, says Snow, physicists of genius. The 1920s was a marvelous decade. Among other great feats of physics, Heisenberg produced one of the most dramatic, the "uncertainty principle"— "meaning that the exact position and precise velocity of an electron could not be determined at the same time." And this led to something more disturbing, "that, in the sub-atomic world, causality broke down. It would never (literally never) be possible to predict exactly where an individual electron would be." It was now possible to say "that the fundamental laws of physics and chemistry were now laid down for ever." Dirac crowned the achievement of that great decade by combining many of the ideas of Heisenberg, Born, and several others with the relativity theory of Einstein. In 1928, Dirac pulled all the strings together and showed that incorporating relativity removed the last of the atom's puzzles. He explained the rather odd fact "that individual electrons spin around on their own axes, like miniature tops, as they orbit within the atom."

Snow, a man of letters as well as of science, concludes the chapter with an interesting literary analogy: "As well as the great names, there were many other men of talent milling around in those dazzling days of modern physics. It was a bit like the Elizabethan-Jacobean theatre. Then, anyone who could write at all could add something. The major genius of Shakespeare, and perhaps the genius of another—Christopher Marlowe —would have triumphed in any period. Others were lucky just to be borne on the collective wave."

This period of scientific explosion was a time of triumph and hope. But it did not last long. The very next chapter is called "The Clouds Gather," and its first paragraph explains the meaning of this ominous title: "The 1930s saw a convulsion in Europe which the scientists did not anticipate, and which then disrupted many of their lives. They were forced into the greatest emigration of intellectuals since the collapse of Byzantium, and one far more dramatic and influential than that" (79). Since many of the physicists were Jewish, they found themselves ultimately homeless under the Hitler regime. The great Einstein left Europe and came to America. Bohr arranged for Copenhagen to be a staging post, though one too near to the Reich for long-term safety. The great faculty at Göttingen was broken up. The United States received a high proportion of the Jewish scientists.

By the summer of 1939 it was known all over the scientific world that a new atom or uranium bomb was a distinct possibility, with all its awful possibilities. One of the appendixes to *The Physicists* is the now-famous editorial by Snow in the magazine he edited, *Discovery*, of September 1939. It is entitled "A New Means of Destruction." In discussing whether the bomb would ever be used, Snow wrote these ominous words: "We have seen too much of human selfishness and frailty to pretend that men can be trusted with a new weapon of gigantic power. Most scientists are by temperament fairly hopeful and simple-minded about political things; but in the last eight years that hope has been drained away. In our time, at least, life has been impoverished, and not enriched, by the invention of flight. We cannot delude ourselves that this new invention will be better used" (177).

In the chapter called "This Will Never Happen" Snow tells of the growing apprehension of some of the scientists about the possibility that Germany would acquire the means of making the bomb. In England several of the scientists were urging their government to acquire the uranium ore in the Belgian Congo. In America three scientists of high class, Hungarian refugees, were campaigning for urgent action; they were Eugene Wigner, who would soon receive the Nobel Prize; Leo Szilard; and Edward Teller. To them the "prospect of a fission bomb in Hitler's control meant nothing short of doom" (103). It was they who decided to go to Einstein and persuade him to write a letter to President Roosevelt. The letter was drafted by Szilard, but Einstein signed it. This probably most famous letter of the twentieth century is also an appendix to Snow's book (178–79). It urged Roosevelt to speed up the experimental work by providing more funds and by helping to obtain the cooperation of industrial laboratories; it warned of the danger to the world if Germany obtained the means to make the bomb.

Once again, Snow takes issue with the "romantic myth that Einstein was ultimately responsible for the atomic bomb." He admits, "It is true that much later he expressed some guilt about signing the famous letter, but that was taking an unnecessary burden on his conscience. What is not in doubt is that he felt as strongly as the others that bitter necessity dictated that the bomb should be made." For most of his life, he had been a pacifist. But with "the advent of Hitler he accepted that he had been wrong" (104).

In the chapter on the Manhattan project and the making of the bomb, Snow pays a special tribute to the chief scientific administrator, Robert Oppenheimer. "Among a mass of very clever men, he was probably the cleverest. . . . He had genuine scientific talent, and could talk on equal terms with the greatest scientists in the place. . . . The curious thing was that Oppenheimer had no great scientific achievement to his name.

. . . There was his tragedy, probably much more deeply wounding than the political misfortunes which later happened to him" (107). On the other hand, according to Snow, the Manhattan project was hampered by its supreme administrator, General Leslie Groves. The prevailing guess was that it would take the Soviet Union about five years to catch up, though others thought that was an overestimate. "General Groves gave contemptuous snorts. He told his political masters that the United States had at least a twenty-year lead, probably much more. That was believed by those who wanted to believe, and produced some political dangers. General Groves was a singularly bad choice for his job" (112).

Another one who comes off poorly in Snow's chapter on the making of the bomb is Admiral Leahy, President Roosevelt's chief of staff during the war; "with his habitual lack of judgment" he "was certain that the bomb would be a fiasco and wouldn't go off at all" (116).

Surprisingly, it is Prime Minister Churchill who is pictured with the most scorn in the chapter on the making of the bomb. Niels Bohr, the great Danish physicist and the one most close to Rutherford, conceived the idea that to avert the postwar perils of the West with the Soviet Union it would be wise to give the Russians an indication of the bomb. "Even a tentative disclosure, Bohr thought, might make for international confidence." He revealed his thoughts to Halifax, the British ambassador to Washington, and to Felix Frankfurter, a Supreme Court justice and close adviser to Roosevelt. Both men gave him considerable sympathy. Bohr's encounter with Churchill, says Snow, "was one of the black comedies of the war." For some obscure reason, Churchill was averse to seeing Bohr. But after "very long and discourteous delays, Bohr was granted a discourteous half hour." Brushed off by Churchill, Bohr was granted an audience with Roosevelt, who was "warm, cordial, amiably sympathetic." What the problem seemed to be with Churchill was that he had taken "a personal dislike to Bohr—about the only human being who ever did so." Another bit of black comedy was that during the second Quebec conference in 1945 "Roosevelt surrendered without a struggle to Churchill's view of Bohr." Churchill insisted that no communication about the bomb should be given to the French or the Russians and that Bohr was to be kept under surveillance, and at one point Churchill insisted that Bohr be arrested. "That was, however, too much for the President's advisers and Churchill's own. . . . Why did Roosevelt and Churchill behave like that? Roosevelt was a sick man. . . . But Churchill? There has never been much of an explanation. He had always had a naive faith in 'secrets.' . . . He was only too conscious that British power, and his own, was now just a vestige. So long as the Americans and British had the bomb in sole possession, he could feel that the power hadn't altogether slipped away" (112–16).

Chapter 8, "Nuclear Fusion," which follows, continues the picture of the development of the atom bomb and its aftermath. The German scientists who were in gentlemanly captivity in Cambridge did not believe the report of the bomb's dropping. They thought it was a kind of bluff to frighten the Japanese. After all, if the Germans could not make the bomb, how could the Anglo-Americans have done so? The mystery was the exact opposite. "Why hadn't the Germans come nearer? The answer seems to be that, until late in the war, the German authorities . . . weren't prepared to devote resources to projects which wouldn't guarantee results within a couple of years." There emerged a sweet romantic story that the German scientists had deliberately held back, that they pretended the bomb was not feasible. The story happened to be utterly untrue, Snow declares (122–23).

Very soon after the dropping of the atom bomb on the Japanese cities, teams of scientists both in America and in the Soviet Union busied themselves with the hydrogen bomb, which would be 1,000 times more powerful than the other bomb. "Such a bomb could annihilate the largest of cities, London, Chicago, Moscow" (128). Snow says, "The H-bomb was the last dramatic contribution of high science to the world's military situation. In the 1950s it brought a sense of doom to many men of good sense and good will. It did so to Einstein, who died in 1956. He spent some of his final energies warning humanity about its dangers. . . . He took it as a final duty, having ceased to expect much sensible behaviour from humankind" (131). Einstein, according to Snow, was one of the two greatest minds that natural science has ever known, the other being Newton. In his last years, the only time he ever lost his temper was against Max Born, one of his oldest and most cherished colleagues. Einstein was not a believing Jew; he had no God except an impersonal God of the cosmos, but he had come to feel that he belonged to the Jewish people. He could neither forgive nor forget the Nazi "final solution." He could not agree with Max Born when Born decided he would return to Germany for his final years of retirement. "Einstein couldn't understand or tolerate this. To go and live among those murderers who had slaughtered millions of 'our people' " (133).

In the concluding chapters of the book Snow discusses the younger physicists and the new trends in physics. One of the newer trends is the growth of computers, and Snow is not at all enthusiastic about them, though he admits they do have some value if used properly. There is, he insists, too much mystification about them. "They can perform many tasks which human intelligence can't: but they are of course useless without human intelligence. After all, they can always be unplugged. In memory storage, they can be given masses of facts which no human memory can retain, reproduce them when given the necessary instructions, do with precision what they are told. And yet, even there, they can't have the fluidity and range of a decent human memory, for which, in many commonplace tasks as well as creative ones, there is no substitute" (159).

Snow cautions against being frightened of computers but points out that with the spread of computers and other technological devices, an enormous proportion of all the goods produced on our planet could be made "by not more than 40 per cent of the present labour force." The advanced societies "are already masking a high level of unemployment" (159–60).

The concluding chapter is called "The Double Legacy." This title refers to the triumphs of physics, which Snow predicts will continue; on the other hand, touched on in the preceding chapters is the anxiety under which many people have been living. "Here there has been a recognition, dark, looming, that something really might hit us—the something being, of course, the supreme technical accomplishment, the fusion (hydrogen) bomb." Yet Snow declares that of all the dangers in front of us, it may very well be that nuclear war is the least likely. "It doesn't need saying that our world is precarious. It will remain so. But there is a subdued irony. It might have been more precarious if the hydrogen bomb had never been made." The most glowing prospect from the invention of nuclear fusion, however, is that within the lifetime of today's children humanity will "be certain of their supplies of energy forever." Since forever is a long time, "perhaps it would be better to say until the seas run dry or until the human species has had a transformation." This harnessing of hydrogen for energy "is the most glowing material prospect which has ever been dangled before us" (170–74).

Conclusion

In summing up Snow's work, a literary critic ought to remember the principle of indeterminacy mentioned in the discussion of *The Malcontents* in chapter 8, for in assessing the work of a recent writer, especially one whose work ended within the past decade or two, it is difficult to assert with any certainty what his or her ultimate fate in the eyes of posterity will be. It would be foolish even to hazard a guess as to whether Snow will, ultimately, be considered a major author of fiction or merely a minor one. That he made some kind of mark in his own time there can be little doubt, but opinions differ widely about the nature of that mark.

It is difficult to see much influence of Snow in the work of younger writers. Almost uniformly they have regarded him as old-fashioned, as a kind of twentieth-century Trollope, but one of lesser stature. They view Snow's novels as stodgy, as weak in the pyrotechnical skill they admire; they deplore his lack of literary density in which an accumulation of myths and symbols plays a large part; his writing, they think, has only a surface clarity that bespeaks mental simplicity, rather than complexity and profundity. They may be wrong, but that is the way they feel today.

The surface clarity of Snow's writing—his style—is evident throughout much of his work, his fiction as well as his nonfiction. We have mentioned previously the possible ambiguities in Snow's narration—whether we can wholly believe every statement of or thought attributed to a character, and whether we are being deliberately misled by the first-person narrators of the stories, who seem to be omitting possibly important events in their lives or changing some events around to suit their own convenience or purpose. Ambiguities, however, are almost never evident in the surface writing itself. Snow's style flows on from book to book, almost always seemingly clear, concise, and in language that hardly ever strains our ability to comprehend immediately; if it does not rise to poetic heights and carry us away on gusts of emotion, at the same time it never descends to depths of turgidity or into twisted, involuted syntax that makes us despair of unwinding. This style has been both highly praised[1] and severely condemned,[2] and, of course, each reader must determine whether it is truly excellent, merely adequate, merely inadequate, or terribly inadequate to express the essence of twentieth-century life. Again, it appears that many of the younger readers, writers, and critics, especially in America, think little of it, for not only, they believe, does it lack the dense accumulation of myths and symbols they equate with profundity, but it also seems to them too mechanical a style, monotonous, on too much of an even keel, and very unemotional. They desire to be carried away on excessive waves of emotion when they are not busily searching into a story for the myths and symbols that they believe will unlock for them, once and for all, the ultimate mysteries of the universe and of the nature of the individual and society. They want a writer to experiment with all or most of the various techniques that have been developed in the twentieth century, because they believe these techniques enable a writer to exhibit humanity in all or most of its subtler manifestations. Snow refused to indulge himself in these ways, preferring the direct approach in his style, scorning anything that seemed to be oblique, to be, as he called it, Alexandrian (see chapter 3 for a discussion of Snow's viewpoint in this respect).

Snow's influence has, in the main, been not artistic but intellectual and moral: for the most part he is being read by those of the middle and older generations who have found some approximation in their own lives to his indeterminate and balanced outlook. This outlook is the chief reason— perhaps even more than his lack of the Alexandrian quality in writing— that the young find it difficult to accept Snow, for though his material is, as his admirers say, relevant to their lives, his is not the kind of relevancy to which they are attracted. Is it possible, however, that they may grow into an appreciation of his type of relevancy? To guess about such a reaction at this time would be futile.

By "Snow's kind of relevancy," we mean that no one in our time examined more minutely the nature of power—its uses and abuses—in so many different kinds of situations. Not only did he show it in his fiction, but he also expressed the view that people who seek and accumulate power are apt to abuse it—power in politics, in science and technology, in education, in family and personal relations, in every area of life Snow touched upon. In one of his later novels, *The Malcontents,* he indicated how the young tend to misuse power even before they actually obtain a firm grasp upon it; he also showed how their opponents, the Establishment, resort to inordinate expressions of power when they feel threatened. Again, as in so many of Snow's novels, situations tend to cancel each other out because Snow was determined to examine life objectively and to show several sides of the subject. He did not always completely succeed, but he almost always made the attempt.

This knowledge of power, accumulated over a lifetime, perhaps tended to make Snow a counselor of caution, of tolerance in the understanding of human beings, of reason as opposed to passion: he was counseling against "the sleep of reason," as one of his better novels shows, because it tends to bring forth monstrous things. The sleep of reason, as his long series of novels shows, tends to make men strangers rather than brothers. Snow was thus preaching the gospel of brotherhood, and since he desired to communicate his beliefs, he tried to write as clearly and as tautly as he could. That ambiguities exist in the way he delivered his message can be seen through a close reading of his novels—ambiguities that perhaps he as author and his narrators, particularly Lewis Eliot, did not always fully comprehend.

His novels tend to fall into similarly organized patterns in presentation of subject matter: quiet beginnings; conflict between several individuals or groups; often an intellectual chase, rather than a physical one, after false or misleading clues (the detective story aspect); the resolution of the conflict; the discovery of the truth as the end result of the chase; slow, quiet conclusions embodying, as noted, a consideration of the wreckage of human beings or their affairs; and a consideration of the possibilities lying ahead for the protagonists or for those who have survived. This pattern is usually dramatic, but it is almost always a quiet drama in which much talk and little action are characteristic. The reflective intelligence, as Snow expressed it, is almost always predominant. Many find these novels quite unexciting; probably few are stimulated by them.

Snow's place as a profound thinker is as indeterminate as his position as a writer of fiction is. He caused much intellectual excitement with some of his startling views, particularly his position on the Two Cultures and on Winston Churchill's conduct of World War II. In his nonfiction, Snow's objectivity—his desire to achieve a balanced outlook and to prevent his biases from showing—most definitely is lacking, and he made no apology as he plunged ahead to present and defend what he strongly believed. This difference may be explained by Snow's awareness that fiction has an entirely different kind of authority from nonfiction. When we wonder if these views expressed in his nonfiction are of lasting significance or are merely passing, indeterminacy seems again to be the principle to be applied. We can almost be sure, however, that Snow would agree that in human affairs the possibilities of understanding with complete certainty the past, the present, and the future are limited.

After several years of illness, C. P. Snow died on 1 July 1980. Almost a year later, his wife of 30 years, the novelist Pamela Hansford Johnson, died, on 18 June 1981. Snow's final novel, *A Coat of Varnish*, concludes with the burial of Lady Ashbrook; because of police regulations, she is denied the cremation she desired—her body is to be kept in the refrigerator at the morgue until the case is settled with a definite solution to the mystery of her death. It seemed probable that she might never be cremated. It was fitting, however, that her creator and his wife, the Snows, received the cremation they desired. Snow's ashes a year after his death were incorporated in a memorial urn in the Fellows' Garden at Christ's College at Cambridge, in company with John Milton and three other distinguished members of the college.[3]

There was an outpouring of obituaries in the press following Snow's death. One of the finest of these came a month later in "A Farewell to C. P. Snow," by Herman Wouk, the American novelist. Among the many tributes Wouk pays to Snow are these words: "He was a master at marshaling the ironic ambiguities of life." An excellent example of this trait can again be found in Snow's last novel: the ordinary mystery writer would stick absolutely within the so-called rules of that genre and present his readers with a definite solution no matter how ridiculous it seemed. The murderer must be disclosed. But Snow was a realist and knew that within the ambiguities of life the murderer often could not be found. Wouk points out this failure of the police that often occurs: "We find out who the murderer is—that is, we think we do. Yet it appears that he is going to get away with it—that is, we think he will. Murder mysteries are not like that: murder probably is like that, out in the real world. The real world was Charles Snow's habitat, his study, and his art. That made him rather an unfashionable novelist."

Wouk ends his tribute by calling Snow "the Trollope of his time."[4] Snow would have loved that, because it is apparent that though he admired many other realists, it was Trollope who most captured his heart and imagination, Trollope whom among all authors Snow wrote a whole book about. On that note it is perhaps fitting that this book on the work of C. P. Snow be brought to its conclusion.

Notes and References

Preface

    1. "Interview with C. P. Snow," *Review of English Literature*, (Leeds) 3 (1962): 93.

Chapter One

    1. *The Two Cultures and the Scientific Revolution* (New York: Cambridge University Press, 1962), 27–29.
    2. "Interview with C. P. Snow," *Review of English Literature* (Leeds) 3 (1962): 92–93.
    3. "The First Excitement That Knowledge Gives," *Discovery* 2 (1939): 161–62.
    4. "The Age of Rutherford," *Atlantic Monthly*, 1958, 76.
    5. Ibid.
    6. Ibid., 79.
    7. Ibid., 79.
    8. "Interview with C. P. Snow," 95.
    9. "The Age of Rutherford," 81.

Chapter Two

    1. *The Two Cultures and the Scientific Revolution*, 4–5.
    2. Herbert Read, "Mood of the Month," *London Magazine*, 1959, 39–43.
    3. F. R. Leavis, *The Two Cultures? The Significance of C. P. Snow* (London: Chatto & Windus, 1962), 9–30. The same volume also has an essay against Snow, by Michael Yudkin.
    4. *Science and Government* (Cambridge, Mass.: Harvard University Press, 1961), 10.
    5. Ibid., 48–49.
    6. Ibid., 51.
    7. Ibid., 63.
    8. Ibid., 64.
    9. Ibid., 27.
    10. Ibid., 82–83.
    11. *Appendix to Science and Government* (Cambridge, Mass.: Harvard University Press, 1962), 3, 13, 36.

12. A. J. P. Taylor, "Bombing Germany," *New Statesman,* 6 October 1961, 482–83.

Chapter Three

1. George Steiner, "F. R. Leavis," *Encounter* 18 (May 1962): 37–45. This essay has been reprinted, with a few minor changes, in Steiner's *Language and Silence: Essays on Language, Literature, and the Inhuman* (New York: Atheneum, 1967), 221–38.
2. "Challenge to the Intellect," *Times Literary Supplement,* 15 August 1958, iii ("Books in a Changing World").
3. Ibid.
4. Ibid.
5. Ibid.
6. "Science, Politics, and the Novelist: Or the Fish and the Net," *Kenyon Review* 23 (Winter 1961): 1–17.
7. Ibid.
8. Ibid.
9. Ibid.
10. Ibid.
11. Lionel Trilling, "The Novel Alive or Dead," in *A Gathering of Fugitives* (Boston: Beacon Press, 1956), 125–32.
12. "Which Side of the Atlantic?" *Harper's,* October 1959, 163–66.
13. "The Irregular Right," *Nation,* (24 March 1956), 238–39.
14. Jerome Thale, *C. P. Snow* (New York: Scribner's, 1964), 38.

Chapter Four

1. *Death under Sail* (London: Heinemann, 1959), vii–viii.
2. Alfred Kazin. "A Brilliant Boy from the Midlands," *Contemporaries* (1962), 171–77.
3. William Cooper, *C. P. Snow* (Writers and Their Work, no. 115, rev. ed. (London: 1971), 12.
4. Ibid.
5. Thale, 19–20.
6. "Interview with C. P. Snow," 91–108.
7. Cooper, 13.
8. *New Lives for Old* (London: Gollancz, 1933), 244.
9. Harvey Curtis Webster, "The Sacrifices of Success," *Saturday Review,* 12 July 1958, 8–10, 34.
10. Prefatory note (10 February 1958) to *The Search* (London: Macmillan, 1959).
11. Robert Greacen, *The World of C. P. Snow* (House & Maxwell, 1962), 20.

12. This supposition is strengthened by the fact that Snow rigorously avoided other methods after having used the third-person-omniscient method once (until very late in his career in *The Malcontents*).

13. Sidney Finkelstein, "The Art and Science of C. P. Snow," *Mainstream* 14 (September 1961): 31–57.

14. The most flagrant misreading in this respect is by Frederick R. Karl, *C. P. Snow: The Politics of Conscience* (Carbondale: Southern Illinois University Press, 1963), 22.

15. Robert Gorham Davis, *C. P. Snow* (New York and London: Columbia University Press, 1965: Columbia Essays on Modern Writers, no. 8), 14.

Chapter Five

1. See Author's Note to *The Conscience of the Rich* (London: Macmillan, 1960), and "Interview with C. P. Snow," 91–108.

2. *Time of Hope* (London: 1961), 106.

3. "The final volume will bring the sequence to within a couple of years of the date of writing," Snow says in "Interview with C. P. Snow," 91–108, and *Last Things* concludes in 1968.

4. Henry James, "The Art of Fiction," in *The Art of Fiction and Other Essays by Henry James* (New York: 1948), 11.

5. See "Interview with C. P. Snow": "On the whole my effects are cumulative . . ."—which is the reason, he says, he does not write short stories.

6. *Homecomings* (London: Macmillan, 1961), 353–54.

7. Pamela Hansford Johnson, "The Novelists and the Drawing of Character: C. P. Snow, Joyce Cary, and Ivy Compton-Burnett," *Essays and Studies 1950* (London: 1950), 82–99.

8. Kazin, 171–77.

9. See, for example, R. W. Flint, "The Undying Apocalypse," *Partisan Review* 24 (Winter 1957): 139–45, who says that *Homecomings* is two novels flimsily joined together. This fallacious view is what comes from not really understanding Lewis Eliot's intent and also from considering one of the novels in the sequence in isolation from the others. By Flint's own admission, this was the only novel in the sequence he had read.

10. Bernard Bergonzi, "The World of Lewis Eliot," *Twentieth Century* 167 (March 1960): 214–25.

11. Ibid.

Chapter Six

1. "Interview with C. P. Snow."

2. Cooper, 19.

3. Ibid.

4. *Strangers and Brothers* (London: Macmillan, 1961), 88.

5. *The Conscience of the Rich* (London: Macmillan, 1960).

6. See Edgar Rosenberg, *From Shylock to Svengali: Jewish Stereotypes in English Fiction* (Palo Alto, Calif.: Stanford University Press, 1960), 302–4, who says Snow alone in the twentieth century has avoided the stereotypes of presenting the Jew.

7. *The Light and the Dark* (London: Macmillan, 1961), 165.

8. Karl, 62.

9. Bergonzi, 214–25.

10. Edmund Fuller, "C. P. Snow: Spokesman of Two Communities," *Books with Men behind Them* (New York: Random House, 1962), 117.

11. Karl, 67.

12. Trilling, 125–32.

13. *The Masters* (London: Macmillan, 1961), 54.

14. In this connection, we have another of Eliot's guesses: "I guessed that, in times past, Crawford had been envious of Jago's charm for women. Jago . . . was confident of love . . . whereas Crawford as a young man had wondered in anguish whether any woman would ever love him. For all his contented marriage—on the surface so much more enviable than Jago's—he had never lost that diffidence, and there were still times when he envied such men as Jago from the bottom of his heart" (98). How on earth is Eliot able to guess all this?

15. Karl, p. 68, says Snow is anxious to demonstrate "what reasonable creatures men are and how fine their decisions may be even when their own interests are at stake." I think Karl is wrong; I do not think Snow is anxious to demonstrate anything at all like that, as my discussion in the text shows. Nor does Lewis Eliot so demonstrate. There is a pertinent comment on p. 40 of *The Sleep of Reason* (London: Macmillan, 1968) that indicates not only Eliot's point of view but that his manner has been deceptive: "I had twice heard an elder statesman of science [probably meaning Crawford] announce, with the crystalline satisfaction of someone producing a self-evident truth, that sensible men usually reached sensible conclusions. I had seen my brother cock an eyebrow, in recognition of that astonishing remark. I had myself reported it, dead pan, to others—who promptly came to the conclusion that I believed in it myself." Yet Karl, when he wrote his book, could not have foreseen the ramifications of Eliot's views; nevertheless, his book as a whole illustrates the dangers of judgments based on a superficial, biased reading of an author. In particular, his chapter on *The Masters* is beset with many contradictions and errors of fact.

16. See Bergonzi and, particularly, Kathleen Nott, "The Type to Which the Whole Creation Moves? Further Thoughts on the Snow Saga," *Encounter* 18 (February 1962): 87–88, 94–97.

17. Karl, 82; Davis, 32.

18. Karl, ibid.

19. *The New Men* (London: Macmillan, 1961).

20. Fuller, 108–9.

21. Thale, 56.
22. *The Affair* (London: Macmillan, 1960), 163.
23. Karl, 151–52. So many views expressed by Karl about *The Affair* miss the point of the book that they militate against his occasional flashes of interesting insight; in my opinion, his chapter is basically obtuse and is to be read with caution.
24. *Corridors of Power* (London: Macmillan, 1964)
25. Ibid., vi.
26. Davis, 39.
27. A. J. P. Taylor, "Dark Corridors," *New Statesman,* 6 November 1964, 698.
28. *The Sleep of Reason* (London: Macmillan, 1968).
29. See, for example, D. J. Enright, "Easy Lies the Head," *New Statesman,* 6 November 1964, 698–99.

Chapter Seven

1. I cannot agree at all with Cooper's view, pp. 34–35, in his revised edition, that this book has as much of a plot as any of the others, or that it is patterned by plot. The reader must, of course, judge individually; it may be revealing to note, however, that most of the early reviewers complained of the lack of plot.
2. *Last Things* (London: Macmillan, 1970), 342.
3. "The Future of Man," *Nation,* 13 September 1958, 124–25.
4. "On Magnanimity," *Harper's,* July 1962, 37–41.
5. *The State of Siege* (New York: Scribner's, 1969), 31–32, 41–42.

Chapter Eight

1. Robert K. Morris, "C. P. Snow: Nevertheless," *Nation,* 29 May 1972, 696–97.
2. Christopher Porterfield, *Time,* 12 June 1972, 89–90.
3. *The Malcontents* (New York: Macmillan, 1972), 277.
4. Brom Weber, *Saturday Review,* 17 June 1972, 76–77.
5. Ibid.
6. *In Their Wisdom* (New York: Scribner's, 1974), 16.
7. Philip Snow, *Stranger and Brother: A Portrait of C. P. Snow* (London: Scribner's, 1982), 178.
8. When Lord Snow visited America in 1972 or 1973 (my memory is hazy as to the exact date), one of the places he came to was Louisville, Kentucky, to speak at the University of Louisville. I had occasion to meet Snow for the only time at the home of one of the faculty of that university. He greeted me warmly, for I had been corresponding with him for some time, and we spoke together for about three hours during the course of the evening. Suddenly, in the midst of our talk, Snow told me that life in England was getting much better than it had been

for many years and, among other things, the food was better than at any time in his life. His observation, which seemingly came from nowhere and was not apropos of anything else we had been discussing, bewildered me. When I first read this passage in *In Their Wisdom,* I realized that in a way Snow had been trying it out on me. When we remember that Ryle was patterned after Snow, as Philip Snow later wrote, then the remark begins to make sense.

9. *A Coat of Varnish* (New York: Scribner's, 1979), 4.
10. Russel Davies, *New York Review of Books,* 21 February 1980, 31–33.
11. Ibid.
12. Philip Snow, in the chapter called "Last Things," 174–83.

Chapter Nine

1. Philip Snow, 169
2. *Variety of Men* (New York: Scribner's, 1967), 7–8.
3. G. H. Hardy, *A Mathematician's Apology* (Cambridge: Cambridge University Press, 1969).
4. Philip Snow, 193–95.
5. Ibid., 138. As his brother says, this statement was one of "several *obiter dicta*" that "[h]e came out with almost casually; I used to make a note of them soon afterwards to retain their flavour."
6. For example, there is the curious statement in the preface to *The Realists* (New York: Scribner's, 1978), xii, that Charles Dickens is "obviously not a realist in the sense that Trollope, Jane Austen, George Eliot were. . . . [A]gainst my own inclination, I can't pretend that any of them is of the same stature as the greatest realistic masters." I say "curious" because many critics would think that Jane Austen and George Eliot certainly are of the same stature as the eight novelists dealt with in *The Realists* and also because many statements made about Trollope in Snow's book on him belie such demeaning words in *The Realists.*
7. See Michael Sadleir, *Trollope, a Commentary* (London: Constable & Co., 1927), 141–51.
8. David Kirby, *America* 139 (30 December 1978): 501–2.
9. See chapter 2's discussion of *The Two Cultures.*
10. C. P. Snow, *The Physicists* (Boston and Toronto: Little, Brown, 1981),
8.
11. Review, *Economist,* 7 November 1981, 114–15.

Conclusion

1. For praise, see, for example, Cooper, 41–44, and Michael Millgate, "Structure and Style in the Novels of C. P. Snow," *Review of English Literature* 1 (April 1960), 34–41.
2. For condemnation, the reader can do no better than go to Rubin

Rabinovitz, *The Reaction against Experiment in the English Novel, 1950–1960* (New York and London: Columbia University Press, 1967).

3. Philip Snow, 182.

4. Herman Wouk, "A Farewell to C. P. Snow," *Saturday Review,* August 1980, 16–17, 20.

Selected Bibliography

PRIMARY WORKS

Novels (Listed Chronologically)

Death under Sail. London: Heinemann, 1932; revised and reprinted, 1959.
New Lives for Old. Published anonymously. London: Gollancz, 1933.
The Search. London: Gollancz, 1934; Indianapolis, New York: Bobbs-Merrill, 1935. Revised with preface by the author, London: Macmillan, 1958; New York: Scribner's, 1958.
Strangers and Brothers. London: Faber, 1940; London: Macmillan, 1951; New York: Scribner's, 1960. (Name changed to *George Passant,* 1970, for all subsequent editions.)
The Light and the Dark. London: Faber, 1947; New York, Macmillan, 1948; London: Macmillan, 1951; New York: Scribner's, 1961.
Time of Hope. London, Faber, 1949; New York: Macmillan, 1950; London: Macmillan, 1951; New York: Scribner's, 1961.
The Masters. London: Macmillan, 1951; New York: Macmillan, 1951; New York: Scribner's, 1960.
The New Men. London: Macmillan, 1954; New York: Scribner's, 1954.
Homecomings. London: Macmillan, 1956; published as *Homecoming,* New York: Scribner's, 1956.
The Conscience of the Rich. London: Macmillan, 1958; New York: Scribner's, 1958.
The Affair. London: Macmillan, 1960; New York: Scribner's, 1960.
Corridors of Power. London: Macmillan, 1964; New York: Scribner's, 1964.
The Sleep of Reason. London: Macmillan, 1968; New York: Scribner's, 1968.
Last Things. London: Macmillan, 1970; New York: Scribner's, 1970.
The Malcontents. London: Macmillan, 1972; New York: Scribner's, 1972.
In Their Wisdom. London, Macmillan; 1974; New York: Scribner's, 1974.
A Coat of Varnish. London: Macmillan, 1974; New York; Scribner's, 1974.

Nonfiction Books

The Two Cultures and the Scientific Revolution. London, New York: Cambridge University Press, 1959.

The Two Cultures: And a Second Look. London, New York: Cambridge University Press, 1964. Expanded version of the 1959 volume.

Science and Government. London: Oxford University Press, 1961; Cambridge, Mass.: Harvard University Press, 1961.

Appendix to Science and Government. London: Oxford University Press, 1962; Cambridge, Mass.: Harvard University Press, 1962.

Variety of Men. London: Macmillan, 1966; New York: Scribner's, 1967.

The State of Siege. London: Macmillan, 1969; New York: Scribner's, 1969.

Public Affairs. New York: Scribner's, 1971.

Trollope: His Life and Art. London: Macmillan, 1975; New York: Scribner's, 1975.

The Realists. London: Macmillan, 1978; New York: Scribner's, 1978.

The Physicists. Boston: Little, Brown, 1981.

Essays and Reviews

Snow has written many essays and reviews, and this list represents only a portion of them.

"Challenge to the Intellect." *Times Literary Supplement,* 15 August 1958, iii ("Books in a Changing World").

"Dickens and the Public Service." In *Dickens 1970,* ed. Michael Slater (New York: Stein and Day, 1970), 125–49.

Foreword (1967) to G. H. Hardy, *A Mathematician's Apology* (Cambridge: Cambridge University Press, 1969), 9–58.

"Miasma, Darkness and Torpidity." *New Statesman,* 11 August 1961, 186–87.

"On Magnanimity." *Harper's,* July 1962, 37–41. Address delivered spring 1962 as rector of St. Andrews University, Scotland.

"Science, Politics, and the Novelist: Or the Fish and the Net." *Kenyon Review* 23 (Winter 1961): 1–17.

"The Age of Rutherford." *Atlantic Monthly,* November 1958, 76–81.

"The Case of Leavis and the Serious Case." *Times Literary Supplement,* 9 July 1970, 737–40.

"The Enjoyment of Science." *Spectator,* 12 June 1936, 1074–75.

"The First Excitement That Knowledge Gives." *Discovery,* April 1939, 161–62.

"The Habit of Truth." *New Republic,* 18 August 1958, 26.

"The Irregular Right." *Nation,* 24 March 1946, 238–39.

"The Moral Un-Neutrality of Science." *Science,* 27 January 1961, 256–59.

"The Two Cultures." *New Statesman and Nation,* 6 October 1956, 413–14.

"The 'Two-Cultures' Controversy: Afterthoughts." *Encounter* 14 (February 1960): 64.

"Which Side of the Atlantic?" *Harper's,* October 1959, 163–66.

SECONDARY WORKS

The literature about Snow is becoming very large; the more interesting, important, or provocative, representing differing opinions, are cited.

Bergonzi, Bernard. "The World of Lewis Eliot." *Twentieth Century* 167 (February 1960): 214–25. Though Snow's subject matter is important, finds Snow deficient as an artist, especially in style and the limitations of the narrator.

Cooper, William. *C. P. Snow.* (Writers and Their Work, no. 115). Revised Edition. London: Published for the British Book Council by Longman Group, 1971. Excellent pamphlet, dealing with all the novels; generally good critical perceptions; very sympathetic to Snow.

Cornelius, David K., and Edwin St. Vincent. *Cultures in Conflict: Perspectives on the Snow-Leavis Controversy.* Chicago: Scott, Foresman, 1964. Excellent group of readings; also has excerpts from writers of the past and present on literature and science.

Davis, Robert Gorham. *C. P. Snow.* (Columbia Essays on Modern Writers, no. 8.) New York, London: Columbia University Press, 1965. Deals with Snow's work through 1964; acute analysis.

Fuller, Edmund. "C. P. Snow: Spokesman of Two Communities." In *Books with Men behind Them.* New York: Random House, 1962. Good, objective account of Snow as novelist and thinker.

Gindin, James. "Some Current Fads." In *Postwar British Fiction: New Accents and Attitudes.* Berkeley, Los Angeles: University of California Press, 1962. Calls Snow overrated as a novelist. Gindin's arguments marred by errors, indicating a failure to read Snow carefully.

Greacen, Robert. *The World of C. P. Snow.* With a bibliography by Bernard Stone. New York, London: House & Maxwell, 1962. Very short, sketchy book, but the first on Snow; probably fairly helpful originally, but no longer of much value except possibly for parts of the bibliography.

Green, Martin. *Science and the Shabby Curate of Poetry.* London: Longmans, 1964. Staunch, bellicose defense of Snow's views about the "two cultures" and an examination of the relationship between literary and scientific attitudes in our society.

Karl, Frederick R. *C. P. Snow: The Politics of Conscience.* Preface by Harry T. Moore. Carbondale: Southern Illinois University Press, 1963. Chapters on *The Search* and the first eight novels of the sequence. Has some interesting observations but also some errors and misleading statements; to be read with caution.

————"The Politics of Conscience: The Novels of C. P. Snow." In *A Reader's Guide to the Contemporary English Novel.* London: Thames and Hudson, 1963. Shortened version of Karl's book on Snow, but mainly free of the errors and statements that mar the longer work; in general, a perceptive, good analysis.

Kazin, Alfred. "A Brilliant Boy from the Midlands." In *Contemporaries.* Boston, Toronto: Little, Brown, 1962. Good, reasoned discussion; favorable to Snow.

Leavis, F. R. *Two Cultures? The Significance of C. P. Snow.* London: Chatto & Windus, 1962. The now-notorious attack on Snow. Contains also an essay on Snow's Rede Lecture by Michael Yudkin that is shorter, calmer, and in some respects more perceptive than Leavis's.

Millgate, Michael. "Structure and Style in the Novels of C. P. Snow." *Review of English Literature,* 1 (April 1960): 34–41. Interesting, good discussion.

Nott, Kathleen. "The Type to Which the Whole Creation Moves? Further Thoughts on the Snow Saga." *Encounter* 28 (February 1962): 87–88, 94–97. Shrewd, corrosive attack on the Two Cultures concepts and Snow's derogation of satire.

Rabinovitz, Rubin. *The Reaction against Experiment in the English Novel, 1950–1960.* New York, London: Columbia University Press, 1967. Blast at Snow for not writing the experimental type of novel. Some cogent analysis, but to be read with caution because Rabinovitz's personal bias against nonexperimental writers is evident.

Ramanathan, Suguna. *The Novels of C. P. Snow: A Critical Introduction.* London: Macmillan, 1978; New York, Scribner's, 1978. A very sympathetic critique of most, but not all, of Snow's novels up to 1977. Sees Snow's occasional independence of literary tradition as part of his originality and interest.

Smith, Leroy W. "C. P. Snow as Novelist: A Delimitation." *South Atlantic Quarterly* 64 (Summer 1965): 316–31. Interesting discussion; very unfavorable to Snow, whose moral vision Smith finds limited and pessimistic and whose artistry is inadequate.

Snow, Philip A., O.B.E., J.P., M.A., F.R.S.A. *Stranger and Brother: A Portrait of C. P. Snow.* 2d edition. London: Macmillan, 1983; New York, Scribner's, 1983. Snow's brother, now literary executor, reveals aspects of Snow's family life unable to be found elsewhere. Undoubtedly the best account of Snow's life yet written. Any future biographer of Snow will find this book indispensable.

Stanford, Raney. "The Achievement of C. P. Snow." *Western Humanities Review* 6 (Winter 1962): 43–52. Very favorable to Snow's achievement as a novelist.

Thale, Jerome. *C. P. Snow.* New York: Scribner's, 1965. Excellent, objective presentation of Snow's work through 1964. Probably the best of the earlier discussion on Snow.

Trilling, Lionel. "Science, Literature, and Culture: A Comment on the Leavis-Snow Controversy." *Commentary* 33 (June 1962): 461–77. Reprinted in *Beyond Culture*. New York: Viking Press, 1965. Highly recommended, dispassionate discussion of the controversy by a noted man of letters.

————"The Novel Alive or Dead." In *A Gathering of Fugitives*. Boston: Beacon Press, 1956. Sympathetic appraisal of the novel as written by Snow; mainly about *The New Men*.

Webster, Harvey Curtis. "C. P. Snow: Scientific Humanist." In *After the Trauma: Representative British Novelists Since 1920*. Lexington: University Press of Kentucky, 1970. Extremely sympathetic, perceptive discussion of Snow's novels up to and including *The Sleep of Reason*.

Weintraub, Stanley. *C. P. Snow: A Spectrum*. New York: Scribner's, 1963. A research anthology for students; deals with many facets of Snow's writings on science, criticism, and fiction. Good introduction to Snow's life and works.

Wouk, Herman. "A Farewell to C. P. Snow." *Saturday Review*, August 1980, 16–17, 20. A glowing tribute to Snow by a friend and fellow novelist. Says that Snow was unfashionable as a novelist because his "natural habitat" and "his art," unlike those of other writers, are the "real world." Predicts his books will be read for a long time because they are "consistently entertaining and present the truth behind appearances".

Index

The Author

David Shusterman received his B.A. (1949), M.A. (1950), and Ph.D. (1953) from New York University. He taught at the University of Kansas from 1953 to 1956 and in the English Department of Indiana University Southeast from 1956 until his retirement in 1982. At the latter institution he has held such administrative positions as chairman of English and chairman of the Division of Humanities. He is the author of *The Quest for Certitude in E. M. Forster's Fiction* (1965; reprinted 1973) and has published a number of articles and reviews in such periodicals as *PMLA, Modern Language Notes, Criticism, The Dickensian, Kenyon Review,* and *New England Quarterly.*

Currently professor emeritus of English at Indiana University Southeast, Dr. Shusterman occasionally teaches a course but devotes much of his time to research and writing.